SPECIALTY press

Specialty Press
838 Lake Street South
Forest Lake, MN 55025
Phone: 651-277-1400 or 800-895-4585
Fax: 651-277-1203
www.specialtypress.com

Edit by Mike Machat
Layout by Monica Seiberlich

ISBN 978-1-58007-237-3
Item No. SP237

Library of Congress Cataloging-in-Publication Data

Names: Barbier, Douglas, author.
Title: World's fastest single-engine jet aircraft : the story of
Convair's F-106 Delta Dart Interuptor/Col. Douglas Barbier, USAF (Ret)
Other titles: Story of Convair's F-106 Delta Dart
Description: Forest Lake, MN : Specialty Press, [2017] | Includes
bibliographical references and index.
Identifiers: LCCN 2016043111 | ISBN 9781580072373 (alk. paper)
Subjects: LCSH: Delta Dart (Jet fighter plane)–History.
Classification: LCC UG1242.F5 B368 2017 | DDC 358.4/383–dc23
LC record available at https://lccn.loc.gov/2016043111

Written, edited, and designed in the U.S.A.
Printed in China
10 9 8 7 6 5 4 3 2

Front Cover:
The elegant lines of Convair's sleek F-106 Delta Dart are evident in this dramatic takeoff image as the jet takes to the air in full afterburner. (From a photo by Alec Fuski)

Front Flap:
Two-seat Convair F-106B is shown on the ramp at Edwards AFB, assigned as a high-speed chase aircraft for the Lockheed YF-12 flight test program. (Isham Collection)

Front Endpaper:
This Green Dragons F-106 is armed with the cannon and is seen here during William Tell 1982. (Norman E. Taylor)

Title Page:
Stunning inflight close-up of Convair's F-106 Delta Dart. This Dart belongs to the Massachusetts Air National Guard. (Don Spering/AIR)

Table of Contents:
Undergoing initial Air Force flight testing at Edwards AFB in 1957, the second prototype F-106A displays its sleek lines and unique color scheme. (USAF via Isham)

Back Endpaper:
"Inboard Profile" drawing of the proposed Convair F-102B showing internal components of the aircraft's evolutionary design.

Back Flap:
Author and former USAF Command Pilot, Douglas Barbier, poses with his Michigan ANG F-16.

Back Cover Photos
Top:
Showing what the F-106 was designed for, a California ANG Delta Dart fires a Douglas Genie anti-aircraft missile during the 1980 William Tell competition. (USAF)

Bottom:
This classic 1950s tech art line drawing shows the proposed carrier-based naval version of the F-106 in front view, complete with folding wingtips and vertical stabilizer.

Distributed in the UK and Europe by
Crécy Publishing Ltd
1a Ringway Trading Estate
Shadowmoss Road
Manchester M22 5LH England
Tel: 44 161 499 0024
Fax : 44 161 499 0298
www.crecy.co.uk
enquiries@crecy.co.uk

TABLE OF CONTENTS

ACKNOWLEDGMENTS

An undertaking of this size is never a one-man show. I am indebted to many people for helping make this a far better volume than I could have done alone. First and foremost, I would like to thank Marty Isham, "Mr. ADC." This book is as much his as it is mine and it is only through his lifelong efforts to save the history of Air Defense Command (ADC) and its associated squadrons that this book exists at all. I would be remiss in not mentioning the late SMSGT Erv Smalley in the same regard.

Both Craig Kaston and Brian Rogers went far, far above and beyond the call of duty in assisting me. Craig brought a knowledge of the business and technical sides of military aviation that I was lacking, providing many valuable insights. He also did some serious graphics work. Brian was my "go to" guy for air force lineage. The chapter on squadrons owes a great deal to his input. Both were invaluable in improving the accuracy of the finished product. Likewise, Jennings Heilig spent a great deal of time doing graphics work.

F106deltadart.com webmaster Pat McGee was gracious enough to allow use of materials from the website. Bill Yenne was courteous enough to provide a very historically important shot of the prototype F-106A. John Aldaz was kind enough to allow a portion of his model collection to be photographed for use here, as was Collect-Aire miniatures. Bob "Bobski" Kwiecinski, Ken Wigton of the F-106 reunion committee, and Pat Perry of the 456th FIS all provided valuable contacts, photos, and information. Bill Livesay of the 94th FIS and 171 FIS Six Pack, and Bob Wegeman of the 48th FIS were always there to answer my questions on weapons, and on life as a maintainer as well. Convair rep, and Sacramento ALC manager Joe Sylvia answered many questions about both the wings and the aerial refueling installation on the Sixes. Bruce Gordon and Ray Janes of the 94th FIS were invaluable, helping with both historical information and photography. Dave Kuntz, Tony Chong, and many others provided information and helped keep me straight. Mike Machat of Specialty Press is probably glad to see the end of a seemingly endless series of questions from this "newbie" author but was unstinting in his help as well.

An immense number of people helped with photography. They provided far more than I could use in another dozen books, but every photo helped, if in no other way than to verify markings, modifications, or dates. Ralph Robelado of the Castle Air and Space Museum went far out of his way to take digital photography for me. Don Spering of Aircraft in Review, Bert Kinzey of Detail & Scale, El Mason of BareMetal Decals, Mark Nankivil of the St. Louis Air & Space Museum, Collect-Aire, Ray Leader of Flightleader, Marty Isham, Ron Picciani, Ken Elliott, Ralph Weilant, Baldur Sveinsson, Alec Fushi, Norris Graser, Brian Rogers, Norm Taylor, Frank MacSorley, Terry Love, Jerry Geer, Jack Morris, Charles B. Mayer, Tom Foote, Bill Curry, Mark Frankel, Jack Calloway, Paul Minert, Kirk Minert, Pat Perry, Tom Brewer, Bruce Gordon, Jim Sullivan, Tom and Pat Hildreth, Jack Morris, Phil Friddell, the late Jim Koglin, and Dave Menard all provided photos and assistance.

I would also like to thank my family. Without their help and encouragement this book would never have been written. Little did my wife know what she was in for when we left for pilot training in 1973. Finally, my late aunt spent years trying to get me to write a book, but work, life, and family always got in the way. With this tome, I hope she is happy. Florence, this one is for you.

There will undoubtedly be errors of fact that have crept in, and for those I take full responsibility and offer my apologies.

Publisher's Note: In reporting history, the images required to tell the tale will vary greatly in quality, especially by modern photographic standards. While some images in this volume are not up to those digital standards, we have included them, as we feel they are an important element in telling the story.

ABOUT THE AUTHOR

Douglas Barbier grew up listening to the sound of the 1st FW (AD) Sixes flying out of Selfridge AFB, Michigan. A visit to the base on Armed Forces Day 1962 started a lifelong interest in the jet, while a black-and-white photo taken with a Kodak "Brownie" camera that same day was the first of thousands of aviation photos he has taken. A series of circumstances led to one of his aerial photos ending up on the desk of Gen. "Chappie" James, Commander in Chief of NORAD, who commented, "Who is this guy? He takes better pictures than anything we have!" Shortly after that, Doug had carte blanche to visit any ADC unit in the country and go flying with them.

A USAF command pilot with more than 3,500 hours, he flew the T-38 and T-33, has more than 1,000 hours in the F-4C/D, and finished his military career in the F-16A/ADF. He spent many hours sitting air defense alert and made three intercepts of Soviet Tu-95 Bear bombers along the way. After retiring from the military, Barbier flew for a major international air carrier for 20 years. He has had more than 200 photographs published in half a dozen countries, and this is his first book.

AUTHOR PREFACE

Although the F-106 grew out of the 1954 Interceptor program, attempting to cover its history all the way from the Board of Senior Officers conference in 1948 proved to be too extensive for inclusion in this work. Therefore, I have chosen to begin the story of the F-106 with the successful first flight of the YF-102A. The story of the XF-92 and F-102 belongs in its own book. Likewise, I had always intended to include color images of the various squadron badges of units that flew the Six. Since those images are available in other locations, when cost and production decisions intervened near the end of the project, I opted for more coverage of the aircraft instead. I hope that you will not object too strenuously to that decision. Throughout the work I have chosen to use the popular names of the various corporations. Likewise, I generally use the post-1962 designations for the armament.

Two additional items also should be mentioned here. First, the date a particular aircraft (serial number) was assigned to a unit on paper may have been up to a month either before or after the actual arrival of the jet on the ramp of the gaining squadron. For example, the official USAF aircraft record cards show that at least four F-106s were assigned to the 498th FIS by 1 June 1959, yet the Geiger Field base newspaper gives not only the serial numbers of the first jets to arrive, but also the pilots' names and local arrival times. The first two jets actually arrived on 2 June. Given that it might take anywhere from one day to more than a month to ferry the new jets across the country, paper assignment dates are only good for approximate arrival dates.

Second, security restrictions (especially for those units located on SAC bases), the remote locations of many of the early F-106 squadrons, and sometimes the short length of their existence, led to very few good photographs of some units. In cases where adequate photographs do not exist, the photos shown are the best available.

INTRODUCTION

"FOX 3." One second after rocket motor ignition, this beautiful photo captures what the F-106 was designed for: to shoot down bombers attacking North America. Belonging to the California ANG, this Six was seen during the William Tell 1980 competition. The 2-inch-wide brown band on the Genie indicates a live rocket motor. (USAF)

The F-106 was built for one purpose and one purpose alone, to attack and destroy enemy bombers before they could deliver their weapons. Day or night, clear air or storms, the F-106 was designed to be able to find and destroy the threat. To that end, the Six was the most technologically complicated aircraft ever attempted, and it was armed with an unstoppable nuclear-armed air-to-air rocket.

It was intended to be automatically guided to the vicinity of the target by a network of long-range ground-based radars, which were tied to a computerized command and control network that,

in turn, sent radio guidance signals to the jet. The highly advanced MA-1 Fire Control System (FCS) automatically flew the aircraft in response to those signals. Once near the target, the sophisticated ground-based Semi-Automatic Ground Environment (SAGE) system indicated on the onboard radar screen the rough area where the target should be. The pilot then used the onboard radar to find and "lock on" to the target.

Once the weapons had been manually selected and armed, the onboard electronics flew the interceptor to the proper launch point and, with the pilot's consent, automatically fired the weapons. After manually performing an escape maneuver, the pilot selected a homing point to return to base. By selecting additional points, the F-106 could automatically fly an instrument penetration and approach down to ILS minimums. In theory, all the pilot had to do then was control the speed, put the landing gear down, and flare for landing.

Last to fly, and built in far smaller numbers than any of the other Century Series jets that reached production, the F-106 Delta Dart was the embodiment of a purpose-built aircraft. By demanding capabilities far beyond anything attempted to date, the new aircraft required monumental advances in electronics, aerodynamics, and propulsion. As the most technologically advanced aircraft embarked upon by the air force, in the end, the old adage "If it looks right, it flies right" was never more true than with the F-106.

Its tortuous and prolonged development program finally resulted in an altogether remarkable achievement. The unyielding pursuit of aerodynamic cleanliness resulted in one of the most aesthetically beautiful aircraft ever flown. A joy to fly, the airplane looked as if it were going Mach 2 while sitting still on the ramp.

The Convair Deltas were the first aircraft to be developed under the Weapons System concept where the prime manufacturer was responsible for the development and integration of the whole product (airframe, engines, avionics, test equipment, and publications) versus building just an airframe and then finding out what was available to be used in it. The F-102B, later to become the F-106A, was WS-201B. They were also the first to use the Cook-Craigie production concept, which was an attempt to shorten the time between design and entry into service. Instead of hand-building successive prototypes, refining the design until it was right, and then going into production, Cook-Craigie was to be used where there was a high degree of confidence that the original design was adequate and production assured.

With this concept, all airframes would be built on the production line. One or two airframes would be built initially to verify the design; any fixes would then be incorporated into the following production airframes. The early builds were to undergo rebuilding to final tactical configuration once that had been achieved. Imposing both of these radically new approaches to acquisition, along with simultaneously attempting to set new states-of-the-art in aerodynamics, propulsion, and electronics, led to the extremely long development times and extensive rebuilding programs that both the F-102 and F-106 endured.

In an era when smartphones have more computing power than a building-size vacuum-tube computer of the 1960s, it is hard to realize just how far the concept of the F-106 was in advance of its time, or the available technology. In some ways, it is no idle claim to say that today's fourth- and fifth-generation Stealth fighters are just now catching up to where the Six was in the mid-1960s.

Equipped with a state-of-the-art digital computer (the first true digital computer designed for, or used on, an aircraft) employing a rapid-tuning, frequency-agile radar with world-class electronic countermeasures (ECCM) capability; multiple, integrated sensors; a directional datalink receiver tied in to the automatic flight control system enabling automatic, ground-controlled, emissions silent operation; a "God's-eye view" tactical situation display that showed both target and fighter location; a fuel/range arc as well as geographic location, selectable navigation and airfield information (completely new concepts in cockpit instrumentation that later became a worldwide standard); a variety of internally carried weapons designed for all-weather operation; more than Mach 2.2 speed; more than 60,000-foot altitude capability; and finally, long unrefueled range. That was the F-106 in 1964. Add aerial refueling capability and high-Mach external fuel tanks giving intercontinental range, and you have the Six as it existed in 1968.

The F-106 actually came into existence when the original F-102 program was split into two parts. Initially, the F-102 was designated as WS-201 and known as the 1954 interceptor. It was to have a first-line lifespan of 1954 through 1959. Because technology was unable to meet the demands of the air force, development was far slower than anticipated or desired. Given that, the F-102A was eventually intended to merely be an interim airframe while the FCS and engine matured enough to provide the performance the air force demanded.

The ultimate F-102B version was to have the Hughes MX-1179 FCS and Wright J67 engine while keeping the same airframe as the interim jet. The programs started to diverge when the original YF-102 failed to achieve supersonic speeds and had to be hastily modified to more closely meet the newly proposed "ideal body theory," better known as the "area rule." The wedge was driven wider with cancellation of the J67 turbojet, a further expansion of the area rule theory to cover speeds up to Mach 2, and uncounted delays with the FCS. By the time the F-102B finally flew, virtually all that remained from the interim jet was the delta wing and a broad family resemblance to its XF-92 and F-102 predecessors.

Hun, Deuce, Thud, or Phantom, all aircraft have popular names. But while sometimes described as a Cadillac, it was always simply the Six to all who were associated with it. This is the story of the "Ultimate Interceptor," the F-106 Delta Dart.

Chapter One

BIRTH OF THE F-102B

Four Delta Darts from the Michigan ANG climb to altitude as they head north over the "thumb" of Michigan in April 1978.

When the YF-102A "Hot Rod" successfully completed its first flight on 19 December 1954, there was a huge sigh of relief throughout both Convair and the air force; they finally had an airplane with higher performance than the F-86D. With the ability to meet the interim contractual obligations in sight, thoughts turned toward the long overdue "Ultimate 1954 Interceptor."

But huge hurdles remained. The F-102A was seriously overweight and, in addition to a complete redesign of the entire airframe to accommodate the "ideal body" theory, a simultaneous weight reduction program was begun that eliminated nearly a ton of excess weight that had accumulated. This soaked up much of the money and talent that was supposed to have been spent on the F-102B. Meanwhile, in March 1954, Air Materiel Command (AMC) declared the E-9 FCS inad-

equate for use with the F-102. Requiring Hughes to improve the system resulted in further delay in the far more complicated MX-1179, which was already progressing poorly. In September, Hughes announced a two-year delay with the MX-1179, deferring flight trials until 1957 and production until 1958. Among other changes made at this time, the original electronically scanned 40-inch radar dish was discarded as impractical, and a much smaller 23-inch-diameter antenna, the same size used for the F-102, was settled on.

Meanwhile, in San Diego, large portions of the Convair work force were busy redesigning, tearing out, and replacing more than half of the recently installed production tooling for the F-102. A separate group of engineers also continued to work closely with NACA and Dr. Richard Whitcomb on aerodynamics. Dr. Whitcomb's original area rule theory merely covered operations in the transonic region, but he later expanded his original work to include speeds up to Mach 2. Because of the slap-dash manner in which the original YF-102 was modified into the YF-102A, it was blindingly obvious to everyone concerned that the original concept of the F-102A and F-102B sharing the same airframe and merely having different power plants and avionics was no longer viable. As Dr. Whitcomb refined his theories and wind tunnel tests progressed, the differences between the F-102A and F-102B planforms became more and more

pronounced until it became evident that the F-102B was going to have to start from a fresh sheet of paper.

This played havoc with the Cook-Craigie production philosophy. But with the program already slipping badly and the need increasing, the air force decided to continue along the path originally chosen, accepting the increased costs for, hopefully, a decreased amount of time before the ultimate aircraft could be delivered. As 1954 slipped into 1955, most of Convair's focus was still on trying

Showing a distinct resemblance to the early Lippisch DM-1, this XF-92 nevertheless shows the planform that would evolve into the F-102 and F-106. (USAF via Isham)

Compare the differences between an F-102A and the prototype F-106A. The air inlets are mounted higher and farther aft on the Six. The fuselage is slimmed down, and the upward reflex on the tips of the Case X wing on the Deuce is very evident. The external wing fences also stand out.

Aerodynamic refinements to the F-106 created a much sleeker airframe than the rather portly predecessor. The Six went to a dual nose wheel versus the single wheel of the deuce. (Convair)

On the final version of the Six, the intakes had been thinned and squared off, while slots in the leading edges of the wings replaced the fences.

The hollow nose of the XF-92 has given way to side-mounted air intakes to allow the radar to be placed there, as evidenced here on this very early YF-102-CO. While the weapons bay doors are visible, the metal nose indicates that no radar was installed on this jet; it is simply an aerodynamic test vehicle. (USAF via Isham)

This YF-102 shows the drag chute compartment, original speed brake locations, and high drag exhaust area, as well as the J-57 exhaust nozzle. (USAF via Isham)

The second YF-102 built has been modified with a much longer and rather droopy nose. Compare it to the late big-tail F-102A-60-CO in the background. Significant differences exist in the main landing gear, vertical fin, nose, and canopy, among other changes. (USAF via Isham)

This fiscal year (FY) 1954 F-102A-30-CO is considerably different from the earlier YF-102. It has been changed to make it more closely conform to the area rule. It was easier to add the fillets on the aft fuselage than to widen the fuselage. (NASA)

Compared to the earlier F-102, the fuselage on the F-106 was lengthened, the air inlets were moved aft, the tail was truncated, and the trailing edge swept back. The Six's fuselage has also been area ruled to a much larger extent. While the wings may superficially look the same, there are differences in the camber of the leading edges, and wing tips. (Convair photo 25716 via Isham)

Convair History

In 1943, Consolidated Aircraft and Vultee Aircraft merged to become the Consolidated-Vultee Aircraft Corporation, almost always known as Convair. Largely on the basis of winning the MX-1554 production contract, Convair was bought by the Electric Boat Company and the resulting organization became known as General Dynamics. While Electric Boat continued to build submarines for the U.S. Navy, the Convair division not only designed and produced both experimental and production aircraft for commercial use, for the U.S. Navy, and for the U.S. Air Force, it also moved into missile and rocket projects, producing both the Terrier missile for the navy and the Atlas (intercontinental ballistic missile) ICBM for the air force.

The 1980s-era Convair logo. (Convair via Mike Machat)

to make the F-102A a combat-ready aircraft. However, a nucleus of engineers went to work on the F-102B and were immediately beset with additional problems.

One of the consequences of splitting the F-102 program into two parts was that although the components for the airframe could be financed from production funds, development of the J67 and MX-1179 FCS had to come from far less plentiful research money. But the real problem was that due to all of the previous delays, the F-102A had lost its interim status and was starting to play a larger part in the air defense planning, at the expense of the F-102B.

While Convair engineers feverishly worked to make the new F-102B as aerodynamically "clean" as possible, technical difficulties with the Hughes FCS were standing in the way of timely development. Many of the problems Hughes was facing were due to the fact that existing analog systems were unable to accurately handle the very high closure rates of jet-powered aircraft. That was the reason Hughes decided upon designing the world's first airborne digital computer, which they referred to as the Digitair, for the MX-1179. They felt that only a digital system could make computations rapidly enough to handle the higher speeds.

Although trying to squeeze more speed out of the analog systems was extremely difficult, trying to design a leading-edge digital computer (in an era when digital computers were little more than esoteric research projects) was even more so. As Hughes had earlier forecast, the additional effort they were putting in to making the redesigned E-9 FCS work satisfactorily in the F-102 slowed development of the MX-1179 for the F-102B even further.

Air force indecision on weapons loads and a basic funding problem also slowed progress. While originally specifying the armament capability of the F-102B to be 1 atomic rocket and 2.75-inch Folding Fin Aerial Rockets (FFAR), the air force also wanted an alternate load of 6 Falcons and 40 2.75-inch rockets. But then the influence of the bomber generals and the massed raids of World War II was felt. Since the cost of using nuclear weapons was predicted to be far less than for a conventional defense, the "cost per kill" dictated that all types of defensive weapons employed for air defense be atomic.

According to this theory, nuclear weapons were more desirable than conventional ones because they had a higher "kill" rate against attacking formations, both against the weapons themselves and the aircraft. They would also force dispersal of the enemy attack, thus negating the advantages seen by massed USAAF bomber fleets during World War II. An additional byproduct was the probable psychological demoralization of enemy air crews subject to a nuclear attack.

In the naivety of the time, virtually no concern was given to the negative aftereffects of detonating thousands of defensive nuclear weapons in the skies above the North American continent. To carry out this policy, the Air Defense Command (ADC) issued a requirement that every type of interceptor within the ADC must have nuclear capability by FY 1959. That meant that on top of everything else, Convair was now struggling to find a way to load two of the new unguided Ding Dong rockets onto their new interceptors.

Another source of delay was the engine. In the initial proposal, Convair planned to use the Curtiss-Wright J67 engine, which was

F·102B INBOARD PROFILE

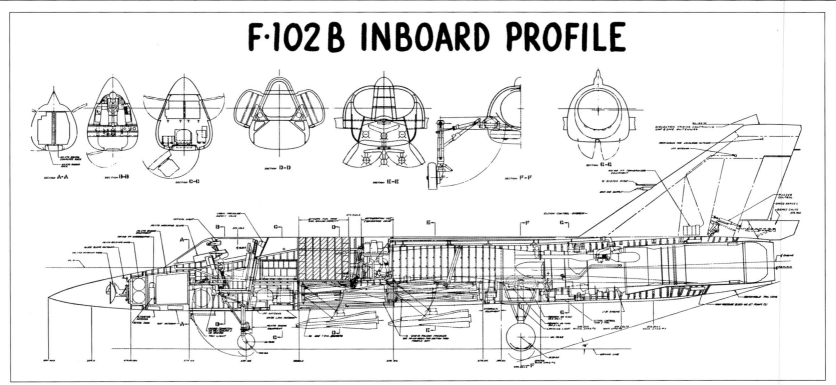

The outlines of the F-106 are starting to become apparent in this drawing of the F-102B. Later refinements included extending the nose to give more volume for the Hughes MA-1, and altering the weapons bay from carrying the six Falcons shown here to four Falcons and a Genie. The speed brakes, tail cone, and engine exhaust were significantly altered as well. The short, single-piece ventral doors lasted through the first two F-106A prototypes before being changed to a longer, bi-fold version. (Via Kaston)

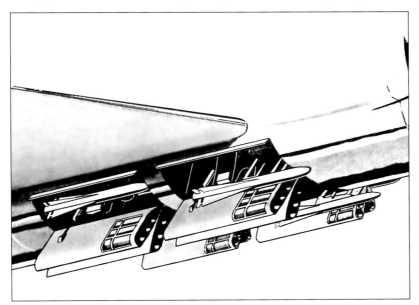

Here is another early proposal for arming the F-102B. Six Falcon missiles and at least 24 2.75-inch FFAR rockets can be seen here in small individual bays. With the advent of the AIR-2 Genie, this proposal was quickly dropped. (USAF via Isham)

An all-too-frequent occurrence during J40 engine testing: This engine disintegrated on the Westinghouse Philadelphia test stand because of metal fatigue in the compressor section. The J40 was intended to be an interim for the F-102 while awaiting the Curtiss-Wright J67. When neither engine was successful, the Pratt & Whitney J57 and J75 were selected to power the F-102A and F-102B. (Westinghouse via Mark Frankel)

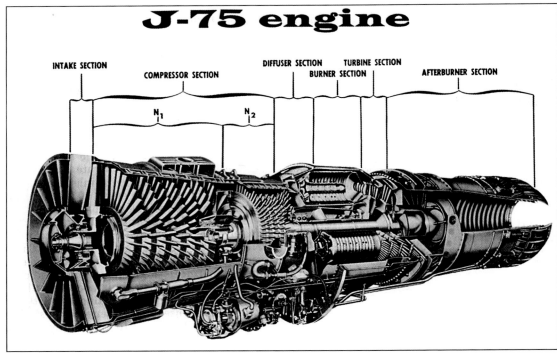

J-75 engine

INTAKE SECTION
COMPRESSOR SECTION
DIFFUSER SECTION
BURNER SECTION
TURBINE SECTION
AFTERBURNER SECTION

N_1

N_2

The all-stainless-steel Pratt & Whitney J75 was virtually indestructible. This illustration shows the basic layout of the twin-spool engine and its afterburner. (USAF)

to be a growth development of the existing Bristol Aero Engines Olympus. But the Bristol engine produced only around 9,500 pounds thrust and needed serious redesign to bring it up to the 15,000-pound class needed by the new interceptor. By August 1953, Wright was well over a year behind in adapting the J67 engine to the future F-102B, and the air force was rapidly losing confidence in it. As Wright's troubles with the J67 continued, the new Pratt & Whitney J75 continued to gain favor.

Because of its superior performance and more favorable production outlook, the first F-102B prototypes were slated to use the J75-P-1 as an interim engine. In April 1955, the air force made the switch permanent and the J75-P-9 was formally substituted for the larger and heavier J67. This decision was more than justified, and it allowed Convair to reduce the fuselage cross section considerably, as the J75 was both smaller and lighter than the J67. However, it resulted in yet another major redesign of the new airframe, which by now showed only a family resemblance to its progenitor.

The cascading delays in the F-102 program finally became too much for the ADC. They needed a new high-speed interceptor and they wanted it yesterday. Partly stemming from a fear of what might happen if all the Convair interceptors were grounded due to some unforeseen problems and partly due to the extended development times, in February 1955, ADC finally received approval from HQ USAF to have the McDonnell F-101 Voodoo developed as an area defense interceptor.

Even though that aircraft was showing some serious deficiencies as well, notably compressor stalls and uncontrolled "pitch-up" events, McDonnell was told to stop development of the IF-101A single-place interceptor and make the new interceptor into a two-man aircraft. Since all Long Range Interceptor proposals had been deemed unsuitable by HQ USAF in a competition in November 1954, the F-101B was slotted to fill the long-range role and the F-102A/B fleet was left filling the medium-range role.

But in a classic case of having to "be careful what you ask for," that approval came with a high price, as the planned purchase of the F-102B was reduced by the same number of F-101Bs that were added. That meant that in 1959, ADC would have 10 fewer squadrons of F-102Bs than previously planned. And the addition of yet another interceptor development program left Hughes completely overwhelmed. As a result, RCA was brought onboard to do a large portion of the work modifying the one-man MG-3 system for use with the much faster, two-man F-101B, as well as to continue development work on the 40-inch radar dish for use on both the F-101 and F-106.

There were straws in the wind that even greater changes were coming. In August 1955, HQ USAF asked ADC to prepare an alternate plan of forces that would reduce the planned 69 squadrons of interceptors to 35. ADC threw a fit, but to no avail.

Meanwhile, the air force general staff and ADC continued to argue about what weapons they wanted the F-102B to carry. Capabilities of the MA-1 had to be designed specifically for the types of weapons to be launched. Since space, carriage, and launching provisions had to be made for the weapons in the new airframe, this indecision caused huge problems for both contractors. The only thing the air force was firm on was that the new interceptor had to be able to carry at least one of the new AIR-2 rockets and that, if carried at all, the new Super Falcon missiles would be used in lieu of the older generation of Falcons.

In July 1955, ADC agreed to change the F-102B armament to a single Ding Dong plus the advanced Falcons (the 4+1 configuration) as long as nothing was done to prevent the F-102B from eventually carrying two of the rockets if it was deemed desirable. ADC also agreed to experiments with a configuration that would permit six Falcons on the F-102B, as long as the experimentation did not further delay the program.

Airplane and Weapon Control Interceptor System

As development progressed, the original MX-1179 project was renamed MA-1. Designed solely for the F-102B, it was more than just an FCS, it was the world's first Aircraft Weapon and Control System (AWCIS). It not only controlled the launching of the armament, but using either ground-based datalink or guidance from the onboard radar, it could also fly the aircraft. The radar and all communication and navigation gear was part of the system as well. Under optimum conditions, the pilot was simply there to make the takeoff, control the interceptor's speed, operate the onboard radar to find and lock on to the target, select the weapons and allow the MA-1 to fire them

when it felt the kill probability was highest, select a homing point, and put the landing gear down and land. The electronics did the rest.

However, although the MA-1 was expected to be a great improvement over the earlier E-series of FCSs, ADC felt that it still fell short of their requirements. The low-altitude capability of the system was far from ideal due to inherent constraints in pulsed radar. Hughes tried to overcome the problem of ground clutter by including an airborne moving target indictor (AMTI). This offered some increase in detection range at low altitudes, but it required exceptional skill for the pilot to operate the radar in this mode. The problem of determining the range to target against a noise jammer, and thus the proper time to launch armament, also had not been solved. Hughes

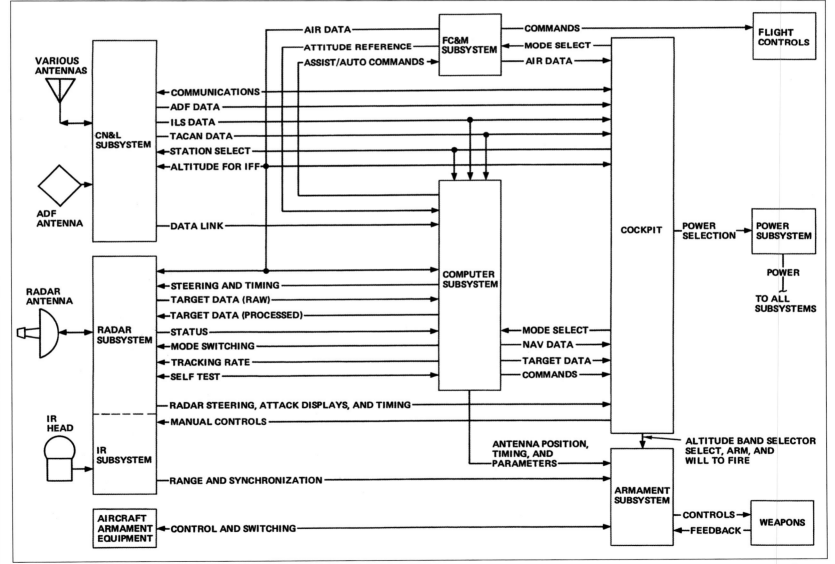

This diagram gives some idea of the complexity of information flow within the Hughes MX-1179/MA-1 Aircraft Weapon and Control System. Everything revolved around the Digitair computer. (USAF)

had built into the system the ability to determine the azimuth and altitude of a target using electronic countermeasures (ECM) but had not yet solved the problem of calculating the range. In view of the fact that the MA-1 had been undergoing development since 1950, ADC thought that a more advanced system should be in the works and urged HQ USAF to make Hughes redouble its efforts to correct the deficiencies in the MA-1.

On 1 November 1955, the Air Research and Development Command (ARDC) issued System Requirement No. 8, which described the mission of WS 201-B as follows: "The F-102B will accomplish interception and destruction of attacking vehicles at all altitudes up to 70,000 feet and within a radius of 375 nautical miles under all weather conditions. The interceptions will be accomplished at speeds up to Mach 2.0 at 35,000 feet and with the flight being under automatic guidance provided by the ground environment (SAGE) and aircraft's fire control system. The destruction of enemy targets will be affected by guided missiles and atomic warhead rockets."

Later that month, the air force finally issued a contract for the first 17 F-102Bs. Hoping to avoid the problems of the F-102A launch, all of the aircraft were allocated for testing. As an example of how far the priority for the F-102B had slipped, there were nearly 750 F-102As on order by the time of the first F-102B contract. The contract specified that the first prototype had to fly by the end of 1956, the second aircraft by January 1957, and the remaining deliveries were to begin in July 1957, a point that was halfway through the projected lifespan of the originally conceived aircraft.

The initial order was for air force serial numbers (S/N) 56-0451 through 56-0467, and these aircraft received Convair Model numbers ranging from 8-20 through 8-23. The first two were considered prototypes and never intended to be more than aerodynamic test vehicles. As such, they had no provisions for either the MA-1 AWCIS or weapons.

The first cockpit mockup inspection of the F-102B, demonstrating the expected layout of the MA-1, was carried out in December 1955 and resulted in serious consternation on the part of the air force. Convair and Hughes displayed a number of ideas that were totally unlike anything ever seen before in an aircraft. Vertical tape flight instruments replaced the conventional round-dial types. And if that was not enough, what really caused the air force to do a double take was that Convair had designed the world's first side-stick–controlled aircraft. The control stick was mounted on the right-side panel of the cockpit, not in the traditional location. This was done to provide an unobstructed view of the equally radical 10-inch-diameter Horizontal Map Display (which was eventually reduced in size by an inch and later known as the Tactical Situation Display). This was located between the bottom of the instrument panel and the floorboard between the pilot's legs where the control stick was traditionally placed. After recovering from their initial astonishment, numerous follow-on discussions between the air force, Hughes, and Convair ensued.

According to Hughes, the MA-1/F-106 system was the first to be designed for operation with continuous-command displays of speed, altitude, and heading. On the new tape instruments, not only was the altitude, speed, and heading of the interceptor shown, but the same parameters were given, via datalink from the SAGE system, for the target aircraft that the interceptor was "paired on" to destroy. In addition, a third set of markers showed the altitude, speed, and heading that the interceptor was directed to fly to complete the intercept.

Extensive research was conducted by Hughes in the early days of the MA-1 development on human interaction with the new instrument displays, but the air force was not satisfied and demanded a flight test demonstration to prove that the new vertical instrumentation was safe and effective. Likewise, they wanted proof that the new side stick controller actually worked. As a result, two early F-102 aircraft (S/N 53-1805 and S/N 53-1813) were modified to use the new cockpit displays and 53-1813 received the new side stick controller as well. Flight testing of the new instrumentation was to be conducted under the auspices of the Wright Air Development Center.

In the interim, the decision was made to develop two cockpit configurations simultaneously in the first 12 aircraft. Of the new interceptors, 6 would have a conventional cockpit with a standard, center-mounted control stick, conventional round instrument gauges, and some non-standard items such as the TSD (this was known as the B cockpit). Provisions would be made for the side stick control, however, and this configuration became known as the Sacred Six.

The other six jets were to have the A cockpit configuration, with side-mounted control sticks (and provisions for a center stick), vertical tape instruments, and the horizontal map display. In both cases, the radar scope would be mounted on the top center of the instrument panel, as with the F-102A.

The March 1956 Cockpit Mockup review reaffirmed the flight test requirements, but since none of the first 12 F-106s had an MA-1 to drive either the vertical instruments or the TSD, the directive was meaningless. In the end, they each received whatever instrumentation they needed for their roles in the flight test program, and testing continued with the two F-102s.

At the end of the cockpit review meeting, recently approved armament changes were again discussed. Like the F-102A, the F-102B suffered from a distinct inability on the part of the air force to finalize the weapons load. Numerous concepts had been put forth by Convair, but competing factions within the air force kept changing the planned weapons. Every time the proposed weapons load changed, it implied redesigns or alterations of the weapons bay, weapons bay door actuators, missile launching equipment, and the associated aircraft wiring, as well as additions or subtractions to the capabilities of the MA-1. This made it virtually impossible to finalize the design of the new interceptor.

Round-Eye Versus Vertical Tape: Advances in Instrumentation

When Convair and Hughes presented their original mockup of what became the F-106 to the air force, one of the many features of the cockpit was the new approach to flight instruments. Until this point, all aircraft had used traditional round gauges, laid out on the instrument panel seemingly without any particular pattern beyond a tendency for engine gauges to be placed on the right. Because fighter aircraft did not engage in combat in the clouds, each manufacturer distributed flight instruments around the cockpit wherever they fit.

The F-106 and Republic F-105 were the first attempts to standardize cockpit instrumentation and use the "T" instrument layout. Realizing the limitations of earlier instrument panel layouts, and since both aircraft were designed to be employed in all-weather conditions, serious efforts were made to make instrument flying safer and easier for the single pilots. Using the concept of "control" and "performance" instruments, a large Attitude Directional Indicator (ADI) was located at the top center of the instrument panel. This instrument not only gave attitude information, it added bars for the instrument landing system and included a turn and slip indicator, combining three separate instruments into one easy-to-interpret instrument.

A Horizontal Situation Indicator (HSI) was mounted directly beneath the attitude indicator and combined the functions of two or three earlier gauges. To the right of the ADI was the altimeter, and below that was the rate-of-climb indicator. To the left were airspeed and Mach indicators.

The "T" concept made instrument flying far easier as the primary attitude indicator was directly in front of the pilot's eyes and the instrument cross check involved simply setting the desired attitude on the ADI and then checking left, right, up, and down. This made flying instruments far more precise, and it eventually became the worldwide standard for flight instrumentation layout.

In addition, both jets were the first to use the radical, vertical tape instrumentation. Instead of having a round gauge with a fixed indicator face, where a rotating pointer rotated to the appropriate speed, heading, or altitude, vertical tape instruments had fixed indices with the tapes moving beneath them to show the appropriate parameter.

The F-106 took that concept a step further. To the right of the ADI was the Altitude-Vertical Velocity Indicator. This instrument had three tapes: One showed the rate of climb or descent, one showed the aircraft's altitude, a third tape showed the target altitude and cabin altitude. To the left of the ADI, the Airspeed-Mach Indicator also had three individual tapes. Moving command markers were

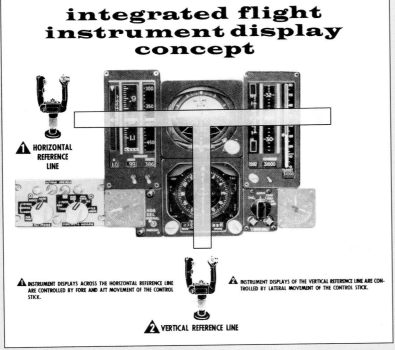

This page out of the pilot's manual for the F-106 graphically illustrates the simplicity of the concept behind the "T" instrument crosscheck, and how the instruments in a vertical-tape-equipped Six were laid out. (USAF)

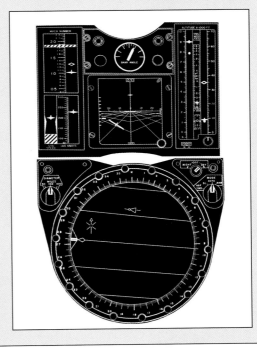

Here is a diagram of a notional Hughes instrument panel. The final configuration was vastly improved over this early (and basically unreadable) attempt. All the information was there, but trying to find it was a nightmare. (Hughes via Kaston)

incorporated and tied into the SAGE system through the datalink and MA-1. Those would visually indicate the target altitude as well as the commanded speed, heading, and altitude for the interceptor, among other functions.

The final new innovation was the inclusion of a Tactical Situation Display. This device was far ahead of its time and would be quite at home inside any current-generation fighter. Originally a 10-inch display, the final configuration shrunk by an inch. Located between the bottom of the instrument panel and the cockpit floor, it sat between the pilot's legs. Maps were automatically selected by tuning in an Ultrahigh-Frequency Tactical Air Navigation (TACAN) station and by a range selector located near the display. They gave a view of either a 50-, 200-, or 400-mile radius, with the selected navaid as the center point. The interceptor was indicated by a small,

triangular "bug" that had a course line extending out in front of it.

If the SAGE system was providing data linked target data to the MA-1, a target symbol also appeared. If no target was provided, the symbol became a homing point indicator. A rotating command heading indicator gave a graphic display of what heading the pilot was supposed to fly. As fuel was burned down, the MA-1 generated a green arc that appeared on the display, showing the available range. The 50-mile display gave a terminal display with information on runways and the airfield. The 200-mile display had data for departure, recovery, and holding points; the 400-mile display was a navigation map and tactical display.

Due to delays in securing air force approval for the new instruments, the first two production aircraft using the vertical tape instrumentation were an F-106A (S/N 57-2465) and an F-106B (S/N

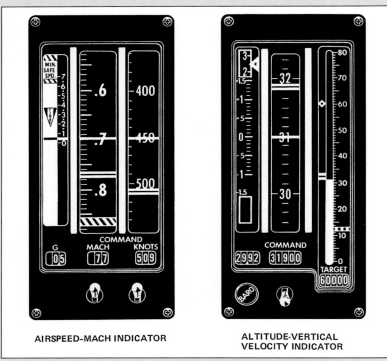

AIRSPEED–MACH INDICATOR

ALTITUDE-VERTICAL VELOCITY INDICATOR

The final vertical tapes used in the F-106. Note how much more legible and intelligible the indications are. Moving diagonal stripes indicate limits. Fixed horizontal lines in the center indicate current aircraft performance. Moving double-line indicators give aircraft commands, and diamond indicators give target information. The left-hand instrument gives Angle of Attack (AOA), Mach, and Airspeed, while the right-hand gauge gives Vertical Velocity and Altitude. The far right indicator graphically displays not only interceptor and target altitude, but cabin altitude as well. (USAF)

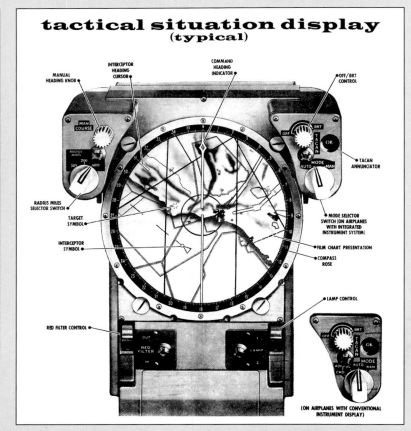

This is what the production Tactical Situation Display looked like. Color film was projected onto the screen from below to show terrain, navigational aids, approach plates, targets, remaining range, and interceptor location. It would be 40 years before something similar made its appearance in a tactical fighter again. (USAF)

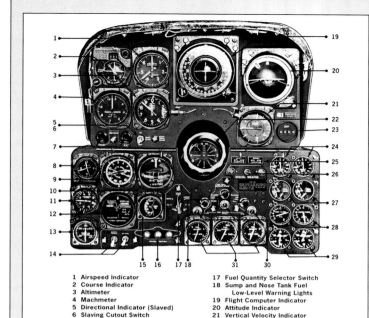

INSTRUMENT PANEL

1 Airspeed Indicator
2 Course Indicator
3 Altimeter
4 Machmeter
5 Directional Indicator (Slaved)
6 Slaving Cutout Switch
7 Oxygen Warning Lights
8 Clock
9 Radio Magnetic Indicator
10 Turn and Slip Indicator
11 Accelerometer
12 Flight Computer Selector Switch
13 Cabin Pressure Altimeter Indicator
14 Cabin Pressure Switches
15 Free Air Temperature Gage
16 Landing Gear Position Indicator
17 Fuel Quantity Selector Switch
18 Sump and Nose Tank Fuel
    Low-Level Warning Lights
19 Flight Computer Indicator
20 Attitude Indicator
21 Vertical Velocity Indicator
22 Pilot's Radar Scope
23 UHF Frequency Indicator
24 Tachometers
25 Special Weapon Warning Lights
26 Special Weapon Selector Switch
27 Exhaust Gas Temperature Gages
28 Fuel Flowmeter Indicators
29 Oil Pressure Gages
30 Fuel Gage Test Switches
31 Fuel Quantity Gages

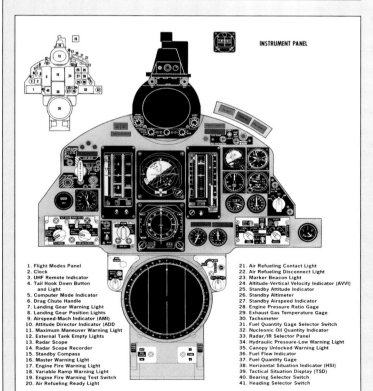

INSTRUMENT PANEL

1. Flight Modes Panel
2. Clock
3. UHF Remote Indicator
4. Tail Hook Down Button
   and Light
5. Computer Mode Indicator
6. Drag Chute Handle
7. Landing Gear Warning Light
8. Landing Gear Position Lights
9. Airspeed-Mach Indicator (AMI)
10. Attitude Director Indicator (ADD)
11. Maximum Maneuver Warning Light
12. External Tank Empty Lights
13. Radar Scope
14. Radar Scope Recorder
15. Standby Compass
16. Master Warning Light
17. Engine Fire Warning Light
18. Variable Ramp Warning Light
19. Engine Fire Warning Test Switch
20. Air Refueling Ready Light
21. Air Refueling Contact Light
22. Air Refueling Disconnect Light
23. Marker Beacon Light
24. Altitude-Vertical Velocity Indicator (AVVI)
25. Standby Attitude Indicator
26. Standby Altimeter
27. Standby Airspeed Indicator
28. Engine Pressure Ratio Gage
29. Exhaust Gas Temperature Gage
30. Tachometer
31. Fuel Quantity Gage Selector Switch
32. Nucleonic Oil Quantity Indicator
33. Radar/IR Selector Panel
34. Hydraulic Pressure-Low Warning Light
35. Canopy Unlocked Warning Light
36. Fuel Flow Indicator
37. Fuel Quantity Gage
38. Horizontal Situation Indicator (HSI)
39. Tactical Situation Display (TSD)
40. Bearing Selector Switch
41. Heading Selector Switch

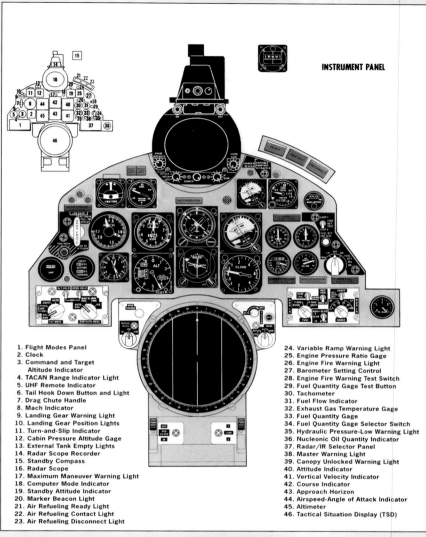

INSTRUMENT PANEL

1. Flight Modes Panel
2. Clock
3. Command and Target
   Altitude Indicator
4. TACAN Range Indicator Light
5. UHF Remote Indicator
6. Tail Hook Down Button and Light
7. Drag Chute Handle
8. Mach Indicator
9. Landing Gear Warning Light
10. Landing Gear Position Lights
11. Turn-and-Slip Indicator
12. Cabin Pressure Altitude Gage
13. External Tank Empty Lights
14. Radar Scope Recorder
15. Standby Compass
16. Radar Scope
17. Maximum Maneuver Warning Light
18. Computer Mode Indicator
19. Standby Attitude Indicator
20. Marker Beacon Light
21. Air Refueling Ready Light
22. Air Refueling Contact Light
23. Air Refueling Disconnect Light
24. Variable Ramp Warning Light
25. Engine Pressure Ratio Gage
26. Engine Fire Warning Light
27. Barometer Setting Control
28. Engine Fire Warning Test Switch
29. Fuel Quantity Gage Test Button
30. Tachometer
31. Fuel Flow Indicator
32. Exhaust Gas Temperature Gage
33. Fuel Quantity Gage
34. Fuel Quantity Gage Selector Switch
35. Hydraulic Pressure-Low Warning Light
36. Nucleonic Oil Quantity Indicator
37. Radar/IR Selector Panel
38. Master Warning Light
39. Canopy Unlocked Warning Light
40. Attitude Indicator
41. Vertical Velocity Indicator
42. Course Indicator
43. Approach Horizon
44. Airspeed-Angle of Attack Indicator
45. Altimeter
46. Tactical Situation Display (TSD)

F-89/round-eye/tape instrument panels. The Hughes Aircraft Company was responsible for bringing flight instruments into the jet age. The "T" crosscheck they designed remains the worldwide standard today. This photo montage provides a graphic illustration of how flight instruments evolved. An instrument panel for a Northrop F-89 Scorpion is on the upper left, the early conventional round-eye instrument panel for the F-106 is above, and the vertical-tape instrument panel is to the left. (Chong/USAF)

Seen here in May 1976 is the early layout of the conventional round-eye instruments. Note how the attitude indicator is not centered and the additional heading and ILS indicators are in the center of the panel. The airspeed indicator is on the upper left, while the vertical velocity is at the lower right. The round-eye Sixes also had a separate Mach indicator, which is the larger instrument on the far left. The ungainly device above the radar scope is a scope recorder that filmed intercepts. The tape would be downloaded after landing and used to debrief the intercepts. Also, note how worn the left handle of the yoke is, as the radar received a lot of use in a Six.

The magnetic compass and G-meter located at the apex of the windscreen in place of the optical sight for the Genie tell us that this photo was taken after the clear canopy was added. This Montana ANG Six has received an updated instrument layout. Compare the changes to the previous photo. (Don Spering/AIR)

57-2523). Both were added to the test fleet in approximately July 1959. Production changeover to the tape cockpits on the F-106A did not occur until another 40 round-eye jets had been built, at the start of the FY 1958 jets (S/N 58-0759). For some reason, the changeover to the new cockpits in the F-106B models was made in the middle of the FY 1957 production, with the 8th subsequent jet (S/N 57-2532).

The early tape-equipped jets were subject to the same electrical and engine failures as the rest of the fleet and added a few new problems of their own. According to one of the early 1st FW (Aair Defense, AD) pilots, "The original altimeter and vertical speed tapes were not in the final configuration and were . . . no good for making an instrument approach so our minimums went to 5,000 and 5! Quarter-size conventional altimeters and vertical speed instruments were installed on the glare shield so we could fly them until new tapes were designed."

This is what the cockpit of a tape-equipped Six looked like between 1968 and 1972. The optical Genie sight rotated down for use but was removed prior to installation of the gunsight. Note that the throttle was gray. (USAF)

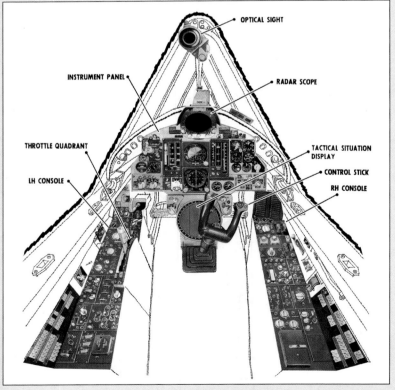

OPTICAL SIGHT

INSTRUMENT PANEL

RADAR SCOPE

THROTTLE QUADRANT

TACTICAL SITUATION DISPLAY

CONTROL STICK

RH CONSOLE

LH CONSOLE

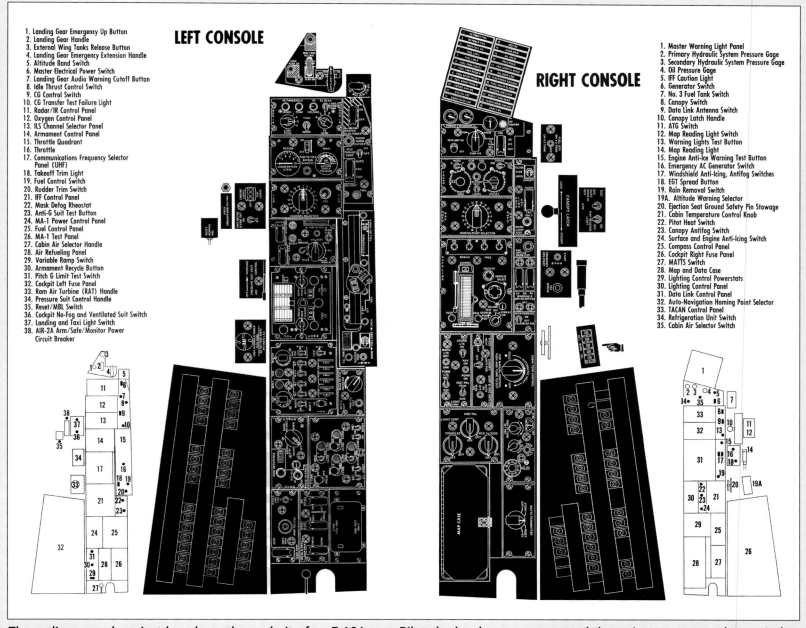

LEFT CONSOLE

1. Landing Gear Emergency Up Button
2. Landing Gear Handle
3. External Wing Tanks Release Button
4. Landing Gear Emergency Extension Handle
5. Altitude Band Switch
6. Master Electrical Power Switch
7. Landing Gear Audio Warning Cutoff Button
8. Idle Thrust Control Switch
9. CG Control Switch
10. CG Transfer Test Failure Light
11. Radar/IR Control Panel
12. Oxygen Control Panel
13. ILS Channel Selector Panel
14. Armament Control Panel
15. Throttle Quadrant
16. Throttle
17. Communications Frequency Selector Panel (UHF)
18. Takeoff Trim Light
19. Fuel Control Switch
20. Rudder Trim Switch
21. IFF Control Panel
22. Mask Defog Rheostat
23. Anti-G Suit Test Button
24. MA-1 Power Control Panel
25. Fuel Control Panel
26. MA-1 Test Panel
27. Cabin Air Selector Handle
28. Air Refueling Panel
29. Variable Ramp Switch
30. Armament Recycle Button
31. Pitch G Limit Test Switch
32. Cockpit Left Fuse Panel
33. Ram Air Turbine (RAT) Handle
34. Pressure Suit Control Handle
35. Reset/MBL Switch
36. Cockpit No-Fog and Ventilated Suit Switch
37. Landing and Taxi Light Switch
38. AIR-2A Arm/Safe/Monitor Power Circuit Breaker

RIGHT CONSOLE

1. Master Warning Light Panel
2. Primary Hydraulic System Pressure Gage
3. Secondary Hydraulic System Pressure Gage
4. Oil Pressure Gage
5. IFF Caution Light
6. Generator Switch
7. No. 3 Fuel Tank Switch
8. Canopy Switch
9. Data Link Antenna Switch
10. Canopy Latch Handle
11. ATG Switch
12. Map Reading Light Switch
13. Warning Lights Test Button
14. Map Reading Light
15. Engine Anti-Ice Warning Test Button
16. Emergency AC Generator Switch
17. Windshield Anti-Icing, Antifog Switches
18. EGT Spread Button
19. Rain Removal Switch
19A. Altitude Warning Selector
20. Ejection Seat Ground Safety Pin Stowage
21. Cabin Temperature Control Knob
22. Pitot Heat Switch
23. Canopy Antifog Switch
24. Surface and Engine Anti-Icing Switch
25. Compass Control Panel
26. Cockpit Right Fuse Panel
27. MATTS Switch
28. Map and Data Case
29. Lighting Control Powerstats
30. Lighting Control Panel
31. Data Link Control Panel
32. Auto-Navigation Homing Point Selector
33. TACAN Control Panel
34. Refrigeration Unit Switch
35. Cabin Air Selector Switch

These diagrams show just how busy the cockpit of an F-106 was. Pilots had to have great manual dexterity to operate the myriad radar and weapons switches, especially if they were also hand flying the jet. Both sides of the rear bulkhead were covered with fuses. (USAF)

Chapter Two

EARLY DEVELOPMENT

Over Edwards AFB, California, in 1957, the prototype Six is entering the traffic pattern after a test flight. The short ventral bay doors are evident, and it has been repainted in a high-visibility scheme, indicating that this is later in the test program, but the sleek lines of the jet are very evident. (Convair)

Meanwhile, design work, tooling, and preparations for production of the new F-102B continued. In July 1956, a modified F-102A (S/N 53-1813) became the first aircraft to be flown using a side stick controller when Convair test pilots Richard Johnson and Joe Fitzpatrick test flew the aircraft. Gen. Albert Boyd, Deputy Commander of ARDC, flew the aircraft the following month. These initial test flights resulted in reducing the size of the control grip, adding an armrest behind the stick grip due to arm fatigue (something that had to be relearned a generation later during the F-16 program), and some other minor changes.

Although a decision to retain the side stick as standard on production models of the F-106 was reached during a configuration meeting in December 1955, a possible indication of changes to come was evident in a Convair publicity film of Gen. Boyd's flight: The body language and gestures of the general showed that he did not appear at all happy after flying the unusual jet.

Convair engineers continued to work closely with NACA on high-speed aerodynamics and refining the wing for high-speed capability. As with the F-102, two wings were applied to the F-106. Continued wind tunnel testing showed that by adding a "conical camber" to the wing (which increasingly "rolled" the leading edge down as you moved from the fuselage to the tip), both low-speed handling and high-altitude capabilities were increased.

The original wing installed on the F-102 was known as the Case X wing. It was replaced with a Case XX wing toward the end of the fiscal year (FY) 1956 F-102 production run and flight tested by

Side-by-side comparison in 1965 showing the differences between the Case XIV wing on the left and the Case XXIX wing on the right. Note how the tip of the early wing flips upward slightly near the aileron joint and how the later wing rolls farther downward near the wingtip. Both jets have the later-style main wheels. (Terry Love Collection)

the Air Force Flight Test Center (AFFTC) in July and August 1957. The Case XX wing had increased conical camber, larger elevons, and eliminated the reflex (the flare, or bend, upward at the tip) that was present on the Case X wing. The initial F-106 builds received the Case XIV wing, which was a middle ground between the two types of F-102 wings and had a minimal upward reflex on the tip, which is very difficult to see in photographs.

Even before the first aircraft rolled off the assembly line, plans were underway to go to the final Case XXIX wing. This wing added a 10-percent conical camber to the semi-span and, as with the Case XX wing, eliminated the slight upward reflex at the tip, leaving the wingtip flush with the elevons when they were neutral. However, unlike the Case XX wing, the elevons remained the same size as on the early wing. According to Sacramento Air Logistics Center (ALC) engineers, once an airframe had been built with a given wing, it retained that wing configuration for the remainder of its lifetime.

As with the F-102, Convair was apparently quite unconcerned about the flight quality of the different wings and absolutely nothing was written into the F-106 pilot's manual explaining the change. Furthermore, there was no change in either block number or manufacturer designation when the change occurred. In fact, exactly which aircraft received the first Case XXIX wing is still a mystery. Convair planning documents from August 1956 clearly show that S/N 57-0237 (model 8-24, number six) was intended to be the first jet to receive the wing, but other evidence points to S/N 56-0467 (the last of the FY 1956 aircraft built) actually being the first. Because there was no published guidance explaining the differences, in later years, some pilots, noticing the slight reflex on the tip of the Case XIV wings during preflight, thought that the wings had been overstressed and refused to fly the aircraft.

The wings fitted to roughly the first two dozen aircraft built also initially included the same type of external wing fences as the F-102. These were intended to control the span-wise flow of air. Air flowing over the tops of the wings had a tendency to be deflected toward the wingtips, leading to early airflow separation and buffeting. However, wind tunnel testing showed that the fences had excessive drag, vibration, and fatigue problems at the higher speeds the F-102B was expected to achieve. A simple solution was devised that added a slot, or notch, in the leading edge of the wing. This allowed an energized airflow to effectively control the airflow with both less weight and far less drag.

Once testing showed this elegant solution to be effective, the fences were removed from those initial F-106As (S/Ns 56-0451 through 57-0237) and F-106Bs (S/Ns 57-2507 through 57-2515) test aircraft that had them installed. Removing the fences simply involved removing the screws that held the fences onto the wings, filling the resulting holes, and replacing approximately an 18-inch section of the leading edge. The second prototype (S/N 56-0452) was the first to have the external fences replaced with the leading-edge slots, and this change was made in December 1957.

Many of the remaining FY 1956 jets had the changes made in the April and May 1958 timeframe. The 34th airframe completed (S/N 57-0238) was the first to roll off the assembly line without them.

In addition to the aerodynamics work, Convair also worked closely with Hughes to ensure that the new airframe mated with the MA-1 FCS and the newly designed Super Falcon missiles. By this time, the differences between the interim and ultimate versions of the aircraft were so significant that Maj. Gen. Thetus C. Odom, Commander of the San Antonio Air Material Area (which handled air force logistics for both aircraft) recommended that the F-102B

The third F-106A was the last to carry F-102–style "buzz numbers" on the fuselage and the last one to carry them in the forward location. It was the first Six with full-length weapons bay doors and hot air exhaust (seen here as a small notch) vent in the upper spine on the fuselage. The external fences on the wings have been removed and replaced with the slot, and it is sporting a replacement ejector in this October 1958 photo. (USAF via Isham)

aircraft be redesignated due to its (now pronounced) dissimilarity to the F-102A.

His proposal was based on the fact that only about 12 percent of the parts were then common between the two aircraft and that the percentage was continuing to decline. HQ USAF accepted the recommendation and on 29 June 1956, with construction of the first aircraft well underway, the F-102B became the F-106A. With that, the program split that began five years previously became final.

In September 1956 the air force added to the previously issued ARDC System Requirement by stating that the new F-106 would carry guided missiles and rockets with atomic warheads (later known as the 4+1 configuration) and it must be available by August 1958, some four years past the original deadline of the original Ultimate Interceptor plan. HQ USAF also re-endorsed the Cook-Craigie production concept for the F-106 and issued a System Development Directive calling for concurrent development and production of the new aircraft. At roughly the same time, and in recognition of now vast differences between the F-102 and F-106, and the difficulties that the earlier jet was having, the number of aircraft planned for the test fleet was increased from 17 to 39.

Both prime manufacturers were still paying only partial attention to the F-106 because difficulties with the F-102A were taking a great deal of time, talent, and money away from the new system.

Engineering Change Proposals for both production line changes and post-production modifications for the F-102 fleet were burgeoning as both Convair and Hughes tried to get the F-102 ready for introduction into ADC squadron service. In an ominous foreshadowing of the future, the Convair and Hughes forces at Palmdale were busy rebuilding the first 458 F-102As into a standardized configuration and trying to replace the early MG-3 FCS with the updated MG-10 version.

The San Antonio Air Materiel Area (SAAMA) staff was also showing the strain, as they were overwhelmed trying to keep the F-102 program under control and take on the F-106 at the same time. In addition to trying to keep configuration control over all of the changes being introduced on both jets, SAAMA and Convair were working on several major modification programs to the F-102. In addition, SAAMA was trying to set up programmed Inspect and Repair as Necessary (IRAN) maintenance lines for the F-102 fleet.

For the F-106, SAMMA was still trying to determine exactly what the maintenance and logistics plans for the new aircraft were going to be. Continual turf wars between the ARDC and the AMC, along with inputs from both ADC and HQ USAF made managing development of both aircraft exceptionally difficult.

Regardless of heroic attempts to keep parts standardization under control, the literally "aircraft-by-aircraft" differences made

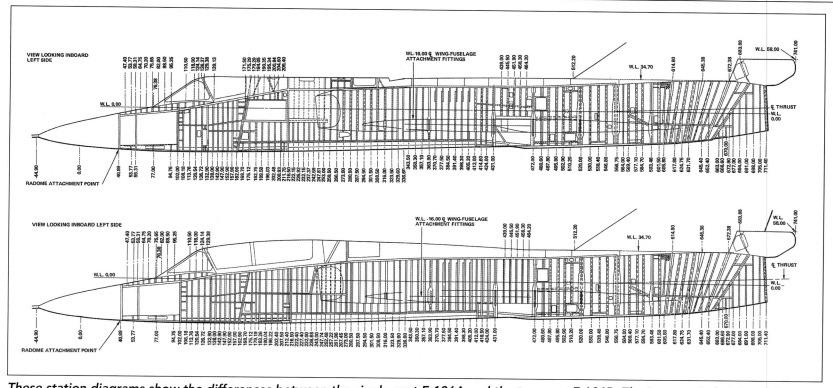

These station diagrams show the differences between the single-seat F-106A and the two-seat F-106B. The increase in height of the spine does not start directly at the base of the tail, but rather a few feet forward. Adding and raising the second seat did not change the overall length of the fuselage but did require redesigning the aft avionics bays, weapons bay, and forward weapons launchers. (USAF)

configuration control virtually a hopeless task. This issue seriously complicated the introduction of both the F-102 and F-106 into squadron service and resulted in several very expensive and extensive rebuild and modification programs over the years.

Even so, the first mockup inspection of the F-106B was held in September 1956 at the Convair Fort Worth, Texas, plant, where the forward fuselage for the new jet would be built. Due to the addition of the second cockpit, many of the MA-1 electronic components had to be relocated, so the F-106B fuselage, weapons bay, and forward missile displacement gear were extensively redesigned to accommodate them. Although functionally equivalent, the many physical location changes of the "black boxes" resulted in the FCS for the F-106B being redesignated from the MA-1 to the AN/ASQ-25.

Other differences between the two aircraft were in the fuel system, with the two-seater having slightly less fuel capacity and some minor plumbing changes in the wings, and in the addition of the second cockpit, which was raised slightly to give the rear-seat pilot a better view. This raised the vertical profile of the spine when compared to the F-106A. Development Engineering Inspections for both the F-106A and F-106B were also held in the middle of the month. Meanwhile, Hughes was progressing with development of the new Super Falcon air-to-air missiles, and construction of the first prototype MA-1 system was finally underway.

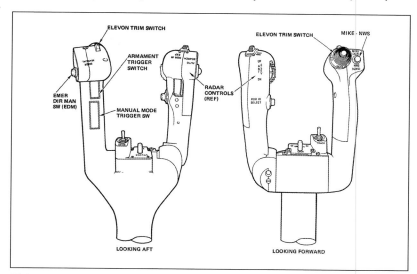

This unique two-handed yoke was derived from that used on the F-102, and had additional controls for MA-1 operation added. When unlocked, the left-hand portion could move both side to side, and fore and aft to operate the radar. Elevation of the radar beam was controlled by the thumbwheel. Operating both sides of the yoke independently while hand flying the aircraft required plenty of practice in the "piccolo drill." (USAF)

Air force and Convair photographers alike were out to record the first flight of the F-106 Delta Dart. The stubby ejector for the exhaust, wide natural metal band on the tail cone, and the communications antenna mounted behind the nose wheel are evident in this 26 December 1956 shot. (USAF via Isham)

With the dual nose wheels about to touch down, the prototype F-106A is landing after its shortened maiden flight.

The air force threw the F-106A program another curve ball during the cockpit mockup inspection held 8–9 November 1956. At that time, the air force changed its mind and decided that all F-106s delivered to "using agencies" should revert from the side stick back to the center control stick and use a two-handled yoke design, similar to that on the F-102. Further, conventional instrumentation would be used in all of the aircraft, pending further development of the unconventional instruments.

This decision resulted in a complete physical redesign of the cockpits, as the consoles for the side stick were much lower than those needed for the center stick, and the design of a new control yoke. It also resulted in designing an entirely new instrument panel using standard round gauges, which resulted in yet more changes to the MA-1 design. Fortunately, few aircraft were actually under construction at the time, but it added yet more redesign work, cost, and time to a program that could scarcely afford it.

December 1956 was a huge month for the F-106 program. The second mockup inspection of the F-106B, held at Fort Worth mid-month, was an anti-climax. The big news was that Hughes finally managed to test fly the first prototype MA-1 FCS, using a modified NT-29B propeller-driven passenger aircraft, and that after nearly eight years of development, the prototype F-106A (S/N 56-0451) was completed on 14 December.

Because the aircraft was still shrouded in secrecy and time was running out on the contractual requirement to successfully complete the first flight before the end of the year, the new airframe was simply covered in canvas, rolled out of the plant in San Diego, loaded onto a truck, and driven to Edwards AFB, California, with no public announcement at all. In fact, secrecy was so tight that no public references to the Mach 2 speed capability were allowed until well after the aircraft was in ADC squadron service.

After arrival at Edwards and initial ground checkout, a minimal number of taxi tests began on 22 December. After taking Christmas Day off, the Convair crew was back to work and Convair chief test pilot Richard L. Johnson made the first flight of the F-106 on 26 December 1956. Getting airborne at 1450L in the afternoon, the maiden flight did not use the afterburner of the barely flight-qualified Pratt & Whitney YJ75-P-1 engine for takeoff. Even so, the takeoff was considered equal to that of an F-102A using the afterburner. After reaching an altitude of about 30,000 feet and a speed of Mach 0.8, the flight had to be cut short when the speed brakes stuck in the open position and the air turbine motor that generated electricity for the prototype aircraft started fluctuating in frequency.

Regardless of whether or not the initial test objectives were completely met, that successful flight resulted in a large Christmas present for Convair, as the air force authorized production of 18 more F-106s and then gave Convair a New Year's present as well, when a new contract for the first large-production batch of F-106s was inked on the last day of the year. The contract for the 18 aircraft was issued

as a supplement to the existing contract that authorized the first 17 F-106s and covered S/N 57-0229 through 57-0246, all of which were slotted for flight test and development work. The production contract for 54 aircraft was a new contract that covered the first tactical aircraft, S/N 57-2453 through 57-2506.

However, even with success finally in sight, any thought of celebration was premature as major hurdles still loomed. Both military and political leaders were looking at the maturation of the Convair Atlas ICBM and thinking the age of manned aircraft was nearing an end. Development of the hugely expensive Boeing and Michigan Aeronautical Research Center (BOMARC) missile system, called an unmanned interceptor and initially designated F-99, and the large number of F-101 and F-102 interceptors already purchased in lieu of the delayed F-106 loomed large in the halls of Congress as a severe budget crisis loomed. The continued wrangling and indecision by the air force meant that major problems still loomed for the F-106.

Two Convair products sit side by side on the Geiger Field ramp in 1959. Just as the F-106 became operational, the threat it was designed to counter was diminished due to the introduction of ICBMs. The Six is from the 498th FIS, and the Atlas missile has been trucked somewhat out of its way, en route to delivery to the first Strategic Air Command (SAC) Atlas missile wing at F. E. Warren AFB, Wyoming, to stage this photo. (USAF)

Chapter Three

FLIGHT TESTING THE NEW INTERCEPTOR

Shown in typical test paint markings, S/N 56-0462 sits next to a Convair B-58 during this display. Between 2 and 15 May 1958, this jet toured the country to demonstrate the new interceptor. The ejection seat warning triangle is a decal, and note how the paint has been masked around the "U" of the "U.S. AIR FORCE" on the fuselage. (Via Don Spering/AIR)

The second F-106A (S/N 56-0452), also powered with a Pratt & Whitney YJ75-P-1 engine, was trucked to Edwards on 5 February 1957 and first flown on 26 February, a month behind the original contractual requirement. But once available, it immediately joined Convair's Category I (manufacturer testing) flight test program. Both jets examined the flight characteristics of the new airframes, and the test pilots and engineers tried to find design flaws that needed immediate attention. Ignoring the Cook-Craigie dictum that all airframes were to be identical, both Convair and the air force considered both of the two first airframes to be prototypes.

Because the MA-1 was so badly delayed, neither prototype had provisions for any form of FCS or weapons bay equipment. In fact, both had unique electrical systems, minimal flight instrumentation and communications gear, and no navigation aids at all. Electronics compartments were simply stuffed with large amounts of ballast to maintain center of gravity (CG) requirements. In addition to having unique tail cones, the doors covering the ventral bay on these two prototypes were unlike those on any of the other F-106s. They did not fold; used flush hinges; and at 11 feet, 1 inch long, were far shorter than the 16-foot-long doors of the remainder of the F-106

Displaying the 11-foot-long, one-piece, ventral bay doors to good effect, the prototype F-106A undergoes maintenance. The doors on the first two Sixes were 5 feet shorter than following jets, did not fold, and had flush hinges. The F-102–style buzz number is displayed in the normal aft position here. (Convair via Yenne)

fleet. They looked more like the bomb bay doors on a B-29 than anything else. But they did allow access to the cavernous bay where test and recording instrumentation was set up as needed.

Aircraft -451 was used as the general systems evaluator and -452 was used as the power plant and performance aircraft; both had their instrumentation altered as needed for the test mission at hand. With two flyable aircraft available, the air force could hardly wait to get their hands on the new jets, but it was not until 29 April 1957 that they could try out the new interceptor. However, prior to turning the air force loose on the new aircraft, Convair was ordered to remove the side control sticks and replace them with conventional center sticks.

With the April 1957 Armament Mockup, the air force settled on the weapons configuration for the F-106 once and for all. They declared that "production airplanes 1 through 4 [S/N 56-0453 through 56-0456] will have full-length folding missile bay doors with capability for retrofit [of weapons launchers]," while "production airplanes from number 5 on [S/N 56-0457] will carry the recommended weapons." This was the so-called 4+1 armament configuration of one newly named Genie rocket and four Super Falcon missiles. But just to keep things difficult, they continued, "Work on a six Falcon configuration will continue on a non-interference basis."

The good news was that this finally allowed Convair and Hughes to finalize the design of the weapons bay, some four months after the first Six had taken to the air. Since even a prototype MA-1 system was not expected to become available until after a dozen airframes

were flying, the first jets were simply ballasted and left space available for the system when it finally became available.

The bad news from the air force decision was that, when added to the requirement to redesign the cockpit to accommodate the center control stick (which involved far more than just moving the location of the stick), this nearly put the final nail in the coffin of the F-106: The bill for the two sets of changes was an additional $10 million. In an era when a severe funds shortage was causing all of the military services to reappraise every development program across the board, the price increase could not have come at a worse time. When HQ USAF was faced with the additional bill, they were ready to either scrap the program entirely or redesign the F-106 into a long-range interceptor.

ADC, however, feared that a redesign would take so long it would also kill the program. Further, the F-106 was the one interceptor that would have the automatic control and high performance needed to take on the new Soviet Tu-22 Blinder and Tu-95 Bear bomber threat and they were adamant about keeping the new interceptor alive. The air force countered that the F-101B might have to be dropped if the F-106 was continued. At this point, ADC was between a rock and a hard place. If they dropped the F-101, the only supersonic interceptors they would have would be the two related Convair aircraft. If either one was grounded for any length of time, ADC would be left with an inadequate force. And if both were grounded simultaneously for some reason, ADC would be left with nothing at all.

But the F-106 was, by far, the most advanced in terms of both performance and capability. So, short of "clear recognition that the F-106/MA-1 program has failed," they wanted the F-106. In an 11 June 1957 message to HQ USAF, ADC stated that if it were necessary to reduce the total number of F-101B and F-106 aircraft procured, ADC favored applying the reductions equally to each type because they were complementary in that the F-106 had a shorter range than the F-101B.

At the conclusion of the debate, the air force agreed with ADC and a large axe was taken to both programs. At a time when ADC plans called for 40 squadrons of F-106s (more than 1,000 aircraft), this total was cut nearly in half, to 26 squadrons. The immediate effect was that 100 airframes were eliminated from the FY 1958 budget. The final blow came the following September, when another 80 planned aircraft were cut from the FY 1959 budget; 350 advanced F-106C/Ds were dropped from further consideration, and no further orders were contemplated. The final result was a fleet of only 340 aircraft, including 63 of the two-place F-106Bs, while 480 of the less expensive and less capable Voodoo's were procured.

The first official air force flight of the newly named Delta Dart recorded a top speed of Mach 1.9 and reached an altitude of 57,000 feet, both close to the contractual performance requirements. However, in reality, things were not progressing well with

Shown here in 1964 are ADC's stable of "Century Series" interceptors. The F-106A is from the 325th Fighter Wing (Air Defense) at McChord AFB. The CF-101B Voodoo is from 409(AW) Sq at Comox, British Columbia, while the F-102A is from the 64th FIS at Paine Field, Washington. Both of the Convair interceptors have the infrared search and track (IRST) seekers, but the first batch of Voodoos to Canada never received the Interceptor Improvement Program modifications. In memory of SMSGT David W. Menard. (USAF via Isham)

Seen here later in the test program, many of the unique features of the prototype F-106A are still evident. The early keel rib stands out while ventral bay doors begin at the demarcation between the gray and red paint, just aft of the air inlets. (USAF via Isham)

Posed for the photographer on 6 June 1957 during the Air Force Phase II evaluation, the second prototype is three months old at this point. The jet has no exhaust vent on the spine, since air conditioning equipment was not installed. It also has the early-style main wheels and a large VHF antenna below the nose. (USAF via Isham)

the test program. After 70 test flights by Convair pilots, aircraft performance was below estimates, with speed and acceleration issues being at the top of the list of problems. With only the two aerodynamic test bed prototypes available and only one additional aircraft under construction, AFFTC began investigating the new aircraft by assigning test pilot and Korean War Ace Captain Iven C. Kincheloe and Flight Engineer Willie L. Allen to a partial and accelerated Category II flight testing program.

Intended to "obtain preliminary performance, stability and control data, and qualitative information on the handling characteristics of the airplane," the program began on 22 May 1957 and continued until 29 June. Capt. Kincheloe flew nine flights in -451 to obtain basic performance data and five flights in -452 to obtain stability and control data. Ten further flights were made by various pilots assigned to the Air Proving Ground Command, Air Defense Command, Air Materiel Command, and Air Force Flight Test Center for a qualitative evaluation of the new aircraft.

The initial Category II Report brought up a number of issues that Convair needed to address, most of which the company was already well aware. Even allowing for the facts that only prototype engines were installed and that production aircraft would be using a slightly different air inlet configuration that canted 5 degrees downward, the F-106 only reached Mach 1.8 at 36,000 feet and the maximum power combat ceiling was only 53,000 feet, hardly better than the existing F-102A. Furthermore, acceleration times were very long and used excessive amounts of fuel. While several smaller items regarding instrumentation needs, nose wheel steering, and brake improvements were discussed, two other significant issues were brought up.

First, as Convair and Hughes were well aware, the cockpit would have to be completely reworked, as it had been developed around the now-canceled side stick controller. Second, and completely in line with conventional air force thinking at the time, Capt. Kincheloe demanded that an adequate supersonic ejection seat be installed. With all of the new high-speed Century Series aircraft under development, the thinking was that high-speed, high-altitude ejections were the most serious threats to pilot survival. It is rather ironic that Capt. Kincheloe lost his life the following year in what eventually was realized to be the real threat: low-altitude, low-speed ejections.

On the bright side, the preliminary test report stated that "except for the lack of performance, the prototype airplane tested has the potential of being an excellent Air Defense Command interceptor. Satisfactory demonstration of stalls, spin recoveries, inertial coupling and dead stick landings, as well as an operational fire control system are required before the aircraft is delivered to operational units."

The F-106 flight test program was the last conducted under a system where the contractor and the air force had separate, mirror-image flight test groups and aircraft, a system that required twice as many test aircraft and resulted in slow progress. When Convair completed a contract test point, the air force mirror aircraft was modified (if necessary) and the air force pilots duplicated the Convair test to verify it.

As further testing got underway, two aircraft were assigned and instrumented for each phase of testing, such as flight loads, heating and cooling, and power plant. For example, S/N 56-0459 was the Convair aircraft used for power plant and speed tests and was modified over time with several exhaust nozzle shapes and variable ramp designs in attempts to reduce high-speed drag and increase the top speed. S/N 56-0467 (the eventual speed record aircraft) was the air force test equivalent and was the one modified by Pratt & Whitney with additional engine and fuel control system instrumentation.

Leaving San Diego after modification in August 1957, -452 now has the fuselage lettering in the normal position and new "Convair F-106A" lettering added to the nose. Major modifications while at the plant included modifying the air intakes and tail cone and installing a cylindrical-divergent ejector to the J75. Simply thinning the air inlet lips reduced drag by 1,200 pounds at Mach 2.0 and 35,000 feet.

The second F-106A prototype is shown airborne after finishing the August 1957 modifications. It now has modified air inlets, but retains the prototype tail cone and wing fences. It took a while for the tech orders to catch up and assign a new buzz-number code to the new interceptor. (USAF via Isham)

Many changes are evident in this composite of the early and late air intakes on the F-106. On the left is the final configuration for the prototype, S/N 56-0451. On the right is the intake of F-106B S/N 59-0158. The early intake is parallel to the aircraft reference line, while the 5-degree droop of the later intake is clearly visible. Note how the later intake is more squared off in both airplanes, as well as the differences in curvature on the upper surface. There is a difference in the placement of the hot air exhaust below the intakes as well. (Author/Kaston)

The perforated version of the vari-ramp is seen here in this photo of F-106B S/N 57-2507. The prototype B model never received updated air intakes or vari-ramps. Note the profile of the B model weapons bay doors as well. The lower avionics coffin required reshaping the doors to fit around it.

While the initial Category II testing was underway by the air force, construction of five more airframes was well underway, with the first expected to be completed by August and the last by the end of the year. But due to continuing delays with J75 engine development and MA-1 problems, the first four were again expected to use the J75-P-1 engine instead of the "final" P-9 version. Because none of the first dozen aircraft had any portion of the MA-1 installed, initial testing was limited to improving the aerodynamics of the Six.

Major developmental testing revolved around the air inlets, vari-ramps, tail cone, and exhaust ejector, as well as trying to find a satisfactory fuel control. The original D-shaped air inlets of the prototypes bore a distinct resemblance to the earlier F-102 and were found to be inadequate, creating large amounts of drag at high speeds. The first two jets had slightly larger inlets that were mounted parallel with the fuselage. It had always been planned to build the following aircraft with ducts that canted 5 degrees downward and reduce them in size from 1,050 square inches to 1,000 square inches in an attempt to match the capture area with the engine demands. But in addition to the drag issue, it was also found that the J75-P-9, and especially the later P-17 engines, had much higher airflow demands than the lower-thrust P-1. As a result, the inlets were modified in various ways to both thin the leading edges and have their shapes refined to a boxier shape. At least three inlet configurations can be seen in early photographs.

At the same time, the variable-intake ramps were undergoing changes. Originally, the ramps had covers over the hinge areas, but after a particularly violent compressor stall blew the cover plates straight out the front of the inlets on one aircraft near Mach 2, word came from San Diego to remove them entirely. Much effort was expended attempting to determine exactly how to schedule movement of the ramps, with some test aircraft receiving automated systems and others manually activated ones.

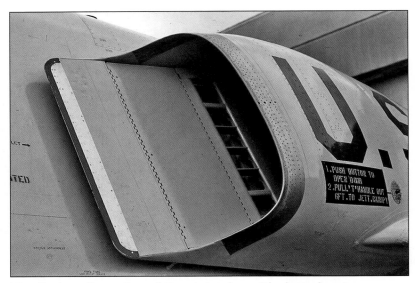
The final configuration of the air intake, with slotted vari-ramp.

that the slotted ramp worked best. The air ingested into the slots was dumped into the engine compartment and then overboard.

The original ejector (afterburner nozzle) and tail cone created excessive amounts of drag at high speed and were also the sources of much engineering effort. Four ejector nozzle variations were tried, including cylindrical, cylindrical-divergent, cylindrical-convergent, and convergent-divergent. The length of the nozzles varied as well. The second prototype made at least 20 test flights using nine combinations of ejectors, vari-ramp configurations, fuel controllers, and engine trims before the engineers finally settled on the slotted vari-ramps and the unusual convergent-divergent exhaust.

The prototype tail cones used on early jets are identifiable by their very wide (15½ inches) natural metal areas at the aft ends and a curved concave profile on the lower surface. They also created large amounts of drag at high speed. In addition to the earlier tests, the second prototype F-106A was equipped with five tail cone configurations. Between 5 March and 29 April 1958, several flights were made in an attempt to find the best configuration.

Configuration I was the prototype tail cone with a 6.4-inch extension, Configuration II was simply the prototype cone, Configuration III was a gloved tail cone with 6.4-inch extension, Configuration IV was the gloved tail cone with no extension over the prototype length, and Configuration V was the prototype tail cone

Three ramp designs were tried in an effort to decrease drag. The original ramp sections were solid, but then perforations and slots were examined. It was finally determined that vents needed to be added to the ramps to bleed off the "dead" boundary layer air and

Compare the differences between the third F-106 and a production jet from the 456th FIS. The short ejector and extended natural metal area on the early jet are quite different. The later aircraft also has the external datalink antennas, tail bumper, and tailhook installation. (Convair/Isham Collection)

By the time drag reduction testing was complete, the ejector on an F-106 was a complex convergent-divergent affair. The small, rectangular "cookie cutter" inserts between the exhaust nozzle and the ejector were only one part of the complicated modifications and were placed there to eliminate yaw during afterburner light-off. Interior details of the speed brakes and drag chute housing are also visible.

In this early view, S/N 56-0453 still has external wing fences, the prototype tail cone and early P-1 engine, and ejector. This was the last Six to carry the FC prefix buzz numbers.

Seen here on 25 September 1958, just 12 days after acceptance, the air inlets have yet to be modified, and it was one of the last Sixes constructed with external wing fences, but the final form of the F-106 was taking shape. This Six has a full MA-1 and a strike camera mounted in front of the windscreen for use during testing. This is the same position as where the IRST was mounted in later years. In about 10 months, this jet will be assigned as a ground training airframe, before being rebuilt during the Test-to-Tactical (T-T-T) program. (USAF via Isham)

shortened by 4.6 inches. This is the one that was finally chosen as the production standard.

While Convair was busy testing and refining the new airframes, Hughes was still trying to *design* the MA-1, much less start constructing one. According to Convair planning documents dated August 1956, the first F-106 anticipated to receive a pre-production MA-1 system was S/N 56-0463, which was expected to become available in late December 1957, a year after the prototype's first flight. The aircraft planned to receive the first "tactical" MA-1 was scheduled to be S/N 57-0232, in March 1958. Production build-up rates were not expected to increase more than one or two aircraft per month until early 1959, the time at which the aircraft was originally supposed to be reaching the end of its service life.

Meanwhile, Convair made Herculean efforts to reduce drag, to the point where even the anti-collision beacons automatically retracted flush to the aircraft skin once the jet reached supersonic speeds. All other navigation lights were also flush-mounted. Not even a radio antenna was allowed to extend beyond the skin and add drag. To their everlasting credit, in their search for speed, the engineers succeeded in creating one of the most aerodynamically clean and aesthetically beautiful aircraft ever flown.

Chapter Four

THE F-106 AIRCRAFT

The numbers "15" on the nose and tail of the jet denote the jet's number within the squadron and serve as a partial basis for the jet's NORAD call sign. The Cape Cod whaling harpoon markings on the external fuel tanks really add to the appeal of the jet. (Photo by Don Spering/AIR)

By the time the new interceptors began flying at Edwards, the external differences between the Six and the F-102 were dramatic. The fuselage had been lengthened and further refined to meet the high-speed "ideal body" theory. Gone were the fillets near the exhaust. The air intakes had been moved around 8 feet farther back on the fuselage, which reduced weight, and increased visibility from the cockpit. Variable geometry ramps inside the ducts controlled airflow to the new YJ75-P-1 engine.

Although the original idea was to retain the F-102A's triangular vertical fin, by 1955 the design had been altered so that the vertical tail was truncated and the rudder hinge line and aft edge swept back. Having been aerodynamically refined to extremes, the new jet was sleek, lithe, and far more visually appealing than its still rather stumpy-looking predecessor. However, other than slightly increasing the amount of conical camber on the leading edges, the size, shape, and construction of the Delta wings remained basically the same.

Regardless of the fact that the F-106 evolved from the F-102, the result was a completely new aircraft, and it led Convair into new areas of manufacturing. Two March 1957 company memos,

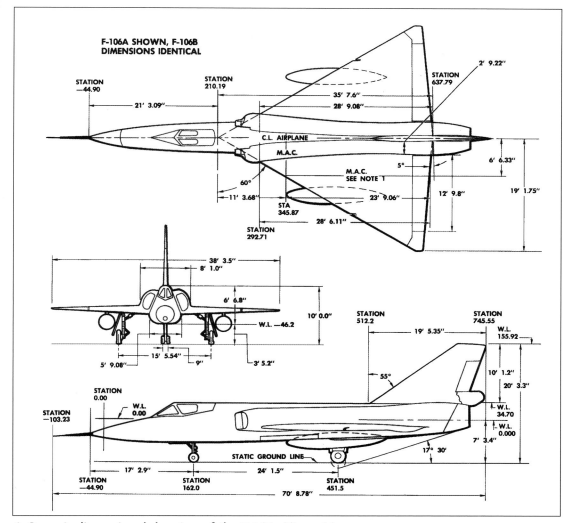

A Convair dimensional drawing of the F-106. (Convair)

fer system or the variable ramps on the air intakes of the F-106, and the missile bay of the new interceptor was far more complicated, needing shrouded wiring harnesses, which were not included on the F-102.

Other changes included the MA-1 encompassing all of the communication and navigation gear, the move from an analog to a digital computer system, an additional 3 miles of wiring over that used in the F-102, and a wiring design that eliminated all terminal posts, which required individually splicing more than 6,000 wires. The memo lists more than two dozen major changes, all of which were sure to increase the manufacturing cost over that of the F-102.

The semi-mechanized production lines of the F-102 were continued, along with use of the USAF Heavy Press program. Rather than assemble the wing spars from various pieces and then rivet them together, heavy presses were used to produce five individual one-piece wing spars. These spars were then machined into final shape. The wet wing was then assembled using patented Straylor rivets and the unique Scotch-weld process, developed in conjunction with the Minnesota Mining and Manufacturing Company (3M). This last feature proved to be both a blessing and the curse that prevented any follow-on sales of the jet to additional customers.

As the wings were assembled, an adhesive was placed on all mating surfaces. Once the wings had been completely riveted together, the entire assembly was placed in a giant oven and baked at 325 degrees F to set the adhesive. The resulting wing was not only leak-proof, it was also virtually unbreakable, as repeated fatigue testing and later operations proved. However, because the inner structure of the wing was used to hold the fuel, it had no self-sealing capability. Fuel was moved via low-pressure air bleed from the engines and any small hole could have resulted in all of the fuel being pumped overboard. Although this was acceptable for an interceptor based over friendly territory, no customer other than ADC was willing to buy a combat aircraft with such a configuration.

Basically an enlarged J57, the newly developed Pratt & Whitney J75 was a two-spool, axial-flow power plant that used eight radially mounted combustion chambers. The YJ75-P-1 was initially used on the first several F-102Bs, with the P-9 replacing it as soon as it was

discussing 1958 procurement cost proposals for 280 follow-on F-106s to AMC and pricing of Engineering Change Proposals (ECP) for both the F-102 and F-106, illuminate some of the differences between the two. Both types of aircraft were built on assembly lines in the same San Diego plant and were then towed across a bridge over an expressway to the airfield. Once there, ballast was placed into the noses for weight and balance purposes, initial power-on and taxi checks were performed, and the aircraft were flown to Air Force Plant 42 at Palmdale, California. Once at Palmdale, Hughes installed the FCS while Convair painted the jets and accomplished the functional flight tests before handing the new interceptors over to the air force.

But whereas a single weight could be placed in the nose of the F-102, the radar compartment of the F-106 was "pigeon-holed" and the required weights had to be sized and placed into the compartments individually. The F-102 did not have either the fuel trans-

If you look closely, the markings on the jets indicate the construction line number, Convair model number, and model sequence number. Although this photo does not show it, all of the jets are coated with a light yellow–green chromate primer. These jets are all from the second contract and are early FY 1957 models. A couple of early F-106B's are visible in the background. (Convair)

ready. The second prototype (S/N 56-0452) had an early P-9 installed in December 1957. By April 1958, it was on its third version of the Hamilton Standard fuel control (though not the last, by any means), and in May 1958, the P-9 engine was modified to increase the area of the first-stage turbine by 4 square inches and the second-stage turbine by 10 square inches.

The engine initially developed 23,500 pounds of afterburning thrust in the P-9 version. The later P-17 engine produced 16,100 pounds of thrust in military power and 24,500 pounds in full afterburner. Inside the aircraft, the engine was surrounded with a cannular titanium shroud to minimize heat transfer to the fuselage structure. Air was forced through the shroud and ejected at the aft end.

Most of the early work on the aircraft revolved around (1) trying to match the size of the intake ducts to match the airflow requirements of the J75 while minimizing drag, (2) determining the proper scheduling of the variable intake ramps, and (3) finding configurations of ejectors, the afterburner nozzle, and tail-cone shapes that would minimize drag and increase thrust.

Unlike on many other engines, the J75 afterburner nozzle was not a variable-position type, it was either fully open or fully closed. That led to the very distinctive "hard light" of the Six. When afterburner was initiated,

Seen here at Michael AAF, Dugway, Utah, in July 1987, this 49th FIS Six pulled more than 16 Gs, and lived. After receiving a set of replacement wings, it continued in service until being shot down as a drone on 18 May 1993. The lucky pilot was sent to Keflavik, Iceland, as a command post officer as penance for his actions.

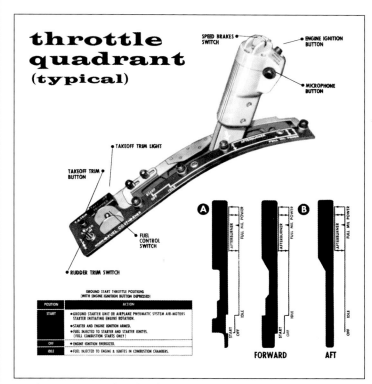

throttle quadrant (typical)

SPEED BRAKES SWITCH

ENGINE IGNITION BUTTON

MICROPHONE BUTTON

TAKEOFF TRIM LIGHT

TAKEOFF TRIM BUTTON

FUEL CONTROL SWITCH

RUDDER TRIM SWITCH

GROUND START THROTTLE POSITIONS
(WITH ENGINE IGNITION BUTTON DEPRESSED)

POSITION	ACTION
START	• GROUND STARTER UNIT OR AIRPLANE PNEUMATIC SYSTEM AIR-MOTORS STARTER INITIATING ENGINE ROTATION. • STARTER AND ENGINE IGNITION ARMED. • FUEL INJECTED TO STARTER AND STARTER IGNITES. (FULL COMBUSTION STARTS ONLY.)
OFF	• ENGINE IGNITION ENERGIZED.
IDLE	• FUEL INJECTED TO ENGINE & IGNITES IN COMBUSTION CHAMBERS.

FORWARD   AFT

Both Convair Deltas had very unusual throttle action. Unlike most throttles, which simply move fore and aft, the throttle on the Six rotated outboard to select afterburner operation. (USAF)

Changing the engine on a Six was very straightforward as it simply rolled aft onto the rails of the specially designed dolly. The titanium cannular shroud that surrounded the J75 and acted as a heat shield between the engine and the aircraft structure is plainly visible in this shot of an early 498th FIS F-106A at the McClellan depot. (USAF)

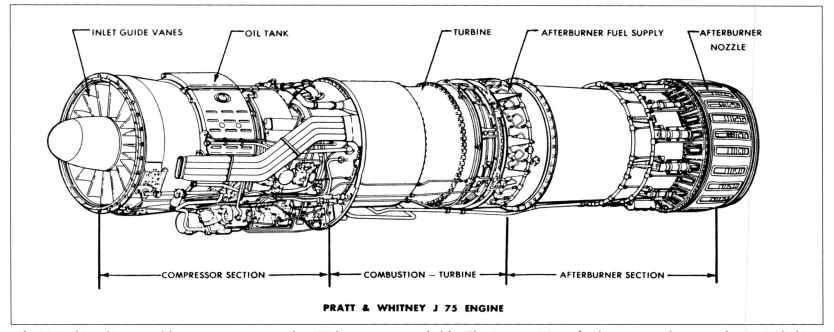

INLET GUIDE VANES   OIL TANK   TURBINE   AFTERBURNER FUEL SUPPLY   AFTERBURNER NOZZLE

COMPRESSOR SECTION ——— COMBUSTION – TURBINE ——— AFTERBURNER SECTION

PRATT & WHITNEY J 75 ENGINE

After initial teething troubles were overcome, the J75 became very reliable. The two-position afterburner nozzle opened prior to light, and the instantaneous "hard light" was a characteristic of the J75. (USAF)

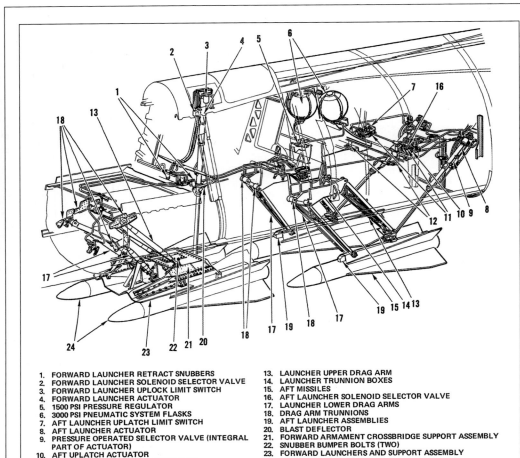

The forward Falcons in an F-106A were supported by a trapeze while the aft launchers were separate, to fit around the Genie launch rack. Both the launchers and the weapons bay doors were powered by high-pressure pneumatic air that was stored in bottles mounted above the bay. "Bubble checkers," or pneumatic troops, spent countless hours trying to trace leaks in the system. The Genie rack is not shown in this diagram. (USAF)

1. FORWARD LAUNCHER RETRACT SNUBBERS
2. FORWARD LAUNCHER SOLENOID SELECTOR VALVE
3. FORWARD LAUNCHER UPLOCK LIMIT SWITCH
4. FORWARD LAUNCHER ACTUATOR
5. 1500 PSI PRESSURE REGULATOR
6. 3000 PSI PNEUMATIC SYSTEM FLASKS
7. AFT LAUNCHER UPLATCH LIMIT SWITCH
8. AFT LAUNCHER ACTUATOR
9. PRESSURE OPERATED SELECTOR VALVE (INTEGRAL PART OF ACTUATOR)
10. AFT UPLATCH ACTUATOR
11. AFT LAUNCHER UPLATCH ASSEMBLIES
12. AFT LAUNCHER RETRACT SNUBBERS
13. LAUNCHER UPPER DRAG ARM
14. LAUNCHER TRUNNION BOXES
15. AFT MISSILES
16. AFT LAUNCHER SOLENOID SELECTOR VALVE
17. LAUNCHER LOWER DRAG ARMS
18. DRAG ARM TRUNNIONS
19. AFT LAUNCHER ASSEMBLIES
20. BLAST DEFLECTOR
21. FORWARD ARMAMENT CROSSBRIDGE SUPPORT ASSEMBLY
22. SNUBBER BUMPER BOLTS (TWO)
23. FORWARD LAUNCHERS AND SUPPORT ASSEMBLY
24. FORWARD MISSILES

1. ACCELEROMETER INSTALLATION
2. REACTOR INSTALLATION
3. FLUX-VALVE INSTALLATION
4. VERTICAL STABILIZER FREE AIR TEMPERATURE BULB INSTALLATION
5. ANTENNA A.A.I.
6. UHF/TACAN ANTENNA
7. FIN TIP WAVE GUIDE ASSEMBLY
8. RADIO TRANSMITTER
9. CONVERTER - AMPLIFIER
10. RECEIVER
11. A.A.I. WAVEGUIDE
12. A.A.I. COUPLER
13. SYNCHRONIZER

the first thing that happened was that the nozzle opened fully, significantly decreasing the available thrust. Then the afterburner lit in an instantaneous fashion, via "hot streak" ignition. This created the very distinctive boom that told everyone within miles that a Six was in the process of taking off. No one who has ever heard that sound is likely to forget it.

After initial teething problems trying to match the engine's air requirements with the intake design of the F-106, and in designing an adequate fuel control system, the all-stainless-steel J75 built a reputation as an exceptionally rugged and dependable engine. It was widely used in commercial aviation as the JT4B.

Internally, the F-106 retained the dual high- and low-pressure pneumatic systems of the F-102. The low-pressure system was fed by bleed air from the compressor section of the J75, while the high-pressure air was stored in spherical containers at 3,000 psi and then metered to 1,500 psi for use. The low-pressure system was primarily used for aircraft and electronics air conditioning and cockpit pressurization systems, as well as for transferring fuel from the external drop tanks into the wing tanks and between the various internal fuel tanks. After serious problems with engine flameouts due to fuel starvation, small hopper retention tanks with electrically powered boost pumps were added to the number-3 fuel tank in each wing to ensure a continued flow of fuel to the engine.

The high-pressure air system did not have an aircraft-driven compressor and was limited to the air available inside the three air flasks. This air was

Even the fin of the Six was used for systems. The two probes on the leading edge were the Ram Air "Q" feel system intakes, while the MA-1 system required a free-air-temperature input to be able to calculate missile launch parameters. (USAF)

40 WORLD'S FASTEST SINGLE-ENGINE JET AIRCRAFT: THE STORY OF CONVAIR'S F-106 DELTA DART INTERCEPTOR

Most aircraft initially received a Weber ejection seat that was a derivative of the earlier F-102 seat. These early ejection seats had neither zero-zero nor high-speed/high-altitude capability and the early Air Force Category II testing called them inadequate.

The early electrical generation and distribution system of the F-106 was exceptionally complex, primarily due to the demands of the Hughes MA-1 system. In essence, the aircraft had two essentially independent power supply systems, one for the Hughes Aircraft Corporation (HAC) MA-1 and one for ship power. The MA-1 required 14 exceptionally stable and pure voltages plus AC frequencies for proper system operation.

Two generators mounted on a Constant Speed Drive (CSD) shaft produced six primary voltages, which were fed to a complicated set of vacuum-tube electronics, which filtered and regulated both AC and DC voltages and generated the additional eight voltages required for the MA-1. Two additional generators, also mounted on CSDs, produced power for the ship systems. Initially, no backup or emergency power supplies were available for the MA-1, but two emergency power sources were provided for ship systems. An Air Turbine Generator initially used engine bleed air to generate backup power, but a hydraulically driven generator was added in the first major set of modifications.

The nose gear trunnion was one of the weak points in the early days of the F-106. Stresses from towing caused frequent strut collapses. The later, off-centerline location for the swept UHF blade antenna, the Total Air Temperature probe, and the fiberglass covering for the AN/ARN-25 direction-finding antenna are also seen here.

primarily used to operate the weapons bay doors and Falcon launchers. It was also used to pressurize the hydraulic reservoirs, raise and retract the infrared (IR) seeker head, and emergency deploy the drag chute. Originally, it was also used to provide an emergency source of cabin pressure for a limited period of time. In later years, it operated the air refueling slipway door.

Due to the limited air supply, the F-106 had only three weapons door opening sequences and weapons launches per flight. This was fine for its designed purpose of shooting down bombers since there was only enough armament for, at most, three firing passes, but it somewhat restricted the pilot's options in a tactical fighter environment.

Both aircraft were unique to the USAF in using pneumatic pressure to operate the brakes on the main wheels. This precluded use of anti-skid braking or parking brakes, features that were sorely missed in operational use. The fore and aft drag struts of the main landing gear contained small air reservoirs for emergency braking in case the main system bled down or had been emptied.

Many of the early problems with the aircraft came from voltage or frequency variations that caused failures in part or all of the MA-1. Because all of the communications and navigation systems were part of the MA-1, the interconnected complexity of the system tended to result in cascading failures that frequently caused loss of communication and navigation capability, or in the worst cases resulted in engine flameouts as even the generators were progressively knocked off line.

The situation in early ADC squadrons was so bad that F-106s were not allowed to fly alone, and the required weather minimums were raised to above Visual Flight Rule standards. Needless to say, this was not ideal for an aircraft that was supposed to provide all-weather defense of the nation. Both Convair and Hughes expended much time and effort trying to fix the situation, and modifications were eventually designed that transferred the communication and navigation gear power source to ship power if the MA-1 failed. Hardly a complete improvement, but at least it let the pilot safely recover the aircraft.

The extended canopy of the F-106B and highly area ruled "wasp" or "coke bottle" waist of the Six are highlighted in this view of the prototype F-106B.

The early canopy was held to the rails with dozens of screws set into dimpled washers. The seldom noticed anti-UV tinting is also apparent in this photo of a 95th FIS jet arriving in Korea in 1970. Note the logbooks stowed on the glare shield for the flight, how the paint for the black anti-glare panel curves around the windshield area, and the multitude of stenciling. (USAF)

Reaching for the sky, the prototype F-106B has just lifted off on its maiden flight at Edwards AFB.

F-106B

With a clear need for a trainer version of the highly automated new aircraft, a two-seat version designated TF-106A was authorized on 3 August 1956. Later that month, the air force decided not to confine it to strictly a training role but to include full tactical capability, and the designation was changed to TF-106B. That designation did not last long either and it was soon changed to F-106B. Convair had already been giving the issue of a two-seat variant considerable thought, and after the fiasco with side-by-side seating in the TF-102 (unflatteringly known as the tub), the choice of the tandem seating configuration was a given. Because space was at a premium in the San Diego plant, production of the new fuselage was outsourced to Convair's Fort Worth Division. The first development engineering inspection was held there on 13 September 1956, along with the first of several cockpit mockup inspections.

This shot of a "bus" illustrates how the rear-cockpit radar tube was mounted to the canopy so as not to impede entry and exit from the rear seat. Just behind the electrically operated canopy actuator strut is the wind blast deflector, which is vertical here. It was designed to protect the rear-seat occupant in the event of canopy loss or ejection and rotated to horizontal as the canopy closed. Removable canopy support struts were normally installed immediately after the canopy was opened. One was used on the A model, and two were used on the B, one on either side of the canopy rail.

Seen here mounted on a railroad flat car, the avionics "coffin" in the forward section of the F-106B weapons bay is clearly visible. All of the weapons launchers have been removed for shipment. (Spering/AIR)

Adding a second cockpit without stretching the existing fuselage meant that a great deal of the MA-1 system electronics had to be relocated. Since the only space available was in the weapons bay, the entire forward half of the weapons bay had to be redesigned, and the missile displacement gear for the forward Falcon missiles had to be changed. A new enclosure was placed between the two front Falcons and filled with the electronics that had formerly been placed in the aft electronics bay of the F-106A. Initially called MA-1T, the physical changes were substantial enough that the system for the F-106B was redesignated as AN/ASQ-25, but the overall capability of the system was identical to that of the A model.

Turning into the echelon, and the low winter sun, the beautiful lines of the F-106 are very apparent in this shot of three 5th FIS jets. Low over Tucson, Arizona, they are flying out of their alert detachment at Davis-Monthan AFB, Arizona. The "gray tail" has recently returned to the unit after depot maintenance at McClellan AFB, California.

This view is looking aft into the weapons bay of an F-106B. The flush-mounted avionics structure, individual forward Falcon launchers, and cut-out weapons bay doors stand out.

Looking forward on the same aircraft. The white rectangle in the upper right is a baggage rack that mounted to the Genie rack. Note how the inner weapons bay doors are shortened to fit behind the avionics structure.

Additional changes to the aircraft included raising the height of the spine slightly so that the rear-seat occupant had a better forward view, doubling the size of the liquid oxygen system to accommodate the second crew member, decreasing the size of the fuselage fuel tank, and minor plumbing changes in the fuel system.

Most of these changes were finalized during the second mockup inspection, held in Fort Worth in mid-December 1956. With construction of the prototype already well underway, a supplement to the original F-106A contract covering seven new two-seat versions of the F-106 was issued in April 1957, finalized on 3 June, and given final approval on 25 June 1957. All of the new two-seat aircraft, plus several more of the next batch, were immediately programmed for flight testing.

The first F-106B (S/N 57-2507) was actually the 13th airframe to come off the production line in San Diego and the only F-106B to have the early Case XIV wing. It was powered with a J75-P-9 engine with perforated duct air inlets and did not have provisions for the MA-1 FCS system. After having been trucked from the Convair plant in San Diego to Edwards, it began taxi tests on 8 April 1958. After landing from the maiden flight on 10 April, Convair test pilot John M. Fitzpatrick said it was "the best first flight I have ever made."

After a short period of Contractors Phase I Flight Testing, -507 was accepted by the air force later that month and immediately put to work. It was initially used for handling quality investigations, which included spin and stall testing. The spin tests began in October 1958, and by then the jet had been modified by removing the F-102–style wing fences with which it was built and replacing them with the later-style slot. It was specially

Another view of the F-106B weapons bay doors.

modified with a spin chute and pilot-deployable nose strakes (which were also used previously on the F-106A spin tests). Emergency backup electric and hydraulic generators were added to the weapons bay to ensure safe recovery.

After completion of the spin tests, it eventually became the test bed aircraft for flight testing of the new Convair "upward rotational" ejection seat, and continued its career as an ejection test bed by proving the Apollo ejection system as well. Only the initial seven F-106Bs were intended to be assigned to flight testing, but an eighth was added after number 7 (S/N 57-2511) crashed during weapons testing at Holloman AFB, New Mexico, after only three months' use. Further, according to a Convair report dated 17 September 1956, F-106Bs numbers 5 through 7 were originally supposed to be assigned to Eglin AFB, Florida, in early 1958 for Air Proving Ground

Command (APGC) weapons testing. Due to the protracted nature of the initial flight and MA-1 testing, these aircraft were actually retained for use at Edwards and Holloman.

Regardless of the initial development problems, in the end Convair produced an aircraft that was a joy to fly. With a roomy cockpit, it was stable and light on the controls. The only real complaint pilots had was that it was so "clean" it was hard to slow down. Like other Deltas, it went into light buffet surprisingly early in turns, but the progression from "pebbles" to "rocks" to "boulders" was very predictable, and it gave plenty of warning that you were approaching the edges of the flight envelope. Once the initial teething problems with the J75 fuel control and fuel supply issues were overcome, the engine became extremely reliable and was virtually immune to foreign object damage.

Chapter Five

MA-1 AND AGE

More than 2,000 pounds of vacuum-tube electronics that comprised the MA-1 AWCIS are displayed here. Due to progressive changes to solid-state electronics, by the end of its life, more than 1,000 pounds of weight had been lost. The AIM-4Fs have the original 10-cm aerodynamic spikes, and a TSD is prominent in the center. That is not an infrared (IR) seeker on the nose of the Six, but rather a strike camera. (Convair)

The MA-1 AWCIS system for the F-106 broke new ground and was, at the time, the most technologically advanced program the USAF had ever initiated. Likewise, the required test and Aerospace Ground Equipment (AGE) were far more complex than anything seen to date.

The Electronic "Heart" of the Six: Hughes MX-1779/MA-1 System

To say that the technological challenges the Hughes Aircraft Company faced when designing what eventually became the MA-1 were nearly impossible to successfully overcome cannot be overstated, especially given the timeframe allowed. The AWCIS was not just a fire control system. It was the first attempt to design a completely integrated system that combined fire control, flight control, navigation, and armament delivery. All functions were intermingled and controlled through the central computer. Nothing like it had ever been attempted before; the concept was well beyond the state of the art when the design was begun.

Today, when a typical cellular telephone contains more computing power and memory than was available to the entire world when design of the MA-1 began, it is hard to comprehend just how much

In this posed photo, Col. William C. Clark, Commander of the ADC joint test project, inspects the MA-1 compartment on an early Six. His hand is on one of the built-in test sets. (Hughes via Isham)

air force required was to build a digital system. Mechanical computers had reached their practical limits and were simply unable to handle the ever increasing speeds of the aircraft and the complexity of the computations needed.

The result was, for the time, a fiendishly complex system that comprised 200 black boxes and weighed 2,520 pounds. Although it worked in the lab, it was very susceptible to temperature or humidity changes, as well as electrical power purity. It was also extremely time intensive to maintain. In the words of one electronics technician who worked on the original system, "When it worked, it was great; you just couldn't get it to work."

To give credit where it is due, Hughes made every attempt to design the system with maintenance in mind. Line-replaceable boxes were placed in racks with rectangular pigeon holes, using gold-plated connectors. Similar systems were grouped together and built-in test programs were used to the greatest extent possible. One unique (and not necessarily successful) part of the original design was that circuit breakers were not used. Instead, banks of ceramic fuses with pop-out pins to indicate which ones had failed were installed.

The Hughes Digitair computer was the heart of the MA-1 and, like the rest of the avionics, used hundreds of subminiature vacuum tubes, each with pins individually hand soldered to the electrical connections. The original computer had only two kilobytes of 18-bit octal (0-7) core memory, and the program was contained in a magnetic drum system (an early form of hard drive). As initially deployed, the MA-1 system was so integrated that the pilot did not have typical frequency selector dials for either the TACAN or ILS. Each interceptor unit chose what frequencies would be used for a given selector switch position, and the data was loaded into the memory drum by maintenance personnel. The pilot then had to cross-reference a printed guide to choose the station or frequencies he desired, using either a 23-position homing point selector switch or a 20-position channel selector switch for the ILS. Eventually, the practical difficulties this presented when flying outside the local area were recognized, and a standard TACAN control panel was installed.

The primary purpose of the computer was to take data from the SAGE datalink signals, azimuth and distance information from the TACAN, and inputs from the air data computer, and then to calculate steering solutions for the two operational modes of the MA-1: navigation or attack. The results were then displayed on the radar scope; command bars on the heading, altitude, and airspeed indicators were displayed on the TSD and if "automatic" was selected, provided to the autopilot to steer the interceptor to the proper point in space.

To make it work, the operations section of each squadron selected up to 23 waypoints, each with an associated latitude, longitude,

of a technological achievement it truly was. Because the primary weapon was unguided, Hughes really had to design a system that was mounted in, and aimed, what was essentially a rifle moving at twice the speed of sound. That system then fired a nuclear-armed, ballistic, rocket-powered "bullet," which traveled at three times the speed of sound, at a target that was also maneuvering in three-dimensional space at Mach 1 or better, and then expecting the bullet to hit the target. Every time. Given the sheer complexity of accomplishing that task, it is little wonder that development took as long as it did.

Since practical transistors were not available until several years after design was begun, the only solution was to use vacuum tubes. The first of three major hurdles that Hughes had to overcome was that tubes are inherently analog. To make a digital computer required first finding a way to ensure digital responses from the tubes. More than 140 digital to analog and analog to digital converters were required to interface with the analog systems of the aircraft, instrumentation, and Falcon missiles.

An even larger challenge was to design a digital computer that was both small enough and light enough to work in an aircraft, and then be able to function at the extremes of temperature, humidity, and pressure that were involved. At the time design began, digital computers were in their infancy and were so large that they occupied the entire floor of a building. But the air force had demanded a completely automatic aircraft, and the only way to get what the

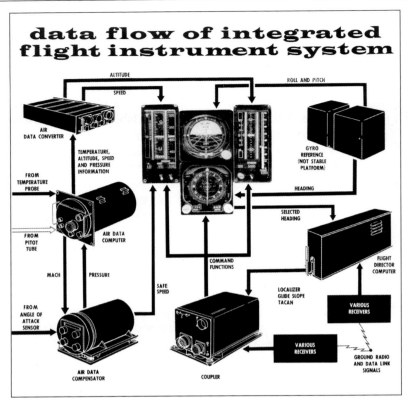

data flow of integrated flight instrument system

This is the data flow just for the flight instruments in an F-106. When the weapons functions were added, the complexity increased exponentially. (USAF)

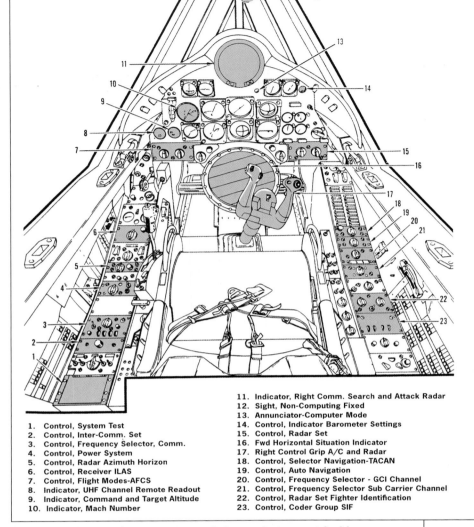

1. Control, System Test
2. Control, Inter-Comm. Set
3. Control, Frequency Selector, Comm.
4. Control, Power System
5. Control, Radar Azimuth Horizon
6. Control, Receiver ILAS
7. Control, Flight Modes-AFCS
8. Indicator, UHF Channel Remote Readout
9. Indicator, Command and Target Altitude
10. Indicator, Mach Number
11. Indicator, Right Comm. Search and Attack Radar
12. Sight, Non-Computing Fixed
13. Annunciator-Computer Mode
14. Control, Indicator Barometer Settings
15. Control, Radar Set
16. Fwd Horizontal Situation Indicator
17. Right Control Grip A/C and Radar
18. Control, Selector Navigation-TACAN
19. Control, Auto Navigation
20. Control, Frequency Selector - GCI Channel
21. Control, Frequency Selector Sub Carrier Channel
22. Control, Radar Set Fighter Identification
23. Control, Coder Group SIF

The toned boxes show portions of the cockpit provided by Hughes. On a vertical tape–equipped jet, there were far more. (USAF)

altitude, and speed. The avionics section of the unit then programmed the drum tape with the requested data. Types of waypoints could be exit points from scramble routes, pre-planned holding points, divert fields, initial approach, or final approach fixes for instrument recoveries, etc. The pilot selected the waypoint to be used and the system calculated the direction (both vertically and horizontally) to fly. If the pilot was using the autopilot, the system dropped back to hold after a waypoint passage and the pilot then had to select the next TACAN station and re-engage the autopilot automatic mode. Since the Six did not have an auto-throttle system, the pilot was still responsible for managing the aircraft's speed.

The attack mode was selected automatically, either by locking the radar or IR seeker onto a target, or by selecting any armament. In this mode, the selected weapon and altitude difference from the target determined which tactics the computer used. As time counted down toward launch, the system automatically prepared the weapons and initiated the firing signal. Since the target was expected to be a large, non-maneuverable bomber, little consideration was given to minimizing the amount of time it took to prepare the weapons for launch, and the original 16 to 20 seconds the system took between radar lock-on and weapon launch made using the Six in a tactical environment much more challenging.

The trigger on the yoke was not a trigger in the usual sense, but a "consent for launch" switch, as the computer, not the pilot, determined when to launch the weapons. Using the datalink and fully automatic mode of flight control, the pilot's job was to control the jet's speed and use the onboard radar to find and lock up the target. With weapons selected and armed, all he had to do then was to hold the trigger depressed until after weapons launch. Of course, if the automatic mode(s) did not work, that meant that the pilot had to take over all of those functions, and trying to fly at supersonic speeds with your head buried inside a radar scope was not an easy task. Trying to do it while at low altitude or in mountainous terrain was even more hazardous and several F-106s were lost this way.

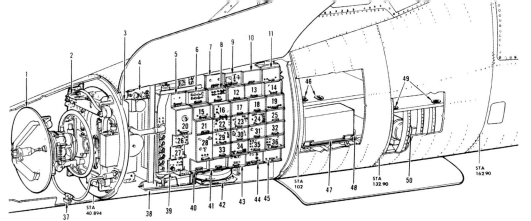

1. MA-1 Radar Antenna
2. Glide Slope Antenna
3. MA-1 Radar Transmitter-Receiver.
4. Radar Pressure Panel
5. Regulator-Voltage, Direct Current -15 Volts
6. Test Set-Radar No. 2
7. Switch Box-Radar Test
8. Computer-Steering Signal
9. Test Set-Radar No. 1
10. Power Supply, Transistor, - 50V D-C
11. Filter-Direct Current, Power + 150 Volts
12. Amplifier-Filter Steering Signal
13. Oscillator-Radio Frequency
14. Converter-Signal Data, Analog Multiplier
15. Filter-Direct Current, Power - 140 Volts
16. Amplifier-Computer, Antenna Control
17. Amplifier-Electrical Control, Elevation Drive
18. Amplifier-Electrical Control, Antenna Tracking
19. Regulator, Voltage + 100v - 140v Ref. To +100v
20. Amplifier-Electrical Control, Transmitter Tuning
21. Amplifier-Torque Generator, Rate Gyro
22. Amplifier-Electrical Control, Antenna Servo
23. Amplifier-Electrical Control, Azimuth Drive
24. Converter-Signal Data, Time Sharing
25. Converter-Signal Data, Attack Display
26. Amplifier-Synchronizer AM-1246/ APX-26
27. Amplifier Oscillator, AM-1243/ APX-26
28. Power Supply, Direct Current -250 Volts
29. Converter-Waveform, AGC and Angle Of Attack
30. Gate-Electrical Clutter
31. Synchronizer-Electrical, Master Timer
32. Amplifier-Modulator, Attack Display
33. Comparator, Signal AMTI
34. Amplifier, Intermediate Frequency
35. Synchronizer, Electrical, Range Tracking
36. Amplifier, Sweep Generator-Indicator Video and Azimuth Sweep
37. Localizer Antenna
38. Marker Beacon Antenna
39. Synchronizer-Electrical SN-126/ APX-26
40. Power Supply, Transistor + 50V D-C
41. Amplifier-Video Synchronizer, AMTI
42. Antenna-Direction Finder Group AN/ ARA-25
43. Amplifier-Video Tracking, Preamplifier
44. Generator-Sweep Indicator
45. Filter-Direct Current, Power +300 Volts
46. Cockpit Floor Feed-Thru Installation
47. Air Data Converter
48. Nose Wheel Well Interphone Receptacle
49. Feed Thru Installation
50. Air Data Compensator

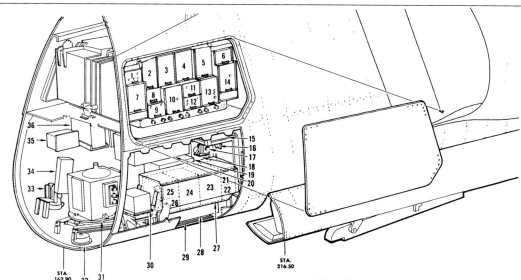

1. Voltage Regulator, 115/55V, 1600 CPS (+300v Ref)
2. Transmitter, Bearing - TACAN
3. Transmitter, Range - TACAN
4. Modulator-Coder, TACAN
5. Receiver- Interrogator, TACAN
6. Power Supply-Communications
7. Voltage Regulator- 400 Cps and 1600 Cps
8. Radio Receiver - Localizer
9. Radio Receiver - AILAS Glide Slope and
   Marker Beacon R-77 / ARN-51
10. Radio Receiver - AM Data Link
11. Tuner, RF-UHF
12. Electronics Control Amplifier - ADF Audio
13. Radio Transmitter - UHF Communications
14. Radio Receiver - UHF Communications
15. J-4 Compass Directional Control Gyro
16. STA. 216.5 Feed-Through Installation -
    Forward Launcher Harness
17. J-4 Compass System Turn Cutout Switch
18. Dehydrator Installation
19. Data Link Receiver Transmitter
20. Power Relay Installation
21. Amplifier-Electronic Control Roll and Pitch
22. Test Set-Stabilization Group
23. Amplifier-Electronic Control Integrator
24. Amplifier-Electronic Control, Azimuth
25. Demodulator Channel
26. Junction Box and Latitude Counter
27. Stable Platform Amplifier Rack Assembly
28. Pitch and Yaw Amplifier
29. Data Link Antenna
30. J-4 Compass Servo Amplifier
31. Stable Platform Generator
32. Lower Annular Slot Antenna
33. Compressor Installation
34. Dehydrator Installation
35. Lobing Switch
36. APX-19 Data Link Coder-Decoder

Avionics bays of the F-106 were heavily packed with electronics. This is a very early MA-1. (USAF)

Late in the Six's career, the air force did a study to determine which aircraft had the highest pilot workload. Only the F-16 was more difficult, and then only by a marginal amount.

To ease the pilot's workload somewhat, under SAGE control the computer generated an ellipse in elevation, range, and azimuth on the radar scope where the target could be expected to appear. The radar was originally built with several advanced modes (such as Coherent On Receive and Airborne Moving Target Indicator) to help find low-altitude targets that were in ground clutter as well as those using electronic countermeasures, or chaff. But these modes tended to be used infrequently, required extensive amounts of test equipment and time to maintain, and were removed within a few years to provide space in the electronics racks to add the IR seeker and other radar modifications.

Unlike any other aircraft built before it, the F-106 Weapons System as a whole was a joint effort between Hughes and Convair. For example, the only portions of the cockpit that Convair was responsible for were literally the sheet metal, ejection seat, and basic engine, fuel, and hydraulic gauges. Everything else was supplied by Hughes. Hughes was responsible for the entire MA-1 system, its power supply, all of the instruments it drove, and the Falcon missiles. Convair was responsible for designing an airframe that would both fit the avionics equipment supplied by Hughes and meet the air force performance requirements. Essentially, Convair designed an airframe that moved the Hughes AWCIS around the sky.

The left aft avionics bay of an early F-106A. Every effort was made to make the electronics accessible. (USAF)

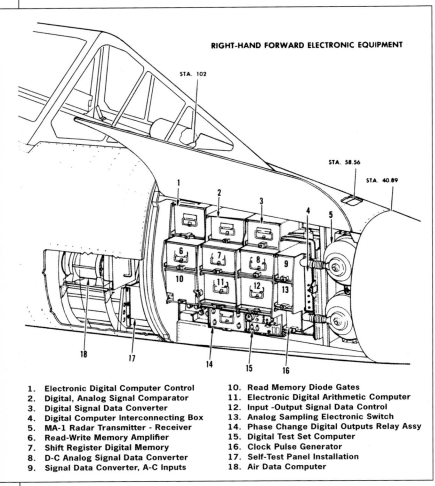

RIGHT-HAND FORWARD ELECTRONIC EQUIPMENT

1. Electronic Digital Computer Control
2. Digital, Analog Signal Comparator
3. Digital Signal Data Converter
4. Digital Computer Interconnecting Box
5. MA-1 Radar Transmitter - Receiver
6. Read-Write Memory Amplifier
7. Shift Register Digital Memory
8. D-C Analog Signal Data Converter
9. Signal Data Converter, A-C Inputs
10. Read Memory Diode Gates
11. Electronic Digital Arithmetic Computer
12. Input -Output Signal Data Control
13. Analog Sampling Electronic Switch
14. Phase Change Digital Outputs Relay Assy
15. Digital Test Set Computer
16. Clock Pulse Generator
17. Self-Test Panel Installation
18. Air Data Computer

Hughes also led the way with built-in test equipment. (USAF)

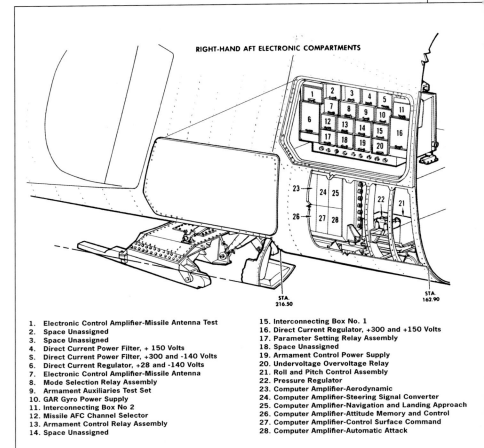

RIGHT-HAND AFT ELECTRONIC COMPARTMENTS

1. Electronic Control Amplifier-Missile Antenna Test
2. Space Unassigned
3. Space Unassigned
4. Direct Current Power Filter, + 150 Volts
5. Direct Current Power Filter, +300 and -140 Volts
6. Direct Current Regulator, +28 and -140 Volts
7. Electronic Control Amplifier-Missile Antenna
8. Mode Selection Relay Assembly
9. Armament Auxiliaries Test Set
10. GAR Gyro Power Supply
11. Interconnecting Box No 2
12. Missile AFC Channel Selector
13. Armament Control Relay Assembly
14. Space Unassigned
15. Interconnecting Box No. 1
16. Direct Current Regulator, +300 and +150 Volts
17. Parameter Setting Relay Assembly
18. Space Unassigned
19. Armament Control Power Supply
20. Undervoltage Overvoltage Relay
21. Roll and Pitch Control Assembly
22. Pressure Regulator
23. Computer Amplifier-Aerodynamic
24. Computer Amplifier-Steering Signal Converter
25. Computer Amplifier-Navigation and Landing Approach
26. Computer Amplifier-Attitude Memory and Control
27. Computer Amplifier-Control Surface Command
28. Computer Amplifier-Automatic Attack

When the IRST was added, some little-used functions of the radar were deleted to make space for the seeker and its electronics. (USAF)

Cook-Craigie + Concurrency = Configuration Control Nightmare

In attempting to get the F-106 working properly, both Convair and Hughes took the Cook-Craigie and Concurrency philosophies to extremes. Each of the first hundred or so aircraft was literally "one of a kind," both in the airframe and the electronics. Due to the scope and complexity of the new electronics, flight testing on the MA-1 continued through early 1961. Throughout testing, as problems were identified, and solved, the resulting changes were then applied as quickly as possible to airframes that were under construction.

Due to time constraints, parts that had not been approved by San Antonio were frequently used. Changes were made so frequently that maintenance documents available to the users were far behind the configuration of the actual aircraft, and could only be described as rough guides. Users, both test and operational, frequently had to call the SAAMA for help in determining what parts were actually needed, or if they were even available. This resulted in a telephone call to Convair, and possibly a subsequent call to HAC to determine exactly which configuration the aircraft had.

Many times, Convair and Hughes technical reps had to tear down an aircraft to be able to find out exactly what was inside. Between Convair, Hughes, and the overall systems manager at San Antonio, Configuration Control (the knowledge of exactly what part was in use on what aircraft) was essentially lost. As such, the overall reliability of both the MA-1 system and the aircraft was abysmal when the F-106 first entered service. Several years of modifications, improvements, and upgrades were required to achieve adequate results.

The entire process was made even more complicated because, at the same time all of this was happening, the air force was changing the entire way it handled inventories. The Air Material Areas were trying to evaluate and approve proposed new parts while simultaneously trying to design and implement an entirely new "top to bottom" catalogue change of every part in existence. Given these conditions, it is little wonder that serious problems existed.

Ground Support Equipment for the Six

Given the complexity of the MA-1 AWCIS, existing Aerospace Ground Equipment (AGE) was utterly inadequate to maintain it. Convair and Hughes therefore had to design many new pieces of test equipment. Some of the new components of AGE were: the M32A-13 engine-driven electrical power unit and its 440V electrically powered ECU-10M counterpart; the massive gas-powered MA-3 and electrically powered MA-3M air conditioning units; a bench mockup of the MA-1; a Mobile Automatic Radio Test (MART) set; a mobile Fault Detection Tester (FDT) that fit over the radome of an F-106; a tow-through radar calibration or "cal" barn; and many others. Falcon missiles and Genie rockets also required not only new test equipment, but specialized transport and storage equipment, to say nothing of specially designed maintenance and storage buildings, as well.

To minimize scramble times, the original concept for the Six was to have automatic pull-out plugs for both the electrical and air carts. The M32 was designed to fit underneath the wing of an F-106, which precluded having to move it during a launch. The MC-11 high-pressure air cart, used for starting the engine, was usually parked at the eight o'clock position in relation to the jet, and outside the wing.

The plan was that the Six would start up and taxi away, the power cable and high-pressure air hose would simply pull out of their respective receptacles on the aircraft, and spring-loaded doors would close up; all without assistance from the crew chief. As with many grand plans, however, this one failed. Pulling out a plug on a nice Southern California day was quite different from doing the same thing on a 30-degrees-below-zero day at Minot AFB, North

On the ramp at Elmendorf, 21 September 1967, this 11th FIS Six shows the later-style alar on the tail, minus the usual Red Bulls squadron badge. The original external fuel tanks limited the Six to subsonic speeds but did increase the range. That massive M32A-13 electrical power unit with the thick 56-wire connecting cable was ubiquitous around the Six prior to the Power Upgrade Program (PUP) modification. (Norman E. Taylor)

Dakota. It did not take long to see just how much damage occurred to the 56-wire power cables and 3,000-psi air hoses before that idea was scrapped.

Because the Six was so maintenance-intensive during its early years, some bases actually received 440VAC power lines buried under the concrete ramp areas, with supposedly weather-protected caps, so that the electrically powered ECU-10M units could be used on the ramp. That idea also proved to be impractical, but when the large aircraft shelters were constructed on northern-tier bases, all were provided with 440VAC power.

So much heat was generated by the MA-1 system that, unlike the F-101 or F-102, which could simply use ventilating air, the Six had to have an air conditioner to undergo any electronics maintenance. A massive, 12-ton air conditioner. By way of comparison, a one- or two-ton unit cools a normal house. Those densely packed miniature tubes needed a lot of cold air to keep from overheating and failing. Since the original ground air and electrical units were so large,

With a 94th FIS Six in the background, this 1960 photo shows some of the specialized AGE equipment needed. From left to right are: M32A-13, MC-11, MA-3, and a LOX cart. When the IRST was added, a similar cart was used to service the system with liquid nitrogen. (USAF via El Mason)

Seen taxiing off the air force ramp at Duluth, Minnesota, in September 1967, this 11th FIS Six shows the later red alar unit markings. On the right is one of the buried 440V electrical outlets. (USAF)

In practice, the MART was rarely used. Although it verified proper operation of the TACAN, ILS, and some of the datalink systems, it was, in the words of one avionics specialist, "normally broken and useless." The tester was maintained by the communication/navigation shops, but spare parts were hard to come by, and both the operating instructions and troubleshooting guides for it were considered to be very poor by the line maintainers.

The Fault Detection Tester (FDT), on the other hand, was a very sophisticated piece of test equipment. It was used to test operation and target tracking of the radar and infrared search and track (IRST) systems, as well as verifying proper operation of a good portion of the missile control system. According to avionics personnel who used it, when the unit first came out it was laden with bugs, and it took several years and modifications before the unit was considered useful. Even after the problems were solved, it was still very time consuming to hook up the unit.

First, the tester was towed to the Six in question and backed up so that the hood fit over the radome of the jet. Then cables had to be connected from the FDT to a connection inside the nose wheelwell of the jet. Finally, air conditioning and electrical power had to be supplied to the aircraft, the IRST extended, and the radar placed into operation. However, once the system matured, it capably did the job it was designed for.

Moisture caused serious problems. And once again, "Murphy" entered the scene. The designers apparently did not consider what would happen when the equipment was used in the high humidity of Florida or other damp locations. As soon as the dew point started to climb, the evaporators started to freeze up. When all of the ice

they were designed to be self-powered to make them easier to move. After many injuries to maintenance personnel, that function was deactivated, which eased maintenance on the units somewhat, as well.

A scene that was a daily occurrence but rarely documented. This Six from the 84th FIS at Castle AFB, California, has a Fault Detection Tester placed over its radome. With ground power and air conditioning running, the Six's radar would be radiating, and the IRST active as well. Keeping the Six's avionics running took a lot of specialized test equipment and highly trained technicians, as well as a lot of hours.

in the MA-1 system eventually melted, it shorted out both the hardware and coaxial cables carrying radio and radar signals. The fix for that was not a short one.

The original computer on the F-106 had several rows of line-removable electrical boxes that plugged into racks. Vibration or G-forces frequently caused intermittent or failed contacts. When maintenance was called for MA-1 malfunctions, the normal "quick fix" was to take a rubber mallet and tap all the boxes, which would, with luck, fix the problem. Until the advent of the transistorized computer, at many Six bases, pilots started their aircraft and taxied, not to a "last chance" inspection, but to a quick-fix area to get the MA-1 system working prior to takeoff. Code 1 (no malfunctions) returns were exceptionally rare.

For a prospective MA-1 maintainer, the road was daunting. Not only was a security clearance required, but the MA-1 school was the longest tech school in the air force. Once the new maintenance man arrived on his assigned base, he immediately started a minimum of six months of on-the-job training to become qualified. By the time an enlisted man completed his four-year tour in the air force, he was just becoming competent at keeping the MA-1 system operational. Since re-enlistments after spending a few years on remote and freezing north country air bases were rare, the air force had a difficult time keeping qualified electronics maintenance people on the job.

Maintaining the AGE equipment was just as difficult. That required a six-month tech school followed by at least six months on base to learn the F-106–unique equipment that was not taught at the tech school. Not only was knowledge of gasoline and diesel engines required, but also electronics, air conditioning, and pneumatics. Because adequate manuals and spare parts were in short supply or non-existent in the early years, keeping the AGE equipment operational was just as difficult as keeping the MA-1 system up and running.

Who said working inside was warmer? The heavy parkas on these maintainers show that whatever heat was available inside the aircraft shelter was inadequate. The massive 56-wire electrical cable is locked into the aircraft's external power jack. With cables running up into the lower aft electronics compartment, maybe the stable table is being tested. Photo of S/N 59-0013 of the 5th FIS at Minot AFB, North Dakota, circa 1964. (USAF via Isham)

Watching them come home. As one Six rolls out on landing, a crew chief watches another 4-ship come up initial and waits for his jet to return. 49 FIS at Griffiss AFB, New York, April 1973.

Chapter Six

WEAPONS FOR THE SIX

NORAD defenders await review by the brass. In front of one of the older-style Butler alert hangars, this Six keeps a NIKE Hercules, an F-102, and an F-104A company. The Genie is sitting on its MF-9 dolly next to an AIM-4E. The date is either 1959 or 1960. (USAF)

In September 1962, most USAF military equipment was re-designated into one joint listing. For example, the Genie rocket, originally known as the MB-1, became the AIR-2A. The Super Falcon missile family, originally known as the GAR-3/-3A and -4, was renamed as the AIM-4E, -4F, and -4G. (Rather than confuse the issue, I generally have used the later designations.)

One of the first weapons proposals for the F-106 consisted of a large number of 2.75-inch folding-fin aerial rockets (FFAR). At least in concept, these were derived from the R4M aerial rockets used by Luftwaffe Bf-109s and FW-190s in attacking Allied bombers over Germany in World War II and were widely used by early USAF interceptors. Unguided, they were launched in groups of between 6 and more than 40 and were aimed by the interceptors' FCS. While even one hit could bring down an aircraft, they were notorious for going off in any direction but that of the target, and early gun camera films showed target banners flying unscathed through a cloud of rockets during attack after attack. Given the rapid advances in missile technology, unguided rockets were rapidly consigned to backup status. Fortunately, they were discarded altogether prior to the F-106 reaching the advanced construction stage.

Posing in an early pressure suit, this pilot from the 498th FIS stands next to an AIM-4E Falcon missile and an AIR-2A (MB-1) Genie rocket. The early pressure suits seriously impeded mobility for the pilots. (USAF)

The Douglas Genie

Nearly as soon as the first nuclear device had been detonated, the possibility of shrinking the warhead to a size small enough to be used in an aerial rocket was considered. With existing USAF leadership coming from a background of massed heavy bomber formations, they were well aware of the difficulties in stopping such an attack before it incurred massive damage to targets on the ground. A nuclear warhead seemed to be a much more effective way of eliminating large numbers of bombers at once than attacking each bomber individually.

Initially, it was impossible to shrink the nuclear device to a size small enough to be carried onboard a fighter-type aircraft. But technological progress was rapid, and by the early 1950s, feasibility studies conducted by the air force, the Rand Corporation, and others had concluded that such a weapon was possible. As a result, the Douglas Aircraft Company (later McDonnell Douglas Astronautics) was tasked to design and develop such a weapon. Work began in December 1954 and was carried out in secret. Several code names were used to describe the project, including Bird Dog, Ding Dong, High Card, and eventually, Genie.

Because the weapon was unguided, extensive research was conducted on launch simulations to determine what corrections had to be designed into the FCS. For the F-106, much of this research was carried out by the Langley Pilotless Aircraft Research Station at Wallops Island, Virginia. Simulated ejections with fins open, fins closed, fins closed with a shroud around the fins, and fins folded with a "boat tail" placed between the fins were carried out at simulated altitudes between 12,000 and 40,000 feet, at both subsonic and supersonic airspeeds.

The first dummy test drop of a Genie occurred at Holloman AFB on 8 March 1956, and several methods of carriage and launching of the rocket were investigated for use on both the F-102 and F-106. One method that was live tested used an excess YF-102 (S/N 53-1781), *sans* engine, that was inclined at a 45-degree angle while suspended from a test sling on the ground. A fixed pylon on the centerline of the fuselage was used for the rocket. YF-102 S/N 53-1797 had a retractable Genie launcher installed in the weapons bay, while YF-102C S/N 53-1806 had its weapons bay rebuilt and modified with an internal rack of the type later used on the F-106. This aircraft

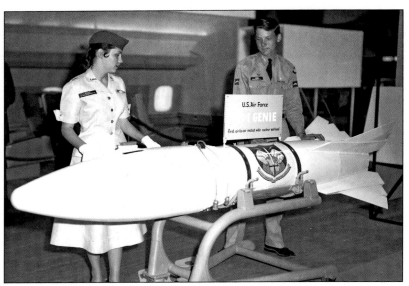

Civil Air Patrol cadets stand by a dummy Genie on display in May 1959. The fins are in the extended, flight position.

was used for airborne drop tests and performed at least one live test launch in the 1956–1957 time period. After a little more than two years of intensive effort, the MB-1 Genie rocket became operational in January 1957 with the F-89J interceptor. When the U.S. military designations were redone in 1962, the weapon became the AIR-2A.

The W-25 warhead for the Genie was live tested twice, the second time after the weapon was already in service. The first test was an underground one, and resulted in an explosive equivalent of 2.2 kilotons (Kt). The second was the only live air-to-air test ever concluded with a nuclear armed rocket. That test gave a result of around 1.5 Kt, so the average yield was considered to be 1.8 Kt.

Air Defense Command had initially planned on testing the Genie on a drone B-47 target but Gen. Curtis E. LeMay, Commander of the Strategic Air Command (SAC), was vehemently opposed to the idea because he felt that it would completely demoralize the aircrews within SAC if they saw one of their first-line aircraft destroyed in that manner. A remote-controlled B-17 was also proposed, but that idea was rejected and serious objections regarding the practical difficulties in measuring the data needed with a moving target were also raised. In the end, the time of flight for the rocket was manually set prior to takeoff, and the rocket was simply fired at a highly instrumented point in space with no target present.

The tests were part of Operation Plumbob, and the aerial test, known as "Shot John," occurred on 19 July 1957. Carried out over the Yucca Flats test range outside Indian Springs, Nevada, this test was performed to determine the weapon's yield, fallout characteristics, and the level of radiation that would reach the launching aircraft. Three F-89J Scorpions were instrumented for the test, and two were subsequently flown; one to actually launch the rocket, and the second to photograph the launch and provide a second set of test data.

In addition, five USAF officers and a cameraman volunteered to stand directly beneath the point of detonation. The intent was to prove that neither the shock wave, heat, nor radiation from the blast that occurred overhead was dangerous and that the Genie would be safe to use over populated civilian areas. Various descriptions have been given about the height of the blast, but the best evidence seems to be that it was actually launched at 19,000-feet MSL and detonated between 18,500- and 20,000-feet MSL, or about 15,000 feet above the ground.

The warhead was designed to produce a large neutron flux that would theoretically destroy any aircraft within approximately a mile of the detonation and would render an enemy warhead incapable of detonation for several minutes. The intent was to preclude a large nuclear ground burst in the event that enemy aircraft were shot down and enemy weapons were salvage fused to detonate on ground impact. In effect, this actually made the Genie the first neutron bomb. As an additional advantage, the SAC generals in charge of the air force also felt that the thought of facing such a weapon would have a very negative effect on the morale of enemy airmen.

Two load-crew members remove the tarp covering this ATR-2 while the team chief reviews the checklist, a scene repeated countless times.

The Genie rocket was extremely simple, with the casing containing little more than the warhead, a safety/fusing mechanism, and the rather massive Thiokol-built rocket motor, which produced 36,000 pounds of thrust. The external case had a pullout plug for electrical connections to the FCS, attachment lugs to hold the rocket securely on the aircraft's launching rack, and stabilizing fins. On the F-106, these fins were held in the retracted position by nylon cords. When the rocket motor ignited, the exhaust burned the cords, allowing the fins to snap-out to the extended position. The rocket was completely unguided and had to be aimed by the launching aircraft. The warhead was fused by a timing signal that was also provided by the carrier aircraft prior to weapon launch.

Several training versions were also supplied to the air force. The ATR-2A carried a high-explosive spotting charge and was the usual round launched for annual nuclear certification and weapons meets. These usually had yellow dots painted over the circular access panels on the nose and were also known as MB-1-T. An AJT was a live training round that had four radio transponders, for tracking purposes, set behind the circular access panels. These were only used when the Multiple Airborne Target Trajectory Scoring (MATTS) system at Tyndall AFB, Florida, was inoperative for long periods of time and were considered much less accurate, as far as scoring capability.

The Anchor Gold rockets were live AIR-2As that had their nuclear warhead removed and replaced with the high-explosive spotting charge. As the stocks of ATR-2s were depleted, only a few of the Anchor Gold rounds were converted. Eventually the propellant in the original rocket motors aged to the point where they were replaced with new Thiokol SR49-TC-1 motors (later re-designated TDU-289). When Congress cut funding in 1984, the Genies were retired.

Practice weapons loads were daily events at operational squadrons, and the inert-load training version of the Genie, known as the

A great view of the MF-9 dolly and load trainer Genie. Small crank handles could move the cradle slightly side to side, or fore and aft, to correctly position the rocket to the rack in the Six's weapons bay. The forward latch and pullout plug location are clearly visible in this May 1969 view. (El Mason)

With checklist in hand, the load-team chief oversees uploading an ATR-2N into the weapons bay of this 87th FIS F-106A at K. I. Sawyer AFB in March 1978. Blue paint denotes a training round.

ATR-2N, was a frequent sight on the flight line or in the aircraft shelters at all F-106 units. Finally, the McDonnell Simulator Rocket (MSR) was an instrumented package that was fixed onto the Genie launching rack on the F-106. This training device recorded various parameters at the simulated launch, which could then be downloaded and used for debriefing purposes at the unit level.

Genie missiles weighed 822 pounds, had a length of 9 feet 8 inches, and had a span of 3 feet 4 inches. It had a speed of around Mach 3.3 and a range in the vicinity of 6 miles, depending upon the launch altitude. Tactical rockets were painted white overall with minimal black stenciling. Training rounds with live rocket motors were generally painted white overall, but sometimes had an orange rocket motor section. Starting in the mid-1970s, a brown band was painted around the circumference of the rocket behind the warhead section to indicate a live motor was installed. Over the years, ground training shapes have been gloss white overall, white forward sections with blue motor sections, and white noses with orange rocket sections.

Hughes Super Falcons

Hughes began developing the Falcon family of missiles during 1946 under project MX-798. This subsonic, tube-launched, bomber defensive weapon rapidly gave way to a supersonic version, project MX-904, in 1947. In 1950, the decision was made to develop the missile to arm interceptor aircraft.

The Super Falcon family of missiles was significantly different from the original Falcons. They had warheads nearly double the size of the originals, were slightly larger in wingspan and length, had forward strakes,

At Kirtland AFB, New Mexico, in 1959, this new Six is on display next to its original weapons load. Prior to introduction of the Super Falcons, the Six could use only the Genie and four of the transitional AIM-4E Falcons. Note the lack of forward strakes on the missiles. Their poor aerodynamics seriously limited their usefulness. (USAF)

Four AIM-4E Falcons are displayed in front of this 94th FIS F-106A on Armed Forces Day 1969. By this time, these early Falcons had been relegated to war reserve spares and load training. The thin red stripes between the yellow and black band on the fin of the Six are barely visible. (Mason)

An AIM-4F Super Falcon. The thin white rectangles on the leading edges of the aft fins are the contact fuses. At least two of these had to be crushed for the small H.E. warhead to explode. There was a great deal of stenciling on these missiles. (Mason)

and were more technologically advanced. The single-stage rocket motor of the originals gave way to a new Thiokol M46 two-stage boost-sustain variant and, whereas the original Falcons could not begin guidance until after motor burnout, the Super Falcons began guiding once the motor went into the sustain mode. The differences in guidance and size made it impossible for either the F-101B or the F-102 to use any of the Super Falcons. Likewise, the F-106 could not carry or employ any of the original series of Falcons.

A full load of four, either radar- or IR-guided, Falcons could be carried in the Six, but because they always fired in pairs from either the fore or aft launchers, different types could not be mixed side by side. Since the aft launchers fired first, the AIM-4G IR missiles were always loaded aft in a mixed radar/IR load. This prevented the IR missiles from guiding on the rocket motors of the radar-guided AIM-4Fs. The missiles required a great deal of information from the MA-1 and final missile preparation prior to firing started at least 20 seconds before actual launch. That was the time the pilot had to press and then hold the "launch consent switch" (aka, trigger). In later years, the normal alert Falcon load was two radar-guided missiles on the forward launchers and two IR–guided missiles on the aft launchers.

The initial Super Falcon used semi-active radar guidance and was a transitional vehicle. It was known as the AIM-4E (GAR-3/HAC Model EPa) and, although lacking the forward lateral strakes that were found on the later AIM-4F and -G versions, it did have the increased wingspan of the later missiles. The -E model scored its first air-to-air hit in 1955 and was deemed ready for service in 1958, but testing with the F-106 was delayed until enough aircraft with suitably equipped MA-1 systems were available. As a result, flight tests of the AIM-4E with the F-106 did not begin until March 1959, continuing through November. During testing at Holloman, the AIM-4E was found to be inadequate and the Six was very restricted as to the flight conditions under which the AIM-4E could be successfully launched.

Guidance also proved to be a problem since, to save space and weight, all of the Falcons were only equipped with contact fusing. Thus, not only was a direct hit required, but a direct hit that allowed the missile to penetrate the target far enough to crush the fuses that were contained in the leading edges of the wings. Given the restricted launch parameters for the AIM-4E, the air force decided to replace the AIM-4E with the AIM-4F in January 1959, before one was even fired from an F-106. Only 300 of these missiles were produced, and although lasting in the field through at least 1968, they were rapidly consigned to backup war reserve status with the units that received them.

The follow-on AIM-4F (GAR-3A/HAC model EPb), introduced in 1960, had the forward lateral strakes that characterized the Super Falcon family. Seeker electronics were also improved to have greater accuracy and increased immunity to jamming. As originally built, the radome of the missile had a 10-cm-long spike that was intended to improve the aerodynamics and aid with ECCM. However, these were found to be quite fragile, and they were so frequently broken off during handling that the air force began removing them almost immediately after they entered service with ADC, trading slightly decreased performance for much increased ease of handling.

Given the differences in flight and guidance characteristics between the AIM-4E and AIM-4F, additional modifications to the MA-1 automatic weapon control system (AWCS) were required. Negotiations between Convair, Hughes, and the air force led to a determination that all aircraft produced after November 1959 would have the capability to carry the AIM-4F, while all F-106s built prior to that would have the capability added during programmed maintenance scheduled for June and July 1960, a date well after the first squadrons were to be equipped and operational.

Initial test firings of the AIM-4F from the F-106 were accomplished at Eglin in July 1959. Once enough F-106s had received MA-1s modified to guide the newer generation of Super Falcons, further testing was accomplished in 1960 at both Holloman and Tyndall. This was the long-delayed Category III testing (Operational Test and Evaluation), and much of it was carried out by the 539th FIS, based at McGuire AFB, New Jersey, the first operational squadron to receive the F-106. Convair considered this portion of testing complete in September 1960, but ADC was of a different mindset.

The IR–guided AIM-4G was actually built in two versions. The initial version (HAC model GPa) used the IR seeker of the earlier AIM-4C Falcon on the body of the later AIM-4F and was known as the GAR-4. The early seekers were rapidly replaced with improved versions, and the resulting missiles were known as the GAR-4A (HAC model GPb). Apparently, by the 1962 re-designation, none of the early GAR-4s were left in service, so the IR-guided version became known as the AIM-4G. Only very small quantities of the original GAR-4 were procured before being replaced with the later version.

The AIM-4G was unique for its time, using a cooled seeker head that made it much more sensitive. As a matter of comparison, the AIM-9 Sidewinder series of IR-guided missiles did not feature a cooled seeker head for nearly 15 years after the AIM-4G went into service. Although no attempt to specifically engineer an all-aspect capability into the missile was made, Maj. Bruce Gordon of the 94th FIS registered a direct hit on the engine of a BOMARC target missile in March 1967, using a head-on attack pass. At missile launch, the closing speed was nearly Mach 5, and the single Falcon hit the missile in its left engine.

AIM-4Es were 86 inches long and had a span of 24 inches. They were originally painted red overall with white radomes. AIM-4F missiles had the same length and span but were painted with white forward sections and red aft sections. They had light gray ceramic radomes. The AIM-4Gs were only 81 inches long and had

This AIM-4G IR-guided Super Falcon in its storage container was seen at William Tell 1984. A plastic nose cover protected the fragile glass nose. (Bert Kinzey/Detail & Scale)

Towing a trailer full of Falcons out for a weapons load; this was a typical scene at any F-106 base. The handling dolly is strapped to the back of the trailer. When this photo was taken in 1970, the tractor and trailer were yellow. The Falcon coffins were always natural aluminum. (USAF)

AIM-4G missiles were rarely seen without their protective nose covers in place. Thirty seconds after the covers came off here, the missiles were out of sight.

Falcons were stored and transported in these specially designed containers, frequently known as "coffins." Seen here during their Korean deployment, these two 95th FIS armament troops are about to use the unique carrying handle to lift the missile out of the coffin. (USAF)

A WSEM loaded on the right forward launcher of an F-106A. Normally painted FS 15102 blue with a light gray ceramic nose cone, they were used to record firing parameters for post-mission analysis.

round-glass IR seekers on the nose. They had the same paint colors and wingspan as the AIM-4F. The Super Falcons weighed around 150 pounds each, had a maximum speed of Mach 3, and had a nominal range of 7 miles.

Unlike the "unstoppable" Genie, the same could not be said of the AIM-4 Falcon family. Given the air force's requirement to carry four of them inside the F-106's weapons bay, Hughes had to cut many corners. To save weight and volume, they were equipped with simple contact fusing, instead of a proximity fuse. Likewise, they were not able to use a blast-fragmentation warhead to increase lethality; there was only room for a small, explosive blast–type warhead. The missile's small size meant that only small rocket motors could be used, which seriously degraded the range. When finally given the chance to do what it wanted, Hughes responded by enlarging the basic design, resulting in the Long Range (X) AIM-47 for the Mach-3.2 Lockheed YF-12 Blackbird. That missile eventually morphed into

the incomparable AIM-54 Phoenix, which armed the navy's legendary Grumman F-14 Tomcat fighter.

A flight training version of the Super Falcons, known as a Weapons System Evaluator Missile (WSEM), could be loaded and captive-carried on any of the launch rails of an F-106. This training device had truncated fins and no rocket motor. They were painted FS 15109 blue (the standard air force color denoting inert weapons) and carried a tape that recorded all of the launch parameters and guidance information fed to the missile at simulated launch. After landing, the tape was downloaded from the WSEM and the intercept was graded back in the operations building.

Because guns were considered passé in the new world of automated, missile-firing interceptors, no thought was given to arming the F-106 with a gun. It was nearly 20 years before serious attempts were made in that direction and a quarter of a century before the General Electric Vulcan cannon was regularly seen on the Six.

Not in a Vacuum: The History of SAGE

Convair's interceptors were not developed in a vacuum. At the beginning of the Korean War, the U.S. Air Force leadership was dominated by "bomber generals," those who had run the massed bomber attacks on Germany and Japan in World War II. Gadflies who believed in fighter airpower had either been shown the door (Claire Chennault) or moved to relatively meaningless occupations (Gen. Elwood "Pete" Queseda). Although the bomber generals believed that only the massive application of strategic air power would result in victory, they also understood that the carnage their bombers had wreaked on Germany and Japan could not be allowed to happen to the United States.

When it became evident that the Soviet Union had also attained nuclear weapons, the generals saw a critical need to keep even a single enemy bomber from reaching the United States. Following the nearly total post–World War II demobilization, however, the United States had virtually no defenses left. It was quite clear to the air force hierarchy that large numbers of capable all-weather interceptors were needed. It was equally clear that just having the best interceptor force in the world was not going be enough.

There also had to be a radar net to detect enemy bombers and a control system to guide the interceptors to the vicinity of their targets. Thus, the rise of a hostile Soviet Union led to the frantic development of SAGE (Semi-Automatic Ground Environment Air Defense System). Taking as its starting point the Royal Air Force's line of "chain home" radar sites, and the centralized plotting and control centers that were established just prior to the Battle of Britain, the SAGE system eventually linked hundreds of manned and unmanned radars, Texas Tower offshore radar platforms, U.S. Navy radar picket ships, and the first airborne early warning system in history. Combat units of the Air Defense Command, the Army Air Defense Artillery Command, and the Royal Canadian Air Force were integrated into an air defense system that covered not only the entire North American continent, but stretched across the entire Atlantic and halfway across the Pacific Ocean.

But the SAGE control centers were the heart of the network. It took seven years of development for MIT's Lincoln Laboratory, IBM, and the Rand Corporation to develop the AN/FSQ-7 computer and the software that ran the system. Digital computing was barely in its infancy in the early 1950s, and vacuum tubes were the only means of providing internal memory. These tubes were slow and unreliable. In attempting to solve the problem, one of the greatest technological breakthroughs in computing occurred: the invention of reliable, magnetic-core memory. This became a watershed moment in the development of both SAGE and commercial computing, as not only did reliability improve by several orders of magnitude, but performance improvement was significant as well, thus allowing digital computing to become practical.

In the case of the SAGE computers, operating speed doubled, the data input rate quadrupled, maintenance time on the memory dropped from four hours per day to two hours per week, and the mean time between memory failures (MTBF) jumped from two hours to two weeks. It is no idle claim to say that today's computing devices owe their existence to the development of the SAGE computer.

The first FSQ-7 was declared operational at McGuire on 1 July 1958. Eventually, 24 FSQ-7s were installed. Each weighed 250 tons, had a 3,000-kW power supply, and used 60,000 vacuum tubes. To ensure continuous operation each computer was duplexed. It actually consisted of two machines operating simultaneously, one being primary and the second acting as a real-time backup. Because of the immense amount of heat generated by all those tubes, the concrete-reinforced blockhouses in which they were installed were not heated, only cooled.

Targets seen by any of the radars were quickly and automatically linked to the Air Defense Regional Centers and Direction Centers. Warnings were passed up the chain of command and defensive forces alerted. Interceptors were sent aloft to identify unknown targets at any time of day or night and in any weather conditions. Ground Controlled Intercept (GCI) controllers assigned the destruction of a hostile track to either manned interceptors, U.S. Army Air Defense Command (ARADCOM), Nike surface-to-air missiles, or unmanned BOMARC missiles. Most of the Nikes and all of the air force systems carried nuclear warheads. This was the automatic ground system that the 1954 interceptor was designed to work with.

When the final radar site was completed in 1962, the SAGE system was finally operational. However, technology was moving so fast that it was already obsolete. The air force was looking beyond manned aircraft. Boeing and the University of Michigan were busy designing the first unmanned interceptor missile, which later became the BOMARC. Faced with the multi-layered nuclear defensive shield that surrounded the North American continent, the Soviet leadership concluded that ICBMs were a much more cost-effective offensive weapon. While they maintained enough of a long-range aviation bomber force to be a significant threat, their efforts turned toward a weapon the SAGE system could neither address nor defeat.

A typical 1950s-era wooden squadron operations building is in the background here at Castle AFB in March 1978. Weapons loading was a daily task at interceptor squadrons, and live weapons were commonly used. Security was tight. Unless you wanted a gun in your back while eating cement, you had better be wearing a restricted-area access badge if you crossed the red line on the ramp.

Chapter Seven

CONTINUED FLIGHT AND WEAPONS TESTING

The rectangular warning placards on the bifold-type weapons bay doors, the ventral keel, and lack of arresting hook are typical of this early tactical F-106A. The camber applied to the leading edges of the Case XXIX wings is also apparent. (USAF via Isham)

Slow development of the Hughes MA-1 led to a very drawn out flight test program for the F-106. Fortunately, that delay allowed Convair engineers the time they needed to optimize the aerodynamics of the airframe. Indecision and other factors within the air force also led to far slower than desired progress.

Continued Flight Testing

Lack of flight-ready MA-1 systems began to seriously impact the F-106 program in late 1957. When the November 1957 configuration board meeting decided to revert to a standard center control stick, it did not help matters. Hughes engineers had to redesign the yoke of the F-102 to accommodate the additional functions of the MA-1 system for the F-106, and it took time for the changes to be incorporated, new grips to be produced, and aircraft wiring modified. In the meantime, aircraft continued to come off the assembly line with nothing more than a standard control stick and no electronics.

Nine additional F-106As had come off the assembly lines with space provisions for only the MA-1 and weapons launchers by the time the first F-106B flew, and they were added to the Convair test fleet at Edwards as they became available. As it turned out, delays and difficulties with the J75 (particularly the fuel control), as well as investigation of alternative configurations of the air inlets, variable-ramp design, and exhaust nozzles, ate up most of the time while waiting

S/N 56-0462 was used at Edwards for a little more than a year, primarily to investigate stability and control issues. It was placed into flyable storage on 9 June 1959 to await T-T-T rebuild. It still has the wing fences and early air intakes here. (USAF via Isham)

The prototype F-106A engages the barrier cable in 1959 during initial tests of the proposed tailhook modification. (Via Isham)

for a useable MA-1 to arrive anyhow. The J75-P-9 replaced the P-1 of the first few aircraft but proved to be less reliable than desired, and replacement with the newer, higher-thrust J75-P-17 was a high priority.

As additional aircraft came off the assembly lines in San Diego, they were loaded onto a specially designed dolly. They were then towed along a dedicated access road that crossed an expressway, before reaching the flight line on Lindbergh Field, where they were prepared for flight to Palmdale, California. There, at Air Force Plant 42, Convair and Hughes installed the MA-1 fire control system, installed the armament launchers, tested all systems, painted the aircraft, and readied them for delivery to the air force. At the same time and location, nearly 1,000 F-102s were either being modified or undergoing preparations for delivery to the air force. The addition of the F-106s to the mix considerably increased the workload there. The F-102 was still not a mature system at this time, and AFFFTC was still busy conducting flight testing on the earlier aircraft.

Air Force Phase VI testing (Functional Development) began at Edwards in April 1958 with S/N 56-0467. It was immediately instrumented for performance and engine evaluation, while S/N 56-0462, which was the first aircraft with the finalized center-stick cockpit configuration, became the stability and control test airframe. These were followed by S/N 57-0235 and F-106Bs S/N 57-2511 and 57-2512.

The Air Force Flight Test Center originally planned to start a comprehensive Phase II (Contractor Compliance) Flight Test early in 1958. It was intended "to perform a functional and operational evaluation to determine the capabilities and limitations of the F-106 Weapon System; to determine that the system is compatible within

Convair launched most of the existing F-106A fleet as a publicity stunt in July 1958. Seen here on a flyover of the F-106 Joint Test Force sign at Edwards, the formation also did flybys at the Palmdale final assembly plant. (Via Isham)

tailhook installation. The prototype F-106 (S/N 56-0451) was used for both the tailhook and initial external fuel tank performance evaluations before being donated to the Air Force Museum in March 1960. Once completely configured aircraft were available and serviceable, preliminary performance evaluation and tactics development finally began.

By the time the full Phase II evaluation was completed on 31 May 1959, the 24 F-106A and F-106B aircraft that were eventually assigned to the testing had completed 833 test flights and just under 1,000 hours of flight time. Test progress was repeatedly delayed by time compliance technical order changes, "excessive" unscheduled maintenance on the MA-1 system, and participation in aerial demonstrations. All of the aircraft delivered to the program prior to February 1959 required both an engine change and variable-ramp actuator replacement every 25 hours. Finally, the aircraft were grounded for extended periods in both November 1958 and May 1959 for inspection and modification of the fuel transfer line located within the air-conditioning bay.

Further groundings occurred in January and April 1959 for special inspections of the ejection seats. Of the 833 test flights, 89 were flown for directed aerial demonstrations and other test support, 193 were for pilot familiarization/checkout, 58 were for aircraft systems evaluation, 221 were for MA-1 AWCS systems performance determination, 96 were devoted to preliminary tactics development, 13 were for the angle-of-attack indicator evaluation, and 62 were required maintenance test flights. Maintenance on the MA-1 soaked up the majority of the ground effort, requiring more than 36 man-hours per hour of flight time.

By the conclusion of the testing, 17 AFFTC pilots, 18 ADC pilots, and 4 Cambridge Research Center (Hanscom Field, Massachusetts) pilots had qualified on the aircraft. Unfortunately, due to the low utilization rates, late delivery of properly configured aircraft, and in spite of nearly 1,000 hours of flight testing, several important objectives were not achieved. Those areas included armament firings, automatic attack counter-countermeasures, "snap up" attacks, (rocket) escape maneuvers, and combat radius determinations, all of which were deferred for evaluation during follow-on Category III testing.

Slowing progress even further, the final report recommended more than 135 changes to overcome deficiencies and improve the capabilities of the new interceptor. Virtually all systems were assessed as needing help. Eight recommendations were made for the MA-1: The power subsystem received 9, the computer 5, the radar 14, the airframe 21, electrical and lighting 14, power plant 11, and so on.

the supporting environment required for its operational use; and to determine the preliminary employment suitability and capability in meeting an established operational requirement."

Lack of aircraft with the MA-1 installed kept the program from starting until 1 August 1958 when S/N 57-0229 and S/N 57-0231, both containing pre-production versions of the MA-1 AWCIS, were finally handed over. Because of difficulties with the initial checkout of the MA-1 AWCIS, and non-availability of adequate AGE, it was not until December 1958 that MA-1 system testing actually began. Meanwhile, some secondary testing was accomplished.

During the first four months of testing in early 1958, primary emphasis was placed upon aircraft subsystem evaluation and pilot familiarization. Other testing included GCI-modified close control tactics development, a runway overrun barrier compatibility test, an angle-of-attack indicator evaluation, and evaluating the proposed

Just off the assembly line, S/N 56-0454 already has a camera mounted on the nose. Since it is flying in primer paint, it has not yet been delivered to the air force. The B-58 was built in Fort Worth, Texas, while the two interceptors were built in San Diego and finished at Palmdale. (Convair photo 2806 via Isham)

One of the more disconcerting items that rapidly became apparent during early testing was that the main tires, supposedly good for only four flights to begin with, generally lasted an average of only 2½ flights before needing replacement. To save the expensive new interceptors from serious damage, tires were changed after every two flights.

Cold-Weather Testing

One F-106A (S/N 56-0466) was assigned to Phase V (All Weather) of the test program, exposing the aircraft, weapons, and ground support equipment to severe cold-weather conditions. Assigned to the Wright Air Development Center at Wright-Patterson AFB, Ohio, the jet was sent to Eglin where it was thoroughly cold soaked in the environmental test hangar. After the initial testing, Wright Air Development Center (WADC) test

Dart -236 was assigned to the 3499th Flying Training Wing at George AFB, California, for a year starting on 14 July 1959, and used by the Air Training Command for ground instruction while awaiting entry to the T-T-T program. The strike camera mounted on the upper nose is noticeably different from the later IRST, which was located in the same position. (USAF via Isham).

Cold weather testing is always a major part of evaluating a new aircraft. F-106A S/N 56-0466 shivers inside the climate test hangar at Eglin AFB, Florida. Both the aircraft and the newly designed ground equipment had to be tested to ensure proper functioning during cold weather conditions. (Via Isham)

Preparations for flight are underway during cold weather testing carried out at Eielson AFB, Alaska, in early 1959. Heater hoses have been connected to thaw out the delicate electronics. The wings have canvas covers installed, but the snow on the fuselage is being brushed away by hand. (USAF)

After completion of cold weather testing, S/N 56-0466 returned to W-P AFB and received orange and white stripes on the tail. A Wright Air Development Center badge and ARDC badges were also added.

pilot T. R. Bogan flew -466 from Wright-Patterson to Eielson AFB, Alaska, on 21 December 1958 to begin the flight test portion of the cold-weather testing. This testing included missile firings and evaluated how well the jet could be maintained in arctic conditions. A C-97 support aircraft loaded with all of the ground support equipment and additional technicians followed the F-106 from Dayton to Alaska. This testing continued for two months.

Cambridge Research Center

Between roughly March 1959 and April 1960, two aircraft (S/N 57-0244 and S/N 57-0245) were assigned to the 6520th Test Group at Hanscom Field. They were used to research SAGE datalink integration and received the prototype Time Division Data Link (TDDL) antennas. When they were returned to Convair for the Test-to-Tactical (T-T-T) rebuild, they were replaced by S/N 57-2490, which continued the work until November 1961.

Initial Weapons Testing at Holloman

Once enough aircraft had an MA-1 installed, at least 14 aircraft were dedicated to the initial joint Convair/Hughes/air force test force at Holloman. Trying to make up lost time, between December 1957 and October 1960 they were used for evaluating weapons separation, ballistics, MA-1 automatic modes, and general characteristics of the Hughes AIM-4E, -F, -G Super Falcon missiles and the Douglas Astronautics AIR-2A Genie rocket. Since the Genie was slightly further along in development, initial trials were begun with the rocket, followed by the AIM-4E.

The test fleet did not receive the necessary modifications to be able to launch and guide the AIM-4F and AIM-4G until the end of 1959, so testing on them continued throughout the first half of 1960. Additional testing was carried out at Eglin in June and July 1959, and the official Category III testing was carried out by the 539th FIS. They deployed aircraft and crews between McGuire and Tyndall from February until May 1960. Weapons testing was finally completed some seven months after the first F-106s assumed operational alert.

Several of the aircraft at Holloman received special paint markings and were temporarily modified with camera installations either in the wing/fuselage joint area or tip of the vertical fin. Some also had strike cameras mounted in blisters that looked very much like later IRST modifications, and most also had data pods mounted on the fuel tank pylons.

S/N 57-2490 was assigned to the 6520th Test Group at Hanscom Field, Massachusetts. This Six replaced two earlier test aircraft when they were sent to the T-T-T mod. All were used to test SAGE datalink integration and antennas. (USAF via Hildreth)

The Weapons Test Fleet

Some of the aircraft assigned to the weapons test facility at Holloman were:

Serial Number	Use
56-0457	general evaluation
56-0460	armament separation testing
56-0464	MB-1/GAR-3 Auto mode testing
56-0465	as above
57-0231	chase and target support
57-0233	MB-1/GAR-3 Auto mode testing
57-0243	as above
F-106B 57-2508	initial IRST evaluation and anti-chaff electronics testing
F-106B 57-2511	assigned to the Holloman test force on 3 October 1958 but crashed shortly thereafter, on 5 January 1959. It was replaced with 57-2514, which was used for armament separation testing.

Bailed to Hughes, S/N 57-0241 was also assigned to the weapons test facility at Holloman. A camera has been mounted to the fin tip, as well as on the upper nose. The jet has production inlets, and this is one of the earliest photos showing the new UHF blade antenna mounted below the nose, added when the one in the fin was judged inadequate. The upper half of the fin and outer wing panels are high-visibility orange. (Via Isham)

S/N 56-0463 was assigned to Hughes for weapons testing and based at Holloman. It is seen here with a documentation camera mounted on the upper nose and test pods underneath the wing pylons. It also has the later ejector. The upward reflex of the Case XIV wing is very evident when compared to the elevons. (USAF via Isham).

Special paint, kill markings on the jet, a camera scabbed onto the leading edge of the wing, special data collection pods on the wing pylons, the interim ejection seat, as well as test versions of the AIM-4E Falcons. This shot provides a wealth of detail of the test force at Holloman. (Via Isham)

One early test firing of the Super Falcon is worthy of mention. On 14 May 1960, Maj. J. D. Fowler was flying S/N 57-0233 on a mission from Holloman to test the automatic flight control mode of the MA-1 and intended to launch two AIM-4F Falcons. For the test, one of the missiles had an inert warhead and the other had a warhead but did not have live fusing. At the same time, a Martin Matador cruise missile was launched from Holloman. The missile was supposed to do a flyby for the Armed Forces Day air show at Holloman prior to being used as a target for two F-106 Falcon data missions, including the one Maj. Fowler was flying.

But the Matador stopped responding to ground commands shortly after takeoff and headed off in the direction of Albuquerque, New Mexico. Self-destruct commands to the missile failed to work, and Range Safety requested permission to use the F-106 to shoot down the drone. The Matador missile (about the size of a jet fighter) was at 27,000 feet, slowly climbing, 45 miles in front of the interceptor and going away when Maj. Fowler was paired on the target in an extended tail chase. Reaching a speed of Mach 1.5 near the town of Belen, New Mexico, he locked on, placed the system in automatic, and launched the Falcons, which hit the wayward Matador in the tail section and caused it to spin into the desert 125 miles north of the original launch site. Unfortunately, even though the Falcons splashed the Matador, the test flight had to be repeated, because the test parameters the test team were seeking to evaluate had not been met!

Through the early 1960s, in addition to testing both the Super Falcons and Genie weapons themselves, the Holloman Joint Test Force also confirmed the compatibility of the Six with its weapons, and evaluated how well the automatic modes worked. Hughes also tested how well modifications that were proposed for the F-106 worked. Some of the items tested included a retractable IRST sensor that Hughes had designed as part of the ASG-18 FCS for the canceled North American F-108 Rapier, a hydraulically tuned magnetron (radar transmitting tube), and various other hardware and software changes to the FCS.

Other Early Tests, the Scalded Cat

Possibly the most unique F-106 test program that reached hardware stages was the initial High Mach modification. During 1957 and 1958, Convair used studies conducted by NACA in the late 1950s to investigate pre-compressor cooling as a method to increase the speed of the F-106. The main goal was to lower the inlet air temperatures and use existing engines at speeds far higher than could otherwise be attained. The theory behind the design was that by spraying minute droplets of water into the air inlets and allowing it to evaporate before it reached the front face of the compressor, it would have the same effect as flying through much cooler, denser air, thus giving higher mass flow and increased thrust, and delaying the point at which the compressor reached its high-temperature

While the wing fences have been removed, the early engine ejector is still evident in this 5 July 1960 view of S/N 57-2510. The jet was assigned to the Wright Air Development Center at the time. In a month it will be rebuilt in the T-T-T program. (Bob Burgess courtesy of the Greater St. Louis Air and Space Museum)

limit. The effect becomes more pronounced as speed increases and allows an aircraft to accelerate more rapidly and reach higher maximum altitudes and top speeds.

Pre-compressor cooling was used by McDonnell on the specially modified F-4 Phantom that took the speed record away from the F-106 and was frequently a part of the Convair proposals for upgrading the F-106. Using the USAF propulsion wind tunnel at the Arnold Engineering Development Center at Tullahoma, Tennessee, Convair used both J57 and J75 engines to test the theories. Testing with the J57 showed that demineralized water was necessary. The J75 engine logged more than 46 hours of maximum afterburner usage, of which 40 hours used pre-compressor cooling (PCC). At the completion of testing, no adverse effects were noted on either the engine or fuel controls.

Following engine testing, Convair-Fort Worth modified one F-106 B model to incorporate pre-compressor cooling. This involved adding a water tank and a delivery system that sprayed water vapor into the air inlet ducts at high Mach numbers. Pilot reports indicated that it "went like a scalded cat," and significantly decreased the acceleration time to Mach 2. As far as I have been able to determine, no attempt was made to find out what the top speed of the modified aircraft was, but somewhere in the vicinity of Mach 3 was certainly within reason, making the world's fastest single-engine aircraft even faster.

However, the air force decided not to go ahead with the modification. The reasons for the reluctance have not been identified.

This is the first F-106 to visit Kelly AFB, Texas. The hot-air exhaust on the upper spine is clearly visible, as is the fact that the spine does not start sloping upward at the leading edge of the fin but rather a couple of feet forward. The deployed Ram Air Turbine (RAT) and early-style main wheels also add interest. (USAF)

Instead of being built as a test aircraft, S/N 57-0246 was the first tactical F-106A. Seen here in 1959, it has the squared-off production air intakes and slotted vari-ramps. It went to the 95th FIS in 1959. (Via Isham)

Setting the Speed Record: How Convair Made Half a Million Dollars by Going Fast

With special thanks to the late Col. Joe Rogers and F-106deltadart.com.

As the F-106's high-speed capabilities became apparent, the air force decided to attempt to regain the world absolute speed record set by Col. G. Mosolov of the USSR on 7 October 1959 using a highly modified MIG-21 (designated Ye-1152-1). Initially, senior Convair management argued vehemently against making the attempt. Although the exact reasons for the disapproval are unknown, they apparently feared that, since the F-106 development program was not progressing as rapidly as desired, deliberately exceeding the design limits of the aircraft for the record attempt was unwise. The fear was that failure to achieve the record or an accident during the attempt would cause irreversible damage to the program. In the end, however, the attempt was approved and Project Firewall was initiated.

The logical choice for this record attempt was F-106 S/N 56-0459, a production aircraft with newer air inlets. Convair had dedicated this aircraft to power plant and performance testing, so it was already heavily instrumented. Aircraft S/N 56-0467 was designated as the backup airplane because it was undergoing the same testing, albeit with the AFFTC. Because the engine was expected to be operated beyond normal limits, Pratt & Whitney provided two specially modified J75 engines with titanium blades, greater blade-to-case distance allowing for expansion due to the higher temperatures, and additional instrumentation. Maj. Joe Rogers of the Flight Test Center was chosen as pilot, and testing began in early December 1959.

The Federation Aeronautique International (FAI) requirements for the record attempt were very rigorous. The course was specially laid out and instrumented to track the aircraft along a 15-km run. To prevent aircraft from descending to gather speed through the course, they had to keep within a 1,500-foot vertical tube from the time they first entered the course until exiting after the second run. In addition, two runs had to be made, in opposite directions, to compensate for any possible variation in wind. Since this was a test aircraft, it did not have the full MA-1 system or avionics. As a result, there was no autopilot or altitude-hold function, so it had to be hand-flown through the course. Because of this, a highly sensitive rate-of-climb indicator was installed with a vertical accelerometer mounted top dead center on the instrument panel due to its importance to the record attempt.

Fuel was also a significant factor. After climbing to 40,000 feet, accelerating to Mach 2, flying through the course, performing a 180-degree turn, and coming back through the course again, there was barely enough fuel to return to Edwards. In fact, fuel was so critical that the aircraft had to be towed back to the ramp at least once after flaming-out on the runway from fuel starvation after landing. This caused the team

Known as the Red Baron, S/N 56-0459 was assigned to Convair and used for power plant development. It was selected for the speed record attempt but had continued problems with compressor stalls at high speed. The honor went to S/N 56-0467 instead. (USAF via Isham)

to switch to higher-density JP-5 and tow the aircraft to the end of the runway for takeoff rather than consume fuel taxiing.

Unfortunately, -459, which Convair was using to test various exhaust nozzle shapes in an attempt to meet the contractually guaranteed speeds, manifested a very unusual problem: speed-induced yaw. The faster it went, the more it yawed to the side. The unfortunate result of that was severe compressor stalls as the aircraft neared Mach 2.0. Suspecting the inlet ramp was the problem, engineers modified the aircraft with a switch on the control stick to change inlet ramp scheduling. Activation by the pilot at about Mach 1.8 increased the amount the ramps moved for a given increase in speed. This was only partially successful; more air was entering one intake than the other, and this unbalanced air pressure across the face of the engine continued to cause stalls.

An attempt was made to determine the source of the yaw, but it remained undiagnosed, and time was running out for the record attempt. One last try was made with -459, and here is what Joe Rogers had to say about that last attempt with the jet: "I was plagued with compressor stalls every day for two weeks. On 14 December [1959] they were so violent at Mach 2.3, the airplane went divergent in yaw, and I thought she was going to break up. She calmed down and I landed." At that point it was obvious to everyone that the record was not going to be claimed by -459. In fact, at dinner that night with Col. Queen [AFFTC CC], they decided they were going to

Shown taking off from Runway 22 at Edwards, Dart -459 was originally destined for the record books, but that was not to be. (WINGS & AIRPOWER Historical Archive via Mike Machat)

Pilot Joe Rogers smiles from the cockpit after flying the F-106 to a new world absolute speed record of Mach 2.39. Note the blistered paint on the ejection seat warning triangle and special test instrumentation installed above the panel. (WINGS & AIRPOWER Historical Archive via Mike Machat)

use an F-104A for the record attempt the following day. That night, however, Convair pulled off a near miracle.

Convair contacted the Air Force Test Group and asked to borrow S/N 56-0467 for the record attempt. When the air force agreed, the Convair night shift pulled all the special test equipment from -459 and installed it on -467. They also completed not one, but three, complete engine changes and trim runs. They pulled the existing engine out of -467 and replaced it with the special race engine. That engine failed to meet specifications on the trim pad, so they pulled it out and installed the second race engine. That engine also failed so they re-installed the first engine. After approval from Pratt & Whitney to raise the temperature limits on the stock engine, it passed the trim check.

On the morning of 15 December 1959, the last possible day for the record attempt, Convair project pilot James Stuart took off in -467 and made a one-way pass through the course, reporting a speed that was "truly spectacular" to the ground crew. Unbeknownst to the Convair crew, Joe Rogers and Col. Queen were standing just outside the radio cubicle in the hangar and overheard the report. They instantly decided to use the Six for the record flight and Joe told the radio operator: "Tell Jim to make sure he puts the landing gear down because we want that aircraft."

Later that day Joe piloted -467, ballasted to full combat weight, through the course to an average speed of 1,525.95 mph at 40,500 feet, and a new absolute speed record. He later reported that "she

With the paint still blistered from the record speed run, S/N 56-0467 has had an Air Force Flight Test Center (AFFTC) emblem and alar added to its tail for post-record photography. With Mt. Whitney in the background, this shot was taken on 13 April 1960. (USAF via Isham)

sailed through the traps at Mach 2.43 and was still accelerating at the end of the course." However, after every major event, there is always "the rest of the story," and here it is:

After landing, the aircraft exhibited graphic physical evidence of its high-speed flight. Paint was burned on the leading edges of the wings and air inlets and was partly missing on the vertical fin. Canopy side panels were slightly deformed from heating. The stock engine was a complete write-off, and it's a wonder it even lasted through landing.

Joe Rogers received the Distinguished Flying Cross and became the 25th recipient of the Thompson Trophy. He later went on to a distinguished air force career.

Serial number 56-0459 was eventually rebuilt during the T-T-T program and received a new forward fuselage section. It always flew straight after the rebuild and survived to become a display aircraft at the McChord Air Museum.

The record-setting aircraft (S/N 56-0467) also went through the T-T-T program and received a special placard on the right side of the cockpit, properly memorializing its record flight.

After rebuilding during the T-T-T program, this historically significant aircraft was assigned to the 329th FIS at George AFB, California, on 5 June 1961. Unfortunately, two months later it was destroyed during an emergency landing on 14 August 1961. That morning, the right main tire blew out on takeoff. Pilot James Wilkinson burned off fuel and was advised to land at Edwards, where they had better crash equipment.

The pilot found he was also unable to open the speed brakes, which meant the drag chute could not be deployed. The crash crew foamed the runway, but with no right tire, no speed brakes, and no drag chute, it would be almost impossible to land safely. As the right wheel contacted the runway, it immediately began to spark and then disintegrated. Pieces flew up through the wing, starting a fire, and the aircraft eventually slid off the runway and into the desert. Although the pilot egressed safely, all he could do was watch as the record-setting jet burned to a charred hulk.

Although the absolute speed record has been raised significantly since 1959, the FAI still recognizes the F-106 as the world's fastest single-engine jet-powered aircraft.

And that money made by Convair? As the official USAF engine test aircraft, the engine in -467 came with special afterburner fuel-flow instrumentation not found on any of the other engines. For the speed run, the limit screws on both engine and afterburner fuel controls were backed out to allow over-limit operation by the pilot. After the flight, review of the data showed the afterburner fuel control schedule was not providing enough fuel for maximum afterburner performance. This discovery allowed Convair to recover about half a million dollars in performance penalties from the air force.

Showing off the newly added AFSC badge on the nose, AFFTC emblem, and alar on the tail, the record-setting Six is seen on 13 April 1960. (USAF via Isham)

One of the very earliest photos of the subsonic 230-gallon external fuel tanks on an F-106. S/N 56-0467 would never have been able to set a speed record while hauling them around. (USAF via Isham).

A sad end to a record-setting aircraft. These are the remains of S/N 56-0467 after its landing accident on 14 Aug 1961. (USAF)

Chapter Eight

DESIGN STUDIES AND PROPOSED F-106 VARIANTS

One early design study, dated 24 November 1954, looked at using two General Electric XJ79-GE engines (either mounted side-by-side in a non-area-ruled fuselage or in a podded configuration under the wings) as a possible alternative in case the proposed J67 engine was not ready. This may have been the first design study to use the translating external compression "spike" inlets that became common on later proposals and was very similar to the pods used on the B-58.

A later study, dated 21 December 1956, looked at powering the F-106 with the Rolls-Royce Conway RCo.11 turbo fan. This may have been the first time a turbo-fan engine was seriously considered for use in a fighter-type aircraft. As developed by Rolls, the Conway was a two-spool, low-bypass (25 percent) engine that developed 16,500 pounds of thrust in military power. The Conway would have increased the maximum altitude obtainable by a few thousand feet while still allowing a Mach 2 design speed and increasing fuel efficiency by at least 8 percent. The heavier engine was expected to increase takeoff gross weight by 373 pounds and require minor changes to the aft fuselage to accommodate the different dimensions of the engine.

Perhaps the most intriguing thing about this study is the list of "unapproved pending changes" to the F-106. As of that date, the Case XXIX wing camber was expected to add 49 pounds, the newly required "Broficon" (Broadcast Fighter Control) radio receiver weighed 30 pounds, a new supersonic ejection seat was expected to add 80 pounds, and the Hughes MA-1 was expected to be 70 pounds overweight. The Rolls-Royce engine ended up being very successful, but Convair could not obtain adequate data on a proposed afterburner for the Conway, and in the end, Rolls never produced an afterburning Conway.

Naval Versions

Given the close relationship between Convair and the U.S. Navy in the flying boat field, navalized versions of the Delta interceptors appeared as design studies early in the development process. The first known study was done in 1954 and was titled *Model 8 Attack Fighter for Carrier Operations*. This encompassed a two-place version

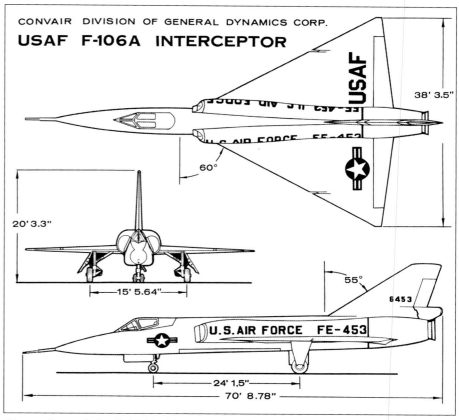

Dimensions of the F-106A. The weapons bay was 16 feet long. (Convair)

of the aircraft, using either a J67 or J75 engine and having a mission of either nuclear strike, conventional ground attack, or as a general-purpose fighter. Modifications to the existing design were made to enable operations from aircraft carriers, including folding wing tips and a tailhook.

A second attempt to interest the navy was a 20 June 1955 proposal for a strike fighter. The Carrier Based High Altitude Fighter Version of the F-102B would have had folding wings and vertical fin; heavier, navalized landing gear with a small-diameter wheel protecting the aft fuselage from deck strikes; a spring-steel tailhook; and a probe-type aerial refueling system. The weapons bay was to be lengthened to accommodate four Sparrow missiles or two "Genie" rockets. Two small, single-piece weapons bay doors would have been

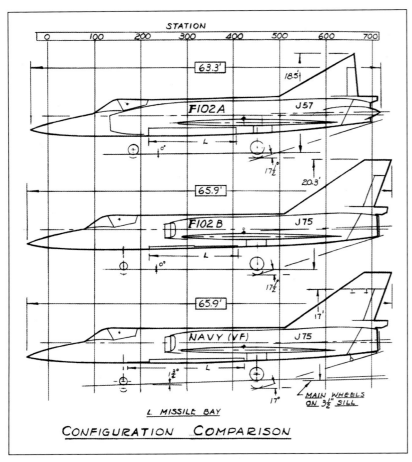

STATION

63.3'
18.5'
F102A   J57
1°
17½°
20.3'

65.9'
F102 B   J75
0°
17½°

65.9'
17'
NAVY (VF)   J75
3¼°
17°

MAIN WHEELS ON 3½" SILL

L MISSILE BAY

CONFIGURATION COMPARISON

added in front of the two lengthened two-piece doors, an Aero 11B FCS would have replaced the MA-1, and a BuOrd Mk 16 combination sight and radar was proposed. Performance was predicted to be Mach 2 at 35,000 feet and Mach 1.77 at 50,000 feet.

A third design study for a navalized Delta was published in 1956, but details of this proposal are no longer available.

One final attempt to interest the U.S. Navy in the F-106 came in two 1957 feasibility studies. In May 1957, the now-familiar advanced design features of canards, flaperons, variable leading-edge camber, and spike inlets made their appearances, but the new *Forrestal*-class super carriers were large enough that no wing-fold mechanisms were needed. A November 1957 study proposed an attack aircraft using a navy-developed PW J58-P-2 (JT11-A-20) power plant that would have produced 26,000 pounds of thrust, enough to give a top speed of Mach 2.5 without using the afterburner. Gross weight was in the 52,000-pound class. As with all of the previous efforts, the navy declined to pursue either option.

Advanced Interceptor Versions

It was clear from the start that a larger radar antenna would significantly improve the contact and lock-on ranges of both the F-102 and F-106, but Hughes was initially unable to get a large antenna to sweep properly. As a result, Convair left enough room in the nose of

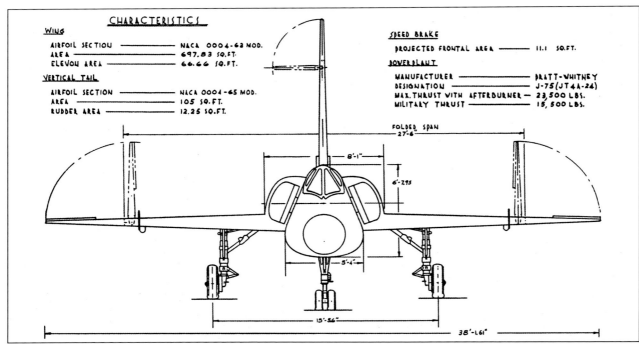

CHARACTERISTICS

WING
AIRFOIL SECTION ———————— NACA 0004-63 MOD.
AREA ———————————————— 697.83 SQ.FT.
ELEVON AREA —————————— 66.66 SQ.FT.

VERTICAL TAIL
AIRFOIL SECTION ———————— NACA 0004-65 MOD.
AREA ———————————————— 105 SQ.FT.
RUDDER AREA ——————————— 12.25 SQ.FT.

SPEED BRAKE
PROJECTED FRONTAL AREA ———— 11.1 SQ.FT.

POWERPLANT
MANUFACTURER ——————————— PRATT-WHITNEY
DESIGNATION —————————————— J-75 (JT4A-24)
MAX. THRUST WITH AFTERBURNER — 23,500 LBS.
MILITARY THRUST ——————————— 15,500 LBS.

FOLDED SPAN 27'-6"
8'-1"
6'-2.95"
5'-4"
15'-5.6"
38'-1.61"

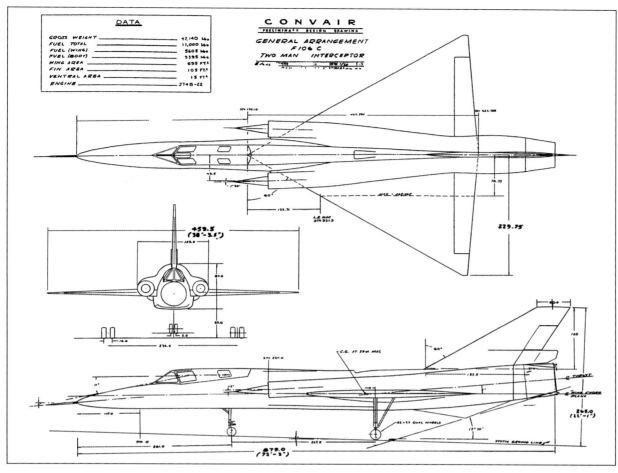

DATA

GROSS WEIGHT	42,140 Lbs
FUEL TOTAL	11,000 Lbs
FUEL (WING)	5605 Lbs
FUEL (BODY)	5395 Lbs
WING AREA	695 FT²
FIN AREA	105 FT²
VENTRAL AREA	15 FT²
ENGINE	JT4B-22

C O N V A I R
PRELIMINARY DESIGN DRAWING
GENERAL ARRANGEMENT
F 106 C
TWO MAN INTERCEPTOR

The initial concept for the F-106C was quite a step forward from the F-102B. All further design studies used some form of canard. (Convair)

---

the F-106 for a 28-inch radar dish, but the same 23-inch-diameter dish of the earlier F-102 ended up being used. Convair and Hughes always intended to add a larger radar dish, but for various reasons, this never occurred.

The idea did not die, however, and virtually all of the dizzying array of follow-on interceptor upgrade proposals became variations on a theme of a larger, 40-inch radar dish, canards, and external compression air inlets to achieve higher speeds and altitudes, along with greater radar ranges. Most of the proposals used some form of uprated Pratt & Whitney JT4A or -B turbojet (JT4 was the civilian designation for the J75). Extensive wind tunnel testing of nose and intake configurations was carried out by Convair and NASA to gain data on which to base hard production decisions.

An early 1956 design study used canards and rectangular intakes similar to those eventually used on the F-15. This morphed into the F-106C proposal. Initially, this was a tandem-seat interceptor using a 40-inch radar antenna, uprated engine, and advanced external compression spikes in the air inlets, and was seen both with and without canards.

Later the proposal was changed to the F-106C having one seat and the F-106D having two. Development of this variation progressed to the point that the air force considered buying 350 of the new models, which had a 50-percent increase in radar detection ranges over the baseline F-106s, but they were canceled on 23 September 1958 when the F-106 program was capped at 340 aircraft.

By that time, however, two F-106As had already been funded for modification into an F-106C configuration.

F-106C RADAR INSTALLATION

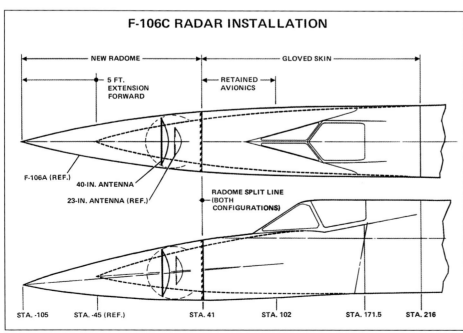

NEW RADOME — GLOVED SKIN

5 FT. EXTENSION FORWARD

RETAINED AVIONICS

F-106A (REF.)

40-IN. ANTENNA

23-IN. ANTENNA (REF.)

RADOME SPLIT LINE (BOTH CONFIGURATIONS)

STA. -105   STA. -45 (REF.)   STA. 41   STA. 102   STA. 171.5   STA. 216

This drawing shows how the nose contours of the F-106A were modified for the two YF-106C aircraft. (Convair)

Looking rather forlorn, the prototype YF-106C sits in storage on the Palmdale ramp. The rather droopy nose, reminiscent of the later F-111, accommodated a 40-inch-diameter radar dish, which increased the range of the radar by 50 percent. Financial considerations resulted in cancellation of at least 350 of these jets. The buzz number is mounted forward in an unusual position. This aircraft was destroyed during fatigue testing shortly after the photo was taken in 1960. (Via Isham)

The second YF-106C was more fortunate than the first. It was rebuilt back to F-106A configuration during the T-T-T program and flew until the Sixes were retired. (Via Isham)

Almost immediately after their delivery on 31 December 1958, two F-106As (S/N 57-0239 and S/N 57-0240) were bailed back to the contractors for modification into YF-106Cs. To allow for the enlarged radar dish, a 5-foot extension was added to the nose and a gloved fairing that went back on the lower fuselage to a point just forward of the engine inlets was added.

Aircraft -0239 was modified for aerodynamic performance testing, and -0240 was modified for radar system testing. Aircraft -0239 was flown 10 times in the spring of 1959. Pilots said it was virtually impossible to tell any performance differences from the F-106A, although rumors of problems with center-of-gravity control have been heard. After the test program ended, -239 was used for destructive fatigue testing, and then written off. Aircraft -240 was rebuilt under the T-T-T program back to F-106A configuration.

Variations on a Theme

Nearly coincident with the F-106C were the first F-106X proposal and a myriad of Advanced Interceptor proposals. Under air force contract in 1956, Convair also conducted studies for advanced Medium Range Interceptors (MRI). The studies considered two all-weather, medium-range, manned weapons systems that were planned to be operational by the start of the 1962–1963 time period, just after the planned retirement date of the F-106 fleet. The MRI was designed for speeds between Mach 2.5 and Mach 4 with a combat ceiling of 100,000 feet, while a lesser performance MRI(X) version was only expected to achieve speeds between Mach 2.5 and Mach 3 at 75,000 feet. Both sets of performance parameters had little to do with actual threat aircraft but much to do with the "higher, farther, faster" mindset of the air force at that time.

As a result, a wide range of "pie in the sky" topics were investigated, including aircraft with up to four engines powered by radical fuels such as hydrogen. As with virtually all of the Convair advanced studies, the aircraft featured canards, internal compression spike air inlets, and uprated engines. A single-engine variant proposed using the new GE J93 (X276A) engine, while the twin-engine concept was a larger airframe that used Allison 701 power plants that produced more than 38,000 pounds of thrust. This version was expected to have a combat range of 350 nautical miles in a clean configuration, and 600 with external fuel tanks. It would have carried new Hughes FCS and GAR-Z (proposed) missiles.

An additional air force research contract, issued as yet another supplement to the original F-106 production contract and dated 30 January 1957, involved improving the capabilities of both the F-102 and the F-106. Both an "Improved" F-106 and an "Advanced" F-106 were to be considered. Only relatively minor structural changes were considered for the Improved variant. The air inlets would have to be enlarged to accommodate the increased airflow requirements of the new engine, the JT4A-27 variant of the J75, that was expected to give an additional 1,000 pounds of thrust. Fuel capacity was significantly increased by enlarging the fuselage fuel tank and filling the T tanks in the aft portion of the wings with fuel as opposed to leaving them

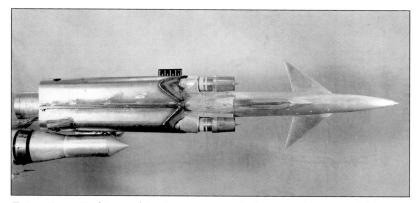

Extensive wind tunnel testing was carried out on the new inlets and canard configurations. This model dates from a NACA test in 1957. (NASA)

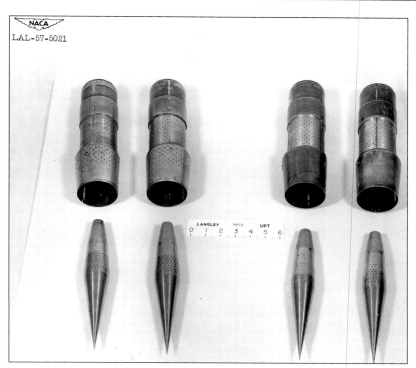

The translating spike inlets, with holes for pre-compressor cooling water spray, were carefully machined for wind tunnel testing. (NASA LAL 57-5021)

empty for takeoff and then using them only for center-of-gravity manipulation.

Provision for the GAR-X missile was planned. The increased weight would have required slightly larger tires and a beef-up of the two wing spars nearest the landing gear. The resulting performance increases were minimal, with top speed only increasing to Mach 2.1, but the combat radius would have seen a large increase.

The Advanced F-106 study resulted in a far different aircraft. The fuselage would have been 4 feet longer, to accommodate the 40-inch radar dish and advanced MA-1, which was expected to give three times the detection range of the existing MA-1 system. An IR seeker would have been added on the tip of the vertical tail, elevons would have become flaperons, and configurations with canards were standard, although a "T" tail plus canard configuration was also proposed. The bi-convex wing camber (variable leading-edge camber) was nearly as radical as the internal compression inlet ducts, pre-compressor cooling, and variable ejector (afterburner nozzle) for the engine. A Stanley Corporation pilot escape capsule finished off the design.

Several power plants were evaluated, including the P-W JT4B-23 engine, a JT4B-22 with pre-compressor cooling, the Allison J89, two GE J79s, and two GE J93s. This time two 500-gallon external fuel tanks were considered, which would have given a combat radius of more than 800 miles.

One version of the Advanced F-106 was envisioned as carrying one of Convair's proposed Sky Scorcher air-to-air missiles. The missile was to use a 2-megaton-yield atomic warhead, would have weighed around 3,400 pounds, and would had a range of up to 140 miles. Convair's plan was to use 80 of the new jets to attack large formations of bombers at great distances from their targets, and then have the standard F-106s pick off any remaining survivors. However, the air force felt that the blast and radiation effects of such large thermonuclear weapons were too significant to allow their use for defensive purposes.

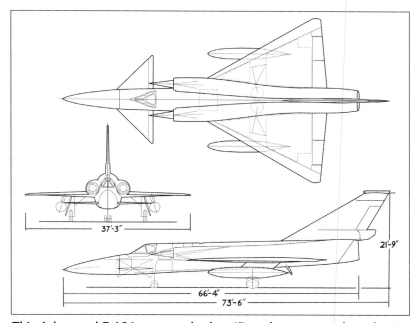

This Advanced F-106 concept had an IR seeker mounted on the tip of the vertical tail, and the typical-for-the-time translating spikes that were derived from B-58 research. It is hard to imagine that airflow from the massive canards would not have seriously degraded the airflow into those inlets. (Convair)

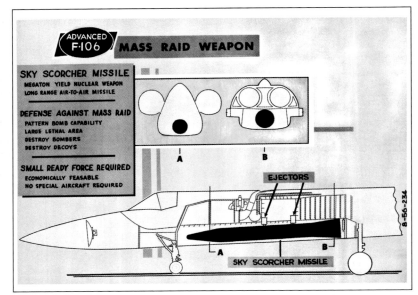

The first F-106X proposal was built around carriage of the 2-megaton-range Sky Scorcher air-to-air missile.

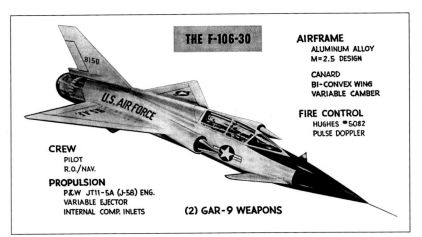

One concept drawing of the F-106-30. Note how the canards change in later versions. (Convair)

Another rendering of the Advanced F-106 proposal. The myriad of proposals were so similar, it was hard to tell them apart. (Convair)

A beautiful wind tunnel model of an F-106-30 proposal that was saved from scrapping. (Collect-Air miniatures)

F-106-30

Formally proposed in March 1958, yet another F-106 design was called the F-106-30. It was a growth concept moving forward from the Advanced F-106 proposal, and was intended to fill the manned interceptor role from 1963 through 1970, after the planned retirement of the F-106A and C models. Using the Hughes AN/ASG-18 pulse Doppler radar and AIM-47 Long Range Falcon (GAR-9) from

the F-108, one version of the new fighter would have used a single 30,600-pound static-thrust Pratt & Whitney J58 engine, which went on to be used in the Lockheed SR-71 family.

Other features would have included the canard control surfaces, internal compression air inlets, and bi-convex variable-camber wing from the Advanced F-106 proposal. The presentation pamphlet stated that all features had already been tested. With a planned gross weight of just under 48,000 pounds, the aircraft was to have

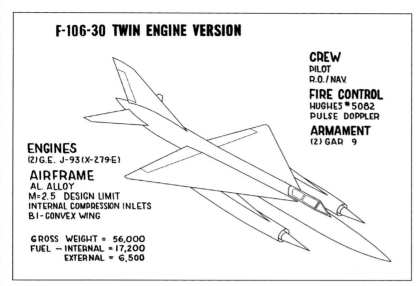

F-106-30 TWIN ENGINE VERSION

CREW
PILOT
R.O./NAV.

FIRE CONTROL
HUGHES #5082
PULSE DOPPLER

ARMAMENT
(2) GAR 9

ENGINES
(2) G.E. J-93 (X-279-E)

AIRFRAME
AL. ALLOY
M=2.5 DESIGN LIMIT
INTERNAL COMPRESSION INLETS
BI-CONVEX WING

GROSS WEIGHT = 56,000
FUEL – INTERNAL = 17,200
EXTERNAL = 6,500

The forward half of this twin-engine version of the F-106-30 looks very much like a modified B-58 design. Doppler radars were now being proposed for the follow-on aircraft. (Convair)

been built conventionally, using aluminum alloy. Performance was expected at a top speed of Mach 2.5, an operational radius of 740 miles at subsonic speeds using external fuel tanks, and a ceiling of 72,000 feet with a zoom climb capability of 88,000 feet.

Using the advanced Hughes radar and missile combination, targets more than 100 miles away and more than 100,000 feet altitude were within the planned lethal capabilities of the jet.

A twin-engine variant was also proposed with a tailed Delta configuration and sporting podded GE J93 engines underneath each wing. The resemblance to a B-58 was noticeable. That configuration had higher drag than the single-engine version, would have weighed around 56,000 pounds, also carried two Long Range Falcons, and was also expected to reach Mach 2.5.

Interestingly, none of the proposals for external fuel tanks came to fruition until late 1967, when the Mach 2–capable, high-lift, 360-gallon tanks were added to the F-106. Had this been done in the early design stage, one of the greatest advantages of the F-101B, that of longer range, would have been nullified. Of all the proposed features that were actually tested, only the IR seeker was eventually added to virtually all of the ADC Century Series interceptors.

After cancellation of the North American Aviation F-108 Rapier in September 1959, ADC was left with nothing in the pipeline for a follow-on interceptor. In response, ARDC asked Convair about a long-range F-106. In November 1959, Convair responded with two proposals, both having two crew members. One version

was a two-place version using the Hughes ASG-18 FCS and GAR-9 (X) AIM-47 Long Range Falcon originally developed for the F-108. With a pulse Doppler radar, long-range "look down, shoot down" capability, and track-while-scan ability, this aircraft would have been a huge improvement over the existing F-106. This would have required very extensive modifications to the existing fleet or newly built aircraft.

The second version would have used a Westinghouse PD radar and Sparrow III missiles. This version would have been a new-construction aircraft, with increased electrical capacity, increased fuel capacity, an enlarged vertical fin (common to almost all of the high-speed aircraft proposals), the 40-inch radar dish, redesigned air intakes to accommodate increased airflow requirements of the pratt & Whitney JT4A-30 engine, and aerial refueling capability.

As with all of the previous studies, nothing concrete came out of the proposals, but in a note of supreme irony, the U.S. Navy saw the potential of the ASG-18/AIM-47 pair and took over development from the air force after cancellation of the YF-12 interceptor. They eventually became the AWG-9 FCS and AIM-54 Phoenix missile, the heart of the F-14, which ended up possessing far greater intercept capabilities than anything the air force had fielded.

Foreign Sales Attempts

Having had no luck selling additional F-106s to the navy, and as prospects for further sales of interceptors to ADC began to look bleaker, Convair turned its attention overseas.

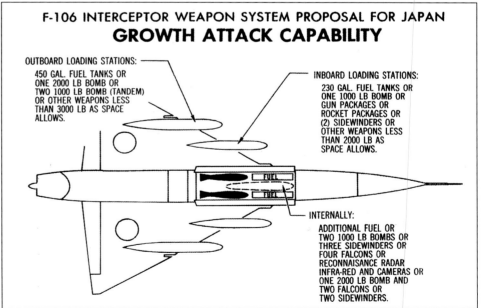

F-106 INTERCEPTOR WEAPON SYSTEM PROPOSAL FOR JAPAN
GROWTH ATTACK CAPABILITY

OUTBOARD LOADING STATIONS:
450 GAL. FUEL TANKS OR
ONE 2000 LB BOMB OR
TWO 1000 LB BOMB (TANDEM)
OR OTHER WEAPONS LESS
THAN 3000 LB AS SPACE
ALLOWS.

INBOARD LOADING STATIONS:
230 GAL. FUEL TANKS OR
ONE 1000 LB BOMB OR
GUN PACKAGES OR
ROCKET PACKAGES OR
(2) SIDEWINDERS OR
OTHER WEAPONS LESS
THAN 2000 LB AS
SPACE ALLOWS.

FUEL
FUEL

INTERNALLY:
ADDITIONAL FUEL OR
TWO 1000 LB BOMBS OR
THREE SIDEWINDERS OR
FOUR FALCONS OR
RECONNAISANCE RADAR
INFRA-RED AND CAMERAS OR
ONE 2000 LB BOMB AND
TWO FALCONS OR
TWO SIDEWINDERS.

Unaware that they were playing fair in a dirty fight, Convair went to great lengths in proposing fighter-bomber variants of the F-106. This was the proposal for the Japanese version. (Convair)

Several additional studies were conducted and serious attempts were made to sell the F-106 as a multi-role fighter to Belgium, Germany, the Netherlands, Canada, and Japan. These proposals involved either the existing MA-1 AWCIS, backdating the aircraft to use the MG-10 of the F-102, or adding an entirely new FCS. Canada was offered domestic production of a multi-purpose F-106 in 1959 but instead chose the Lockheed F-104 for its strike aircraft and accepted used F-101B/F interceptors from ADC for its air defense force, in return for Canadian operation of a portion of the SAGE radar system.

Attempts to sell the F-106 to Japan were equally fruitless. Convair also offered domestic production to the Japanese for an F-106 backdated to use the MG-10 of the F-102, and carrying six Falcon missiles but no Genie. Although Convair thought that the sale was "95 percent in the bag," the Japanese joined the Canadians in choosing the Lockheed F-104.

Sales to Belgium, Germany, and the Netherlands were equally unsuccessful, with Lockheed again winning. It was not until a decade later that the massive bribery of foreign officials that Lockheed engaged in to win the F-104's "Sale of the Century" came to light as one of the largest reasons Lockheed won, but by then it was far too late for the F-106.

Not Invented Here

Convair's first attempt to interest the Tactical Air Command (TAC) in a fighter-bomber version of the F-106 came in July 1957. Both single- and two-place configurations were proposed, both using a variant of the J75 engine. At nearly 47,000 pounds, the single-seater was around 1,000 pounds heavier than the F-106A. The two-seater was slightly heavier still and both were expected to reach Mach 2.1, with a 1,200-mile combat radius. The largest differences came

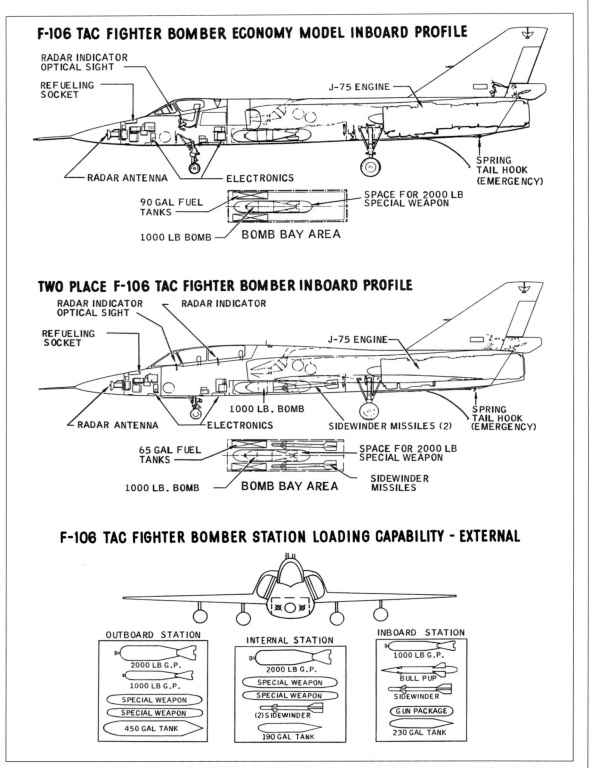

Two of the several variations of a fighter version of the F-106 that were presented to TAC. Problems standing in the way of any sales were the wet wing, insufficient weapons loads, and the fact that TAC had already committed to the F-105. (Convair)

in modifications to the missile bay and wings. The missile bay was to have been divided into a forward and an aft portion. Similar to the F-105D, the forward portion could hold a removable 450-gallon fuel tank. Either a single nuclear weapon or 2 1,000-pound GP bombs could be carried internally, along with either 32 2.75-inch FFAR rockets or 3 Falcon missiles. The Hughes MA-1 would have been replaced with a CV/GE bombing system.

Given that TAC had already committed to the F-105, which carried a much greater payload, this proposal was met with complete disinterest.

Ignoring TAC's very clear attitude of "Not Invented Here" and preference for the F-105 Thunderchief, Convair expanded some of its earlier work and once again proposed several variations of an F-106 tactical aircraft. The years 1959 through early 1961 were marked by repeated efforts to sell additional F-106s. A single-seat F-106A Economy Fighter Bomber, an F-106A/B Fighter Bomber, and an F106B Strike Reconnaissance aircraft were all pitched.

Convair Report ZP-333 dated April 1961 once again laid out the case for the F-106 tactical potential covering all three of the proposals and extolling the advantages of the F-106 and its Delta wing, all the while passing over the lack of self-sealing fuel tanks, and the related downsides of combat damage to the tanks.

The very trouble-prone Hughes MA-1 system was nowhere to be found in this presentation while all-weather navigation using a Doppler system, as well as high-resolution radar bombing capability were touted. Both the world's speed record and the low-level flight demonstration were pointed out, along with the fact that TAC pilots had "performed LABS maneuvers in this aircraft on their first flight, and describe it as a perfect platform for the low-level bombing missions."

Even the Economy fighter was to have several nuclear delivery modes, including either manual or automatic pull-up with computer bomb release, and alternate delivery modes were to be automatically selected whenever "delivery in a particular mode is unsafe or impractical." The weapons bay would be modified to carry a single weapon of up to 2,000 pounds or a 250-gallon ferry tank. The external wing

pylons would be able to carry only the existing 230-gallon fuel tank.

The F-106A/B Fighter-Bomber had additional capabilities. By beefing up the landing gear and using larger tires, the maximum gross weight was expected to increase to 47,000 pounds. The V windshield and heavily barred canopy were to be replaced with a bubble canopy for better visibility. The weapons bay would be reconfigured to hold two Sidewinder missiles, two 85-gallon fuel tanks, plus the 2,000-pound special weapon.

Two additional inboard wing pylons would have been added to hold another pair of 230-gallon external fuel tanks, a gun package, and a Sidewinder missile or Bullpup air-to-ground missiles. The outboard pylons could carry a single bomb weighing up to 2,000 pounds

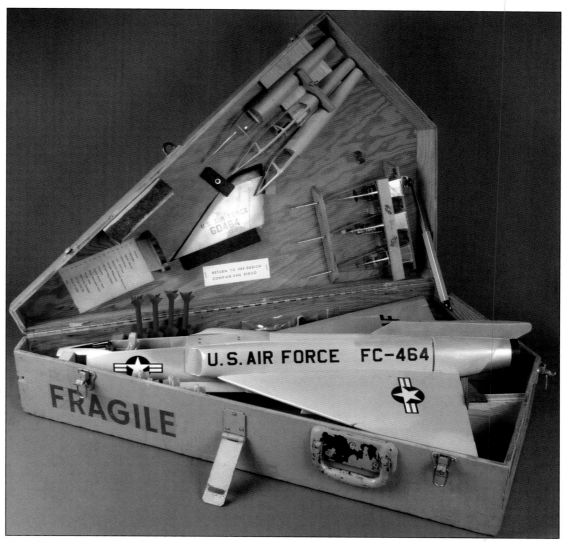

As sales attempts for the Six ramped up, Convair built this "suitcase" model of the Six to show prospective customers different ways that the F-106 could be customized to their specs. Seen here are three different canopies and nose variations, as well as AIM-7 Sparrow and AIM-9 Sidewinder missiles. (Model from John Aldez Collection, photo by Craig Kaston)

The cavernous weapons bay of the Six allowed a huge number of different options for reconnaissance, tactical weapons, or additional fuel. The model could rapidly be reconfigured to show various options. (Model from John Aldaz Collection, photo by Craig Kaston)

Different noses could be attached to the model to demonstrate what the interior configuration would look like. Here is a reconnaissance nose. (Model from John Aldez Collection, photo by Craig Kaston)

or a 450-gallon fuel tank. Additional electronic equipment added over the Economy model was to include an Eastman Kodak TV sight, GE Sidewinder launch computer, Bullpup missile control transmitter, and GE autopilot.

For the F106B Strike Reconnaissance variant, Convair planned to add inertial navigation equipment; side-looking, high-resolution Ka band radar; side-looking IR; a data link; defensive equipment, including RHAW and chaff; an HF radio; data processing equipment; and a unique three KA-8 camera station. The cameras were intended to be carried in pod(s) mounted on one or both of the inboard pylons. Electronic Counter Measures (ECM) pods were also to be loaded on the inboard pylons, either opposite a camera pod or on both stations.

Convair proposed an ambitious production schedule for any of these variants. Delivery of the first aircraft was to be 21 months from program start. Production runs for either 240, 330, or 650 aircraft were planned with delivery rates of up to 26 aircraft per month.

In an effort to show prospective customers different configurations of the F-106, the Convair pre-design team built an approximately 1/24-scale model of the F-106. It featured three canopy configurations, including the conventional single- and dual-seat canopies, and the first representation of a clear-top bubble canopy, one that took another 15 years to become reality. Three separate clear nose sections could be attached, showing the existing nose, an enlarged radar, and a reconnaissance package. Likewise, the weapons bay could accept plug-in reconnaissance loads or missiles. Inner-wing weapons pylons allowed external loading of either AIM-9 Sidewinders or AIM-7 Sparrow missiles.

Continuing in their attempts to demonstrate the tactical capabilities of the F-106 and generate interest in the aircraft, TAC pilots were allowed to fly the F-106 and practice nuclear weapons deliveries. To further generate interest, Convair staged a series of publicity flights. On 23 February 1960, Convair engineering test pilot C. E. "Chuck" Myers flew S/N 57-0230 on a 300-mile-long low-level flight out of Edwards.

Rolling out on final on a cold and dreary Michigan winter day, this Six from the 171st FIS is about to land at Selfridge ANGB in January 1975.

Flying at 700 mph at altitudes between 50 and 300 feet AGL, absolute heights ranged from 8,000 feet MSL while crossing the Panamint Mountains to 100 feet below sea level while flying across Death Valley. The aircraft was ballasted to combat weight and initially loaded with empty 230-gallon external fuel tanks for drag, but in-flight photographs show the jet in a clean configuration.

Convair initially attempted to demonstrate the automatic navigation capability of the F-106 during an early delivery flight to the 539th FIS. However, Operation Longlegs ended up being a failure when the Edwards to McGuire flight turned back over Colorado Springs, Colorado, and returned to Edwards on 4 June 1959. Convair had not publicized the attempt in advance and therefore did not receive any bad publicity for the failure.

Following the initial failed attempt, the publicity flight was successfully completed when Maj. Frank Forsythe flew F-106A S/N 59-0047 on a long-distance, "hands-off" flight to demonstrate the highly automated nature of the F-106/MA-1 combination. After ground crews programmed the entire route of flight into the MA-1 system's memory drum, Maj. Forsythe, the AMC Chief Acceptance pilot for the F-106, took off from Palmdale, California, at 11:48 a.m. on 23 March 1960. As soon as the first TACAN signal was received he went to the automatic mode and let the aircraft navigate itself across the country. To increase range, the 230-gallon external fuel tanks were jettisoned, once empty, over the air force firing range at Yuma, Arizona. After reaching Jacksonville International Airport (IAP), Florida, Maj. Forsythe took over manually and returned to Tyndall for landing.

Perhaps the most unique, or desperate, attempt to sell additional F-106s came in a proposal to use the jet as a high-speed executive transport. VIP seating was to be added in the area originally used for the weapons bay. Like all of the other notions, this one remained a pipe dream.

One further attempt to sell more Sixes came in September 1960, when part of a $100 million funds appropriation was considered to purchase more F-106s to be used as crew trainers for the XB-70 Valkyrie bomber. Cancellation of the XB-70 on 28 March 1961 and USAF preference to use the money for other projects ended that prospect as well.

Chapter Nine

INTO SQUADRON SERVICE: FAILURES AND FIXES

With developmental testing at Edwards and Holloman having been in progress for well over two years, USAF planning turned toward introducing the F-106 into the ADC fleet. Having just been down the same road shortly before with the F-102, ADC was very vocal in its displeasure. They claimed that the F-106 had never adequately completed either Category I or Category II testing; was unreliable and non-maintainable; lacked adequate support equipment, spare parts, and documentation; and was not yet ready for operational service. Given the geopolitical realities of the time, these complaints did not prevail, and the floodgates were opened. The first F-106 to reach an operational squadron was delivered to the 539th FIS at McGuire on 30 May 1959. By the end of the year, four additional combat squadrons as well as the 4750th Test Squadron, stationed at MacDill AFB, Florida, had received the new interceptor.

Tasked with defense of the New York–Washington–Philadelphia triangle, the 539th converted from the much less advanced North American F-86L Sabre. Given that, the conversion was an extended process. And since the Category III Weapons Testing had not yet begun, the 539th did not receive the honor of becoming the first squadron operationally ready with the F-106. Instead, the unit spent most of its time on temporary duty at Tyndall and Eglin performing live-fire tests over the Gulf of Mexico, and trying to complete the delayed testing.

During the week of 20 November 1959, Capt. Tom Goff of the 539th FIS achieved the notable event of becoming the first operational squadron pilot to fire

Brand new Sixes are lined up on the 539th FIS ramp in 1959. The unique tail marking was a stylized dart, with the squadron badge displayed on both sides. Yellow chromate primer was the standard for gear wells in early days, but it went to dark green in later years. (USAF)

With the gear already retracted, this 539th FIS Six hangs on the leader's wing during a formation takeoff from McGuire AFB, New Jersey. The 539th was the first squadron to receive the F-106, but the lack of a buzz number on the aft fuselage and presence of the datalink antennas below the aft fuselage date this photograph to around 1966. (USAF via Isham).

High over western Washington state, this echelon of F-106s is from the 498th FIS. The large "Geiger Tigers" squadron badge and rust-red rudders are a carryover from their F-102 markings. Most jets eventually got a gloss black fin cap. (USAF)

an ATR-2A Genie from an F-106. Due to serious logistical shortages and equally serious problems with water condensation shorting out the MA-1 system (something that never happened during initial testing in the desert), the unit did not complete the Category III testing until early 1961.

The honor of becoming the first combat-ready unit with the F-106 actually went to the second unit to receive the Delta Dart, the 498th FIS at Geiger Field, Washington. This squadron defended the nearby Fairchild SAC base and the Hanford Nuclear Reservation.

Having received the first F-106 simulator and coming from the similar F-102, conversion for the 498th FIS was considerably easier than for the 539th FIS. As a result, the 498th pilots were able to start learning the new jet in the simulator, and after flying to Palmdale in either a T-33 or T-29 support aircraft, they simply received a cockpit checkout and flew their new jets back to home base. Capt. Robert R. Stafford, flying F-106A S/N 57-2461, was the first to arrive at Geiger, landing at 1435L, 2 June 1959. Capt. Allen T. Enslen, flying S/N 57-2463, arrived just three minutes later.

Under the 4700th Air Defense Wing, commanded by the hard-charging Col. Leon W. Gray, the 498th was in a hurry to become operationally ready. Regardless of the fact that they were operating off a relatively short 8,000-foot-long runway that had no barriers, the 498th ran a local checkout program to transition their pilots.

Late in July 1959 the 498th scrambled five F-106As and successfully intercepted several F-102s that were simulating an attack on Spokane. All the targets were intercepted while still more than 75 miles away from the target area.

On 25 September 1959, Capt. Dale E. Downing successfully completed his check ride to become the world's first combat-ready F-106 pilot. At 0600L on 31 October 1959, Capt. Robert R. Stafford and 1st Lt. Jackie E. Moorehart became the first two pilots in history to stand alert with the F-106, as the 498th became the first operational F-106 squadron.

Events soon proved ADC claims to be justified; the F-106 was simply not yet ready for operational use. As the last of the FY 1957 round-eye jets flowed into the 95th FIS at Andrews AFB, Maryland, and the first vertical tape–equipped jets (FY 1958) began to arrive at the 456th FIS at Castle AFB, California, it became very obvious that there were, in fact, serious problems. One of them was that the new vertical tape–equipped jets had instruments that were nearly impossible for pilots to interpret. ADC had to hurriedly install small, conventional gauges until redesigned tape instruments could replace the existing ones.

Issued a full year after introduction to ADC combat squadrons, the interim Category III testing report of late 1960 finally declared the F-106 operationally suitable. However, it was certainly not maintainable. At least four completely different configurations of the MA-1 emerged from the production line. Each jet was literally unique, both

Along with an equally small altimeter, the small airspeed peanut gauge in the center of the photo had to be added to the glare shield of early tape-equipped Sixes. It was retained as a backup instrument when newly designed tapes replaced the originals.

from an electronics and an airframe viewpoint. The differences were so significant that a jet from one squadron could not land at another squadron and expect to receive any support except fuel.

In many cases, spare parts proved to be incompatible with the components they were supposed to replace. Chronic failure of some MA-1 components became commonplace. As an example of how different the jets were, each major electronics configuration was given an alphabetical block number, similar to an airframe receiving a numerical block number for each major structural difference.

When combined with a critical shortage of ground support and testing equipment, lack of spare parts, and inadequate maintenance training, the results were problems of staggering proportions for the ADC squadrons trying to employ the new interceptors.

One of the most serious problems was the fact that the MA-1 system was basically incompatible with its electrical power supply system. The communications, navigation, and landing (CNL) subsystem of the MA-1 failed so often that the aircraft were restricted to flying in pairs in clear weather. During normal operations, the interceptors were required to remain within 15 minutes flying time of a suitable emergency recovery airfield.

An equally serious problem was the high failure rate of the A/C generator. When it failed, it caused the boost pumps that fed fuel to the engine to cease operating. Because there were no provisions for a backup A/C power source, unless the tank was nearly full of fuel, or unless the pilot held a continuous nose-up attitude, an engine flameout due to fuel starvation usually resulted. After several power losses and two crashes, pilots were directed to land with at least 3,000 pounds of fuel remaining, and the offending generators were replaced after only 100 hours of operation. Meanwhile, high priority was given to finding and engineering appropriate fixes.

By mid-1960, ADC went to HQ USAF listing 67 airframe differences and 63 major MA-1 AWCIS differences within the fleet, and flatly concluded that the new aircraft were impossible to maintain. Also, since the F-106 procurement program had been cut short by two-thirds of the number originally envisioned, there were simply not going to be enough of them to do the job. Furthermore, neither the AIM-4F nor AIM-G was compatible with installed MA-1s yet, seriously limiting the combat capability of the jet. As the *Pictorial History of Kelly Air Force Base 1917–1980* eloquently points out:

"Already factions in the U.S. government were pressing for a decision not to develop more manned aircraft. The view was that the F-106, last of the "Century" aircraft, might be the last interceptor in the air force inventory, for [intercontinental ballistic] missiles were making their appearance and the rationale of interception was

When the engine failed in the traffic pattern on 13 Aug 1961, the pilot elected to attempt a dead-stick landing at Selfridge AFB. He could not make it to the concrete and ended up landing in the dirt between the runway and taxiway. An all-too-common occurrence back then. (USAF via Isham)

As the powerless Six crossed the intersecting E-W runway, the transition from muddy infield to concrete tore off the landing gear. This view is looking north and the runway is visible on the far left. The cars are parked on the parallel taxiway. (USAF via Isham)

affected by their characteristics and performance. Thus, the F-106 became more important because it was less important, an equivocal position. If it were to carry the burden of the nation's defense as the last of its line, it must quickly assume that burden, for the time being of the essence for production and equally for modifications. Of course, as has been seen, under the Cook-Craigie concept, there was no leisurely progression from research through development and on to production of combat-ready airplanes. These stages were carried on simultaneously and at tremendous cost."

The Test-to-Tactical Program

A step toward fixing the problem of insufficient numbers of aircraft had already been taken in August 1959, when the air force decided to adhere to the original Cook-Craigie program intent and modify most of the 35 surviving test aircraft to the final tactical configuration. This essentially gave ADC two additional squadrons of Delta Darts. Under this T-T-T rebuilding program (which was also carried out on the previous F-102 fleet), 11 aircraft that were in storage at Palmdale were disassembled and trucked to San Diego, and the remaining aircraft were flown to Convair. Some of the jets still had early engines, some had very early versions of the MA-1 system, and none were anything at all like the last aircraft coming off the assembly line.

For the modifications, the wings were removed and the fuselages were cut in half at the aft end of the 16-foot-long weapons bay. Completely new forward fuselage sections were built, all containing the vertical tape instrumentation and the newly developed Convair supersonic ejection seats. As with the originals, noses for the A models were built in San Diego and noses for the B models were again built by Convair-Fort Worth. Upon arrival at Palmdale, the latest version of the MA-1 was installed before delivery to the USAF. The first of these aircraft was delivered in January 1961 and the final one in June of that year, thus becoming the last F-106s actually delivered to ADC squadrons.

Of the remaining test aircraft, the first two F-106As were considered prototypes, and therefore not considered for modification. The first prototype (S/N 56-0451) was donated to the Air Force Museum (now the National Museum of the Air Force), located at Wright-Patterson AFB in Dayton, Ohio. Because it had no navigation equipment installed, it was led across the country by two F-106s being delivered to the 27th FIS at Loring AFB, Maine.

The second jet (S/N 56-0452) was assigned as a ground training aircraft at Amarillo AFB, Texas, and eventually dropped from the inventory.

Of the remainder, S/N 57-0229 had exploded on 8 April 1959 while assigned to ARDC, S/N 57-0239 had been written off due to destructive fatigue testing after conversion to a YF-106C, and S/N 57-0242 had been lost on 27 October 1958 prior to acceptance by the USAF. Lacking provisions for the ASQ-25, the first F-106B (S/N

57-2507) was used for many years as a test bed before being handed over to NASA, retaining the early air intake configuration until the very end. S/N 57-2511 was lost on 5 January 1959 while serving with the test force at Holloman.

CONVAIR - SD
Form #5-0-55-1
MODEL 8 F-106 A/B MASTER DELIVERY SCHEDULE
MODEL 8 F-106 A/B TEST TO TACTICAL MODIFICATION PROGRAM

Long Range Planning
Issue: 8B-1030F
Date: 8-19-60
Replaces Issue:8B-10...
Dated: 2-12-60
Page 13 of 14

MODEL 8 F-106 A/B TEST TO TACTICAL MODIFICATION PROGRAM

Prod. Line No.	USAF No.	Original Mode-Version No.		New Model-Version No.		Contract No.	Delivery	
		F-106A	F-106B	F-106A	F-106B		Month	Year
1	56-462	8-22-6		8-31-9		AF41(600)11333	Jan	1961
2	57-238	8-24-7		8-31-22		"	"	"
3	56-453	8-21-1		8-31-1		"	"	"
4	56-456	8-21-4		8-31-3		"	"	"
5	56-458	8-22-2		8-31-5		"	Feb	"
6	56-461	8-22-5		8-31-8		"	"	"
7	57-232	8-24-1		8-31-17		"	"	"
8	57-240	8-24-9		8-31-24		"	"	"
9	57-2513		8-27-7		8-32-6	"	"	"
10	56-454	8-21-2		8-31-2		"	"	"
11	57-244	8-24-13		8-31-27		"	Mar	"
12	57-245	8-24-14		8-31-28		"	"	"
13	56-464	8-23-2		8-31-12		"	"	"
14	57-231	8-23-7		8-31-16		"	"	"
15	56-459	8-22-3		8-31-6		"	"	"
16	56-460	8-22-4		8-31-7		"	"	"
17	57-230	8-23-6		8-31-15		"	"	"
18	57-243	8-24-12		8-31-26		"	Apr	"
19	56-457	8-22-1		8-31-4		"	"	"
20	56-465	8-23-3		8-31-13		"	"	"
21	57-236	8-24-5		8-31-20		"	"	"
22	57-2509		8-27-3		8-32-3	"	"	"
23	57-235	8-24-4		8-31-23		"	"	"
24	57-237	8-24-6		8-31-21		"	"	"
25	57-234	8-24-3		8-31-19		"	May	"
26	57-2514		8-27-8		8-32-7	"	"	
27	56-467	8-22-7		8-31-10		"	"	
28	57-233	8-24-2		8-31-18		"	"	
29	57-241	8-24-10		8-31-25		"	"	
30	57-2508		8-27-2		8-32-2	"	"	
31	56-463	8-23-1		8-31-11		AF41(600)11333	May	196?
32	56-466	8-23-4		8-31-14		"	June	
33	57-2512		8-27-6		8-32-5	"	"	
34	57-2510		8-27-4		8-32-4	"	"	
35	57-2507 (replaced 57-2515 2507)		8-27-1		8-32-1	"	"	

Here is the delivery schedule for aircraft modified under the Test-to-Tactical program. The prototype F-106B was initially scheduled for modification, but was replaced by S/N 57-2515. S/N 56-0467 has been lined out, which dates this copy of the document to after mid-August 1961. (Convair)

Phase I of Wild Goose consisted of 20 changes to the CNL system and 6 changes to the airframe. It was an attempt to make the F-106 safe for flight and enable it to resume all-weather flying. Changes to the electrical power distribution system and fuel systems were the major alterations. This phase was completed by the end of the year. Aircraft undergoing the T-T-T program in San Diego received these modifications while still on the production line.

Phase II of Wild Goose began in January 1960, continued through May 1961, and encompassed more than 50 changes to the HAC equipment and 8 changes to the airframe. The final set of modifications were accomplished between May and August 1961, and were solely related to the MA-1. Major changes included an improved power supply system, addition of the TDDL system that allowed electronic integration with the new SAGE system, and the ability to fire AIM-4F and AIM-4G Falcon missiles. Upon completion, all F-106 MA-1/

Upon completion of flight testing, S/N 56-0451 was flown to Wright-Patterson AFB, Ohio, and placed on display at what was then known as the Air Force Museum. Seen here in September 1960, six months after arrival, it still carries an F-102 buzz number and the paint is already starting to fade.

Fixes Begin

The severity of the fleet configuration problems resulted in several inter-related and simultaneous modification programs designed to standardize the fleet into two configurations: those having the conventional round-eye cockpit instrumentation and those having the vertical tape–type instruments. As part of the process, all aircraft were upgraded to the most recent MA-1 configuration as well. The three initial programs were called Wild Goose, Broad Jump, and Dart Board.

Project Wild Goose

Wild Goose was largely a standardization program for the MA-1 AWCIS and was carried out in three phases between September 1960 and August 1961. It involved 131 changes, 800,000 man-hours of work, and cost more than $13 million (1960). Under the auspices of Sacramento Air Materiel Area (SMAMA), most of the work was carried out at ADC squadrons by AMC field teams including from 26 to 59 specialists (electricians, armament specialists, sheet-metal workers, instrument and electronic technicians, and MA-1 specialists) assisted by squadron maintenance and avionics personnel. ADC provided technicians to inspect the completed work and ensure that the MA-1 system operated properly after work was complete. About 90 aircraft had the work done at SMAMA in conjunction with the simultaneous Broad Jump project.

Looking down the Broad Jump modification line in 1961 or 1962, we can see Sixes from many of the early units. The modifications involved a virtual rebuild of the jets. (USAF via Isham)

ASQ-25 systems had been standardized to the latest configuration, then known as Block F.

However, the attempt to make the aircraft reliable fell far short of success. Reports from the ADC Air Divisions revealed that instead of having 84 CNL malfunctions per 200 flights before the program, they had "improved" to only 63 failures per 200 flights, and the flight restrictions remained in place.

Project Broad Jump

The Broad Jump program was a long-term modernization program. It was carried out at the SMAMA depot, and aircraft were carefully scheduled in conjunction with the simultaneous Wild Goose program to ensure that no squadron was left with less than half of its aircraft available. Broad Jump was the first of what became many long-term improvement programs for the F-106, and its goal was to turn out "a completely combat-capable weapon."

Having been made the prime Specialized Repair Facility (SRA) during May 1959, the SMAMA began preparing for the wave of maintenance and modification programs well before contracts were even awarded. They sent hundreds of workers and supervisors to Hughes and Convair for on-the-job training. A huge new maintenance building was constructed, and all of the necessary MA-1 mockups and test equipment to handle the upcoming workload were accumulated. This was a larger job than it may have first appeared.

The main problem was that the many MA-1 system and airframe changes incorporated during factory production were made without consideration for retrofit in the field. The multiple configurations gave SMAMA nearly insurmountable mockup and test equipment problems, since the aircraft came from several squadrons at one time, each with a different configuration. The Wild Goose program helped somewhat, but since virtually no two MA-1s were identical, trying to standardize the fleet required first finding out exactly how each individual MA-1 was configured. In the end, five MA-1 mockups had to be installed to handle the different jets.

The first F-106A arrived for prototyping on 7 December 1959, work started on 12 January 1960, the jet was ready for MA-1 re-installation on 2 May, and work was completed on 5 August. The plan called for 10 aircraft per month to be input, with 60 days allowed for completion of the work over a three-year period. In September 1960, two months before Convair delivered the last newly built F-106, SMAMA began the first of the upgrades.

To do that, all of the F-106 airframes had to be brought up to the most recent standards. Each aircraft that came through had all outstanding Time Compliance Technical Orders (TCTOs) accomplished. Because this program was running in parallel with the Wild Goose program, any aircraft that arrived for Broad Jump that had not been modified under the Wild Goose program had both sets of modifications done at the same time while at the depot. With an overall cost of $15 million and consuming more than 800,000

Seen taxiing at Geiger Field, Washington, this rare shot shows a Six from the 498th that has received a tailhook but has not yet gotten the optical sight for the Genie rocket, so it has only partially completed the three major upgrade programs. The hook has not yet received the point guards, which would be added starting in 1962.

man-hours, the program made a huge improvement to the performance of the F-106 fleet.

During the course of the work, tailhooks were added to those jets that did not receive them on the assembly line (all those prior to S/N 59-001). An optical sight for the Genie rocket was added and many other modifications were made, including altering the rotating beacons so that they no longer retracted at supersonic speeds. The decrease in drag was less of a concern than the decrease in maintenance time needed to keep them working properly.

Of note is that five "peculiar" F-106B models were scheduled for 120 days each for the program, double the amount of time allocated to all of the other aircraft. These were early FY 1957 jets (S/N 57-2516 through S/N 57-2519) that had not received the T-T-T modifications but had been built with the lower cockpit side consoles designed for the side stick controller. Although not receiving new forward fuselages, these five jets did have their cockpits rebuilt in a mini T-T-T to match the rest of the fleet and allow installation of the new Convair B seat.

The overlapping maintenance programs had a serious impact on the ability of the operational squadrons to maintain the required alert commitment and daily training. With up to half of the aircraft out of service for modifications, ADC directed each unit to organize a team of 10 to 15 pilots who would receive priority for training with the available jets to "ensure maximum and reliable combat readiness" during the period. The remaining pilots were often "farmed out" to other on-base organizations in a non-flying capacity. The North American Aerospace Defense Command (NORAD) also cooperated by reducing the alert commitment of the five-minute aircraft from two aircraft to one under normal conditions.

Escaping the fate that many early Sixes suffered, this Six from the 94th FIS did not burn after suffering a tire failure on 13 April 1960. Maybe the notorious Selfridge mud prevented a worse incident. As was typical of the early tire failures, the nose gear has also collapsed. The lack of optical sight and interim ejection seat means that this Six has not yet completed either the Dart Board or Broad Jump programs. (USAF)

The white holes on the left side of the frame show that this image was taken from a print in the safety office. Yet another tire, and nose gear trunnion failure, this time on 6 Mar 1962. It took the depot team about six months to repair the jet and get it back into service. The tailhook has the point guard installed. The Convair B seat and optical sight mean that this jet has already finished the three major modification programs. This Six was later assigned to the ADWC at Tyndall AFB Florida, and became the first Six outfitted with the Vulcan cannon. (USAF via Isham)

As if those problems were not bad enough, the F-106 fleet had to deal with several other issues simultaneously. One involved failure of the nose-gear trunnion support fittings, which were cracking so frequently due to stresses placed on the nose gear by towing the aircraft that they had to be replaced every 200 hours of flying. Along with that, the main wheels still had a tendency to break apart and throw shrapnel through the wing when the unreliable tires blew out on takeoff or landing, causing fires. This problem alone caused the loss of several aircraft. It was finally fixed starting in late 1964 or early 1965, when redesigned main wheels were made available to using organizations.

Category III Weapons Testing, still underway at Tyndall, found yet another unexpected problem: During periods of high temperatures and high humidity, moisture condensed in the MA-1 during flights and caused radar malfunctions. Water frequently saturated coaxial cables in the radar and communications systems, shorting out vitally important systems. As many as 37 cable connectors were found to be waterlogged, and shorted out after a single flight. The situation became so serious that low-level missions had to be suspended until either cooler weather or a fix for the problem became available.

The MA-3 air conditioner was just as poor at putting water into the system, but at least its temperature output could be adjusted to above the dewpoint until the necessary modifications could be made.

The retaining pins for the 230-gallon external fuel tanks were weak and tended to shear accidentally, causing the tank to fall off the jet when the afterburner was lit for takeoff or when Gs were applied, but this was only a minor nuisance.

Another scene from the depot at McClellan, this time from roughly 1964, shows another group of Sixes deep into a modification program. The early hot air exhaust on the spine of the F-106B in the foreground is typical prior to the aerial refueling modification. (USAF via Isham)

given 15 days to complete the work, and a replacement aircraft flown in when the first one was finished. The program had to be extended when the entire F-106 fleet was grounded on 22 September 1961 due to failures of a diaphragm in the fuel control. A temporary fix allowed the jets to return to flying status by November, but a permanent fix was not in place until late February 1962.

Given difficulties in receiving engineering change kits from both CV and HAC (there being so many differences between aircraft that modification kits and scheduling had to be done on an "individual tail number" basis) and scheduling constraints, SMAMA was hard-pressed to process aircraft through the programs in a timely manner. Adding further difficulty was the fact that some aircraft were input for the Dart Board speed line modifications prior to receiving the Broad Jump work.

To make the task nearly impossible, airframes continued to pour off the Convair assembly line, and nine new squadrons were converting to the interceptor while all three modification programs were in progress, and most of these aircraft were required to pass through at least one of the SMAMA retrofits. However, by the time the Dart Board program was complete, the F-106 fleet was finally well on the way to being reliably combat ready, just in time for their first big challenge. Unfortunately, the newly installed Upward Rotational Ejection Seats became problematic almost as soon as they were installed.

Project Dart Board

The Dart Board program, which began in August 1961 and continued into 1962, was yet another retrofit and improvement program that ran in parallel with the latter stages of Broad Jump. Although 35 further modifications to the MA-1 and 3 to the airframe were carried out, the most significant changes made during this program were the addition of a fuel hopper to the number-3 wing fuel tanks that gave the engine an uninterrupted supply of fuel, installation of the new Convair Upward Rotational Ejection Seat in the aircraft that did not have it installed during assembly, addition of an air-driven emergency A/C generator, and upgrading the MA-1 to Block G, if not previously accomplished.

Contrary to published reports, no F-106 ever received the "flash blindness" hood. It was prototyped as TCTO 1F-106-674, dated 16 March 1962, and planned to be part of the Dart Board modifications, but it was deemed impractical due to lack of space in the cockpit and was never installed.

The Dart Board program was run as a "speed line" where one aircraft at a time from a given unit was input,

A three-ship of Sixes from the 48th FIS goes into the break at New Hanover County Airport, Wilmington, North Carolina, in April 1970. These jets have just returned from a mission in the Warning Areas off the coast. (Photo by Jim Sullivan)

Chapter Ten

EJECTION SEATS FOR THE SIX

This 95th FIS Six shows just how sleek the bird really was before all the modification programs started. The original interim ejection seat and lack of optical sight are noteworthy in this 21 May 1960 photo. (Tom Hildreth)

The original ejection seat used in the F-106 was a slightly modified version of that used in the earlier F-102. This so-called interim seat was built by the Weber company. Like virtually all early ejection seats, it was a ballistic catapult seat that used an explosive charge to throw the seat and pilot clear of the aircraft. To be successful, low-speed ejection had to be initiated at least 2,000 feet in the air and at a speed above 120 knots. It was not approved for supersonic ejections.

Air force requirements for a demonstrated supersonic ejection seat resulted in formation of the Industry Crew Escape System Committee (ICESC). Using recommendations from the committee and Convair, the Stanley Aviation Company began development of a new ejection seat that would be useable from zero altitude, zero airspeed ejections through supersonic speeds. The committee came up with two designs: A and B. With Convair taking the lead, both were sled tested using an F-102 forward fuselage mockup on the ARDC's Hurricane Mesa track in Utah. The B design had better aerodynamics and was chosen for development, although extending stabilizing booms had to be added to keep the seat from rolling.

The new rocket-powered seat was known variously as the Convair Upward Rotational B-seat, Supersonic Rotational B-seat, tilt seat, supersonic bobsled, pinball machine, B-seat, and pilot killer. It stands as a classic example of ignoring the "keep it simple" principle.

Built by Aircraft Mechanics Incorporated, the massive seat weighed nearly 420 pounds and was exceptionally complex. The new seat was completely unlike any ejection seat contemplated before, and similar to the original downward-ejecting Lockheed F-104 seat, pilots were required to wear flight boots with specially

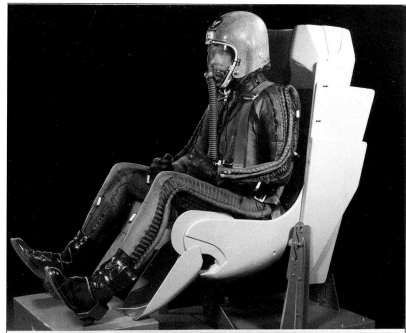

The ICESC A seat design had fold-out wings instead of the booms used on the B seat. But the overall shape and workings of the seat were nearly identical. (Kaston)

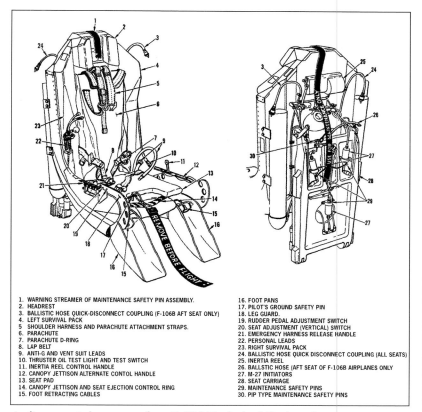

1. WARNING STREAMER OF MAINTENANCE SAFETY PIN ASSEMBLY.	16. FOOT PANS
2. HEADREST	17. PILOT'S GROUND SAFETY PIN
3. BALLISTIC HOSE QUICK-DISCONNECT COUPLING (F-106B AFT SEAT ONLY)	18. LEG GUARD.
4. LEFT SURVIVAL PACK	19. RUDDER PEDAL ADJUSTMENT SWITCH
5. SHOULDER HARNESS AND PARACHUTE ATTACHMENT STRAPS.	20. SEAT ADJUSTMENT (VERTICAL) SWITCH
6. PARACHUTE	21. EMERGENCY HARNESS RELEASE HANDLE
7. PARACHUTE D-RING	22. PERSONAL LEADS
8. LAP BELT	23. RIGHT SURVIVAL PACK
9. ANTI-G AND VENT SUIT LEADS	24. BALLISTIC HOSE QUICK DISCONNECT COUPLING (ALL SEATS)
10. THRUSTER OIL TEST LIGHT AND TEST SWITCH	25. INERTIA REEL
11. INERTIA REEL CONTROL HANDLE	26. BALLSTIC HOSE (AFT SEAT OF F-106B AIRPLANES ONLY
12. CANOPY JETTISON ALTERNATE CONTROL HANDLE	27. M-27 INITIATORS
13. SEAT PAD	28. SEAT CARRIAGE
14. CANOPY JETTISON AND SEAT EJECTION CONTROL RING	29. MAINTENANCE SAFETY PINS
15. FOOT RETRACTING CABLES	30. PIP TYPE MAINTENANCE SAFETY PINS

A diagram taken out of an F-106 Technical Order gives some seldom seen details of the Convair B seat. It certainly failed the "KISS" principle. (USAF)

Being the first USAF ejection seat designed for supersonic escape, and given the radical nature of the seat, it was subjected to more than three years of sled and flight testing before it was cleared for use in the F-106A. Tests continued on the F-106B through 1961, using rocket-powered sleds at both Edwards and Holloman with emphasis on high-speed fin tip clearance, windblast protection, seat stabilization, safe deceleration rates, and "packaging" of the seat occupant and retention of equipment. Thirty-five preliminary tests were accomplished to verify that humans could survive ejections at up to 500 knots.

There were 15 successful test runs using dummies, ranging from a low of 154 knots to one profile simulating a speed of Mach 2.5 at 33,000 feet. F-106B S/N 57-2507 was also used for 11 flight tests and had a camera mounted on the tip of the vertical fin to record the ejection sequences. Ten tests using dummies and a cutout for the rear canopy were accomplished. Speeds between 176 and 733 KIAS were flown at altitudes between 10,000 and 50,000 feet.

Flight tests were flown from Edwards, Holloman, and NAS El Centro, California, home of the naval parachute research center. Humans were used in one sled test and one aerial ejection. On 6 June 1961, TSgt James A. Howell successfully ejected from -507 at

designed spurs that latched to the seat when ejecting. When activated, the system completed typical actions such as jettisoning the canopy and retracting the shoulder harness. But then the seat raised foot pans and leg guards before rising on a set of rails to clear the cockpit, and then rotating 90-degrees aft so that the pilot was lying on his back. At that point, a set of stabilizing booms extended, and only then did the rocket motor fire to separate the whole assembly from the aircraft.

With the stabilizing booms fully extended and the rockets firing, the dummy is going for a ride during this April 1960 B seat sled test. All test runs were filmed with high-speed film cameras so that results could be analyzed later. (USAF)

22,580 feet and 337 KIAS (Mach 0.77). One extremely high-altitude test, presumably using a balloon for a launch vehicle, included dropping the seat with a dummy from an altitude of 84,150 feet to study the effects of long-term free fall.

Considerable difficulty was encountered in trying to ensure successful dual ejections from the F-106B, and the twin seaters were not cleared to have the new seat installed until well after the F-106A. In spite of all the testing, or perhaps because of USAF insistence on supersonic capability, the new seat was not zero-zero capable. Due to diminished aerodynamic stability it was only useable down to 160 knots, and recommended speeds were between 200 and 450 knots.

With testing complete, and having a duly-qualified supersonic seat in hand, the last 37 F-106As, starting at block -130 (S/N 59-0112), received the new seats on the assembly line. Only the last few F-106Bs received the seats during construction. All of the remaining F-106 fleet had the seats replaced under TCTO 1F-106-569, either during the T-T-T rebuild, or during the subsequent Dart Board modification program.

Even before installation of the seats began, however, events were proving the engineers' assertion that low-speed, low-altitude ejections were the larger threat. As the number of low-altitude ejection fatalities grew, Capt. Iven Kincheloe joined other high-scoring aces, including Maj. Lonnie Moore and Maj. Richard I. Bong, in a grim testament to the engineers' foresight.

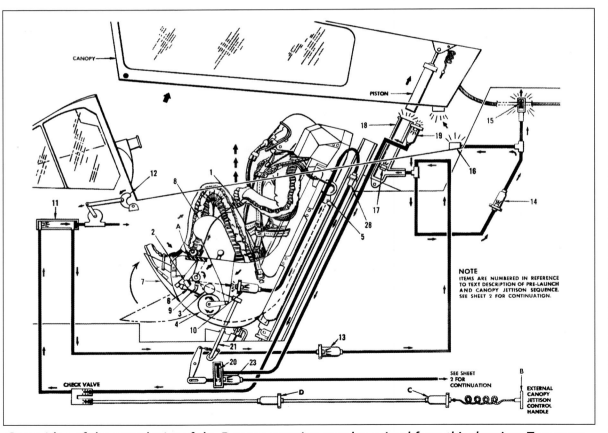

Some idea of the complexity of the B seat operation may be gained from this drawing. Two more drawings were required to list all of the sequences up to parachute deployment. (USAF)

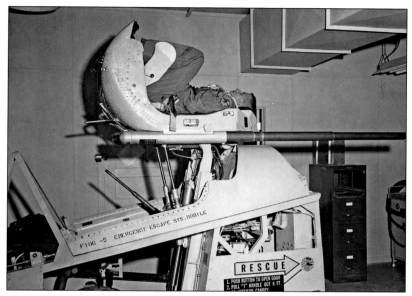

This is where the egress tech normally goes for a cup of coffee. A pilot from the 329th FIS undergoes recurrent emergency training using the B seat mockup. Some idea of the complexity of the system can be seen here. (USAF)

The B seat was not cleared for use with the F-106B until well after it was approved for the F-106A. Problems with seats hitting the tail or one another were apparently difficult to fix. Strict speed limits were imposed for using the seat on the bus. (USAF from November 1960)

Once in the field, serious deficiencies in the B-seat quickly became evident. Among other issues, the intense preparation for contractor testing was not matched with typical in-the-field maintenance.

With more than 30 pyrotechnic actuators, a sequence of some 70-odd events that had to occur, in order, with no malfunctions, and no backups, the B-seat became one of the first deadly examples of what later became known as single-point failure modes. One of the first failure modes to show up allowed the ejection to proceed until the seat rotated to the horizontal position. Then the sequence simply stopped, leaving the pilot lying on his back, unable to disconnect from the seat, and doomed to ride the jet until impact.

Because there was no yaw on the straight sled test track, and the few in-flight tests had been done under carefully controlled straight and level conditions, the possible negative effects of yaw on system performance had apparently been overlooked and were never investigated. Further, the aft canopy was cut out for all of the in-flight tests with the F-106B. However, it quickly became apparent that in operational use, the departing canopy could damage one of the initiator lines, thus preventing successful use of the seat.

The F-106B fleet had additional problems due to the need to separate the two pilots during ejections, and the fleet of two-seaters was not declared operational until 1960. Even after the B-seats were installed, ejections in F-106Bs were limited to under 600 knots. The buses were grounded on 8 August 1962, a year after approval to install the seats was given, in a further attempt to fix the problems.

While efforts were underway to tackle those issues, more arose. On 8 October 1963, F-106A S/N 59-0039 from the 27th FIS expe-

rienced engine failure about 8 minutes after takeoff. The pilot attempted to eject and pulled the D-ring. The canopy left the aircraft, the foot cables retracted his feet, the foot pans and seat pan raised and locked, and the entire sequence simply stopped. The pilot then pulled the emergency harness release and disconnected his seat belt and shoulder harness to give himself enough freedom of movement to either manually bail out or attempt a dead-stick landing with the 40,000-pound glider. But he could not free his left foot from the spur that attached it to the foot cable.

He did the only thing he could: He dropped the landing gear, deployed the Ram Air Turbine (RAT) to provide emergency hydraulic power, and pointed the jet toward an empty potato field. The jet hit the bank of a ditch and started to come apart. The cockpit and engine slid about 300 feet before coming to rest, and the unrestrained pilot suffered very serious injuries while being thrown around inside the cockpit.

Fortunately, the local search-and-rescue helicopter was on the scene almost immediately, and the crew managed to cut the pilot out of his boot and get him free of the burning wreck. The fire was quickly extinguished, and for the first time, there were enough pieces available to conduct a full investigation.

It was found that the vertical thruster squib had fired and struck the primer, but not hard enough to detonate it. Oil was suspected of cushioning the impact enough to prevent the initiator from firing. Additional fixes were rapidly engineered, and several messages to the field about the extreme care required when working on the seat were again sent out.

F-106A S/N 59-0039 suffered an engine failure shortly after takeoff on 8 October 1963. When the Convair B seat failed to function, the pilot had no choice but to dead-stick the crippled jet into an empty potato field. This was the first time investigators had an undamaged seat to examine. (USAF via Isham)

This was one of the few attempted ejections without a pilot fatality, and by then most pilots had lost faith in the complicated seat. In fact, many pilots were flying with the ejection seat safety pins still installed, preferring to attempt a manual bailout if necessary, rather than entrust their lives to a seat with such a high fatality rate.

The final straw came at Minot on 19 December 1963, when F-106A S/N 59-0017 crashed, claiming the 13th fatality directly attributable to the B-seat. The full details of the accident can be found in Col. Jack Broughton's excellent biography *Rupert Red Two: A Fighter Pilot's Life from Thunderbolt to Thunderchief*. After grounding his entire squadron and instituting a nose-to-tail maintenance evaluation of all the aircraft, Col. Broughton was called on the carpet in front of ADC Commander General Herbert Thatcher. That interview resulted in Col. Broughton and his life-support team addressing a large, joint civilian/military conference on the F-106 ejection seat. Chaired by Maj. Gen. W. T. "Red" Hudnell, and held at the Mobile AMA HQ on Brookley AFB, Alabama, Col. Broughton and his team did not receive a warm welcome from the industry representatives.

A graphic demonstration of how it was physically impossible to activate the emergency bailout lanyard while dressed in winter flying gear resulted in silence from the attendees. After a few months of review of ejection statistics, which by then showed the notable failure rate of the B-seat, the clear trend of low-altitude, low-speed ejections, and the near-zero rate of high-speed ejection attempts, the Weber Company was chosen to replace the ICESC seat.

Taking only 45 days to design and deliver the new seat, its zero-zero capability was demonstrated with a live volunteer during Project 90 in late 1965. The replacement seat was an upgraded ver-

sion of the original interim seat, using a rocket catapult instead of a ballistic charge. It weighed only 213 pounds and was rated for safe ejections from zero airspeed to 600 knots. Installed in the fleet between late 1964 and 1965, it was far simpler to maintain and achieved an outstanding safety record.

This 71st FIS jet still has the Convair B seat installed for a mid-1965 hero shot. Note how massive this seat was. Our intrepid pilot has a single visor helmet with a dart-silhouette decoration. The optical genie sight is very nicely shown, along with a wealth of other rarely seen cockpit detail. (USAF)

Strapped in with his helmet resting on the optical sight, this 498th FIS pilot is about to launch on the first deployment to Alaska. The complex 420-pound B seat dominates the cockpit. Note the face shield on the radar scope. The early scopes had poor brightness and the pilots had to fly with their faces up against the tube to be able to see the radar returns. (USAF)

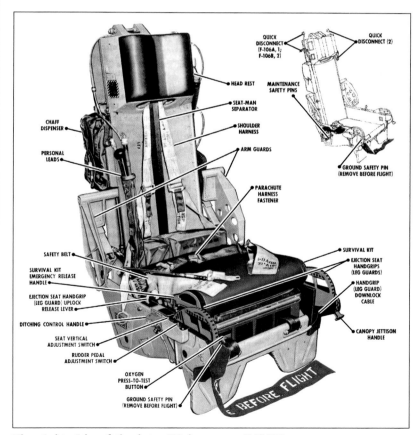

The right side of the later Weber seat. (USAF)

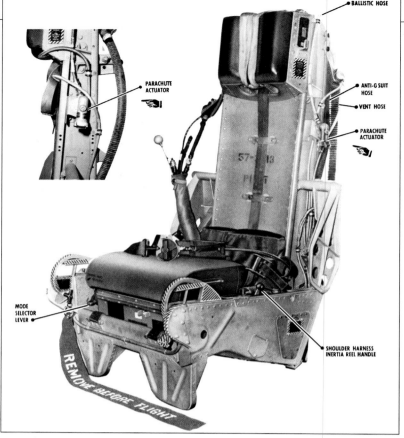

A tech order illustration shows how much simpler the replacement Weber ejection seat was. Not only far more reliable, it worked low and slow where most ejections ended up being made. (USAF)

In a low-speed test, S/N 57-2507 flies straight and level for the ejection on 24 Dec 1969. The cutaway aft canopy section was one reason some of the early Convair B seat failure modes went undetected. After completion of the Apollo capsule ejection seat tests, this jet was handed over to NASA. (USN via Isham)

Chapter Eleven

EARLY PROJECTS

High over Arizona in January 1978, these two Sixes are from the 5th FIS.

Operational use of the U-2 raised questions among ADC and the air staff as to whether the F-106 would be effective against such a high-flying target, or if the MIG-21 would constitute a threat to the new reconnaissance platform. As a result, at least two test programs were run in the early 1960s. The first of these took place during 1960–1961.

Using the U-2s of Operation Crowflight and F-106s from the 5th FIS at Minot, the Sixes made simulated gunnery passes on the U-bird at around 65,000 feet. The gun passes were described as "eye watering." The Sixes flew at about Mach 2 and the U-2 was at a far lower speed, which made it very hard to visually pick up the Dragon Lady. Even with GCI control and a radar lock-on, mere seconds existed to receive a "tally-ho" and get a simulated pipper on target before having to break away to avoid collision.

The biggest concern was that the shockwave from the Mach 2 Dart might cause the U-2, operating at the limits of its flight envelope, to stall, so the Six pilots were briefed to not fly directly past the U-2. In the end it was found that any bank at all by the U-2 was enough to completely negate an attack and it was deemed unlikely that the U-2s would be at risk.

This 5th FIS has an earlier design of markings. Photo from 1967. (USAF)

Project Ice Cube

In approximately 1962, Project Ice Cube was flown by the 329th FIS and was also intended to determine the Six's combat capabilities against extremely high-flying aircraft. The Darts accelerated to Mach 2 at around 45,000 feet, before starting a snap-up Genie attack on a high-flying U-2. Since the afterburner would blow out around 65,000 feet and (at the time) the engine would flame out around 72,000, the Six pilots wore pressure suits.

The F-106 may have been unique in that it was originally designed to bleed high-pressure air into the cockpit to maintain pressurization in the event of a high-altitude flameout. But in this case, the pilots wore the pressure suits as an additional safety measure. (ADC eventually required all F-106 pilots to fly two missions each month wearing the pressure suits, but because they were so uncomfortable and restricted movement so much, it became probably the most detested training requirement imposed, and pilots went to virtually any length to avoid wearing them.)

After armament launch, the Six basically followed a ballistic path until the airspeed started to increase. Once down to around 25,000 feet the engine was restarted and the flight recovered to George. All missions were planned so that simulated armament launch occurred close to Edwards, the thought being that the long, dry lakebed would be available for a dead-stick landing in the event that the J75 could not be started up again. Fortunately, all of the missions landed under power and the test showed that the Six was effective against very high-altitude targets, if the initial vectors were accurate enough to get the Six on, or very near, a head-on intercept.

Project Rough Rider

In 1959 the U.S. Weather Bureau formed the National Severe Storms Project (NSSP). Air force participation was called Project Rough Rider. Because ADC interceptors were tasked to operate in all weather conditions, ADC had a vested interest in supporting this program. The joint civilian/military program involved the USAF, NASA, FAA, colleges, and other research centers in investigating the causes and effects of severe thunderstorms. One F-106A (S/N 57-0234), along with an F-102 and a T-33, was supplied to the project by the Assistant Secretary of Defense (ASD) at Wright-Patterson, and flights were flown from Tinker AFB, Oklahoma, which was in the heart of the severe thunderstorm zone.

For safety's sake, the radar was removed and the fiberglass radome was replaced with solid metal for hail protection. Balsa-wood vanes were mounted on the pitot boom to measure turbulence, and the missile bay was filled with a special instrumentation package that was designed by the NASA Langley research center. ASD wanted to evaluate the all-weather capability of the new interceptors and check out the effects of water and ice ingestion in the jet engines at a high-Mach airspeed. Maj. Jake Knight flew the F-106 through the core of a thunderstorm at Mach 1.22 during one of the 18 thunderstorm penetrations carried out during 1961. In September and October 1961, Rough Rider storm penetrations were carried out from both MacDill and Homestead in Florida. It appears as if the F-106 was only used during 1961 weather testing.

Operation Safe Slide

Probably the most unusual program that the F-106s were involved with was Operation Safe Slide. The rangers at Glacier National Park had been using dynamite to set off controlled avalanches so that the Road to the Sun inside the park could be cleared and kept open during the winter. Unfortunately, the local bear population found dynamite quite tasty, and many of the planned blasts never occurred. By the time the rangers could set the charges and retreat to a safe area, the bears had already consumed them. The park then asked if the air force could help by sending fighters through at supersonic speeds and low altitudes, with the thought

Darts of the 498th over Geiger Field in 1959. (USAF)

that the shockwaves from the sonic booms would dislodge the snow and cause the avalanches.

Beginning in January 1960, the 498th FIS at Geiger was tasked to assist. When requested by the park service, and with acceptable weather conditions, the 498th launched a flight of two F-106s, which "boomed" the locations requested, and left conditions safe for the rotary snow plows to go into action and clear the road.

After the Geiger Tigers left Spokane and moved to the Seattle area, the program was taken over by the 29th FIS flying F-101B Voodoos out of Malmstrom AFB, Montana. When the Voodoos were retired, the task was taken up for a short time by the 71st FIS, by then flying F-106s from Malmstrom. Eventually, the park service began to use cannons to generate the avalanches, and the interceptors lost the chance to go very low and very fast in a good cause.

Project High Speed

Of all of the evaluation projects in which the F-106 participated, Project High Speed was one of the most important for the future

of the Six fleet. In planning for future air defense, both ADC and NORAD had consistently proposed the purchase of additional F-106A aircraft to help cope with the Soviet air threat between 1963 and 1968.

McDonnell had approached the air force as far back as 1958, trying to interest them in a ground-attack version of their new Phantom fighter. Shortly thereafter, a senior ADC colonel flew the new aircraft and was highly impressed. He pushed hard to have the F-4 considered for the air defense role. Then, on 22 April 1961 President John F. Kennedy and Gen. Curtis LeMay attended an air power demonstration at Ft. Bragg, North Carolina, where a navy F-4H dropped 22 live 500-pound bombs for the watching brass.

Regardless of how tactically infeasible the demonstration may have been, Gen. LeMay became an instant fan of the F-4. So when ADC pushed for a competitive evaluation between the F-106 and the F-4 to eliminate doubt as to which of the two could better perform the air defense mission, the Defense Department was happy to accommodate the request. The parameters of the fly-off were to "determine relative system capability, maintainability, and operational effectiveness" in the air defense role. No air-to-air DACT or air-to-ground capabilities were to be considered; it was simply to see which aircraft might be the better interceptor and guide future procurement planning for 1962–1963 budget requests. Convair saw this as the last big chance to sell additional F-106s, and reacted accordingly.

Project High Speed was conducted between 23 October and 17 November 1961, and pitted the 48th FIS out of Langley AFB, Virginia, against VF-74, the navy's first Phantom unit, which was based at NAS Oceana, Virginia. VF-74 was a premier unit, commanded by CDR Julian Gray, a hard-charger who had hand-picked the members of the squadron and who made "beat the air force or you are fired" the overriding goal of the unit.

Westinghouse and Raytheon tech reps maintained the APQ-72 radar of the new jets for the duration of the event, and McDonnell had several factory tech reps on station to help the new unit shine. The 48th FIS, on the other hand, was likely chosen simply because it was the closest F-106 unit to NAS Oceana, and although the entire focus of VF-74 was on the fly-off, the 48th was still required to maintain its air defense alert commitment, and the unit was given no specific reason for the evaluation.

Convair and Hughes sent top tech reps prior to the competition to "peak up" the chosen F-106s, but Hughes sent their people home as soon as the contest started, leaving only the locally assigned tech reps to assist the 48th.

Several altitude profiles were flown, with targets ranging between 500 and 62,000 feet. Since the planned B-58 targets were never made available by SAC, three mission types were not attempted. Some target profiles called for using either electronic countermeasures, or chaff, but no combined chaff and ECM profiles were flown. Tests against a Hound Dog–type ASM were simulated by either an F-104 or an F-4H, neither of which were particularly representative of the actual threat. One of the high-altitude targets was above 50,000 feet and required the crews to wear full pressure suits. That profile used a head-on intercept.

One of the 48th FIS pilots who participated recalls: "I was in the back seat (of an F-106B). The high-altitude target was a small aircraft [sic], and we were supersonic, meaning the closure rate was so high we would only get one chance to lock-on to the target. I believe we got a splash [hit] on the target. I say believe because my attention was diverted by the sight of a navy F-4 slowly passing us low on the port side." The VF-74 guys would not have tried to sabotage the competition, would they?

Live-fire missions were also flown against a towed target. In the words of one of the F-106 participants, "On the live-fire pass we would be firing one radar missile. We were on autopilot, and it made corrections much more abruptly than a pilot would. It was a bit rough, but the steering was superb.

"After we made our break-away maneuver and were heading home we heard the tow plane crew say that part of the dart had broken off as they reeled it in. Later, when we were on the ground, we learned that the referee for the fly-off discovered orange paint scuffs on the remains of the dart, and concluded our missile had made a direct hit.

"We heard that the navy guys were sure they would outshine us, and they were not happy about that result."

The official ADC after-action report stated that "a total of 153 sorties were flown, during which 349 valid interceptions were completed. With few exceptions, the F-4H won the contest easily. The F4H/APQ-72 system repeatedly demonstrated greater reliability, and longer detection and lock-on ranges than the F-106/MA-1 fire control system. Neither performed satisfactorily during low-altitude interceptions. Although the F-4H proved to be capable of neutralizing high-altitude and ASM targets, the F-106A at best demonstrated only a limited capability to engage high-altitude targets and no capability against ASM targets."

Test Results

Type of Target	F-106 (percent)	F-4H (percent)
Below 1,000 feet	56.2	50.0
Below 5,000 feet	58.7	65.6
High Altitude	54.5	93.0
Medium Altitude		
ECM	56.2	75.3
Chaff	57.7	84.8
ASM	0	70.7
Firing Summary		
Attempts	10	7
Fired	7	6
Scored	6	5

Moreover, maintenance man-hours per flying hour were 8.8 for the F-4H and 13.4 hours for the F-106A. The F-4H, it was concluded, was easier to maintain, with its missile control system absorbing only half the man-hours required to maintain the MA-1.

But these results do not tell the whole story. Digging deeper gives a little more perspective. The F-106 was designed to be part of the NORAD SAGE system, using long-range ground-based radars to detect the threat and vector the interceptor into the vicinity of the target, which meant that a large, powerful radar was not built into the F-106.

The F-4 was designed to work at the edge of, or outside, radar coverage from the carrier group. Thus the F-4H had a much larger radar dish (32 versus 23 inches) and much higher output power from the radar, which in turn gave much greater contact and lock-on ranges, easing the strain of high-speed closures. The farther away you could see the target, the more time you had to lock-on and position your aircraft.

Further, VF-74 was full of hand-picked, premier crews, who were chomping at the bit to beat the air force and show just how good their new jet was. To the 48th FIS it was just another HHQ tasking: important, but not the end of the world.

It must also be remembered that the test was run before the F-106 received the IR seeker system, and the F-106 fleet was deep in the throes of several modification programs, one of which involved several ECCM improvements, which eventually rendered it the premier ECCM platform in the air for decades.

Also, weapons philosophy was completely different between the air force, which considered the single nuclear armed Genie as the primary armament, and the navy, which demanded far more conventional engagement capability. As a result, the F-4H did not have the size constraint of the F-106's interior missile bay, and carried up to ten AAMs, four of which were semi-recessed into the fuselage.

An exceptionally rare shot, this 48th FIS Six is returning to parking at Tyndall after a mission during William Tell 1963. (Via Isham)

A classic view of what was once a daily occurrence. While this view is at Tyndall, the 48th FIS did use an F-106B during some of the Project High Speed missions. (Don Spering/AIR)

In addition to the four fuselage launchers, the original F-4Hs could carry one radar-guided Sparrow missile on the bottom of each inboard weapons pylon, as well as four heat-seeking Sidewinders. This gave the F-4H up to ten firing passes versus at most three for the F-106. Not having the size constraints of the Falcons, all of the F-4H armament had much greater ranges, larger warheads, proximity target fusing, and required less preparation time to launch. To top it off, the early Sparrow missiles were at their best on a high-speed, front-aspect pass, whereas the Falcons were better on the beam or in the stern.

Finally, some ill-informed comment has been issued regarding the performance capabilities of the two aircraft. The zoom climb capability difference between the two was meaningless in the real world, and it is widely recognized now that the F-106 was far superior to the F-4 at any altitude above 10,000 feet. In fact, the higher you went the better the F-106 was. Further, the roughly 0.1 or 0.2 Mach difference in top speeds between the two types of aircraft is insignificant when you are talking operational squadron aircraft versus

With two of its squadron mates barely visible in the background, this Six from the 94th FIS is headed home after being deployed to Korea for the "Pueblo" crisis in 1969. (USAF photo by Ken Hackman)

peaked-up, record-setting jets; McDonnell and the navy used special one-off, pre-compressor cooling during the F-4 speed record attempt.

Interestingly, the one area where the F-106 was undoubtedly superior, that of how quickly it could become airborne after a scramble, was never addressed. Although an F-106 could be airborne within 2 minutes of a warning, no F-4 could hope to beat 5 minutes, and 12 to 15 was much more likely, especially in cold weather where you had to wait for what seemed forever for the oil bath in the Inertial Navigation System (INS) to warm up to operating temperature, even with a saved alignment.

In any event, Convair was livid at the "poor" performance of its jet and blamed the air force for putting a "second-rate squadron against the best the navy had," but in the end, money and politics spoke the loudest. In an era of budget austerity, the F-4H cost less than half as much as the F-106 ($1.9 million for an F-4C versus $4.9 million for an F-106A) and cost almost half as much to operate ($924 for 8.8 man-hours versus $1,600 or 13.4 man-hours).

By 1961, the political priority for air defense was lessening, both in the air force and the government, as the ICBM became ascendant. Nuclear armament, especially defensive nuclear armament, was becoming, if not anathema, then certainly politically less acceptable as the undesirable side effects of nuclear detonations were becoming better understood.

Finally, the USAF was being forced back into conventional weapons delivery, partly due to pressure from President Kennedy, who realized that there was no credible conventional backup to the U.S. nuclear arsenal, and partly due to Secretary of Defense Robert McNamara who was beginning his drive for commonality between the services and was very negative on the whole concept of aerial defense of the United States. He believed that there was no use spending money to try to stop the bombers when nothing could be done to stop an ICBM attack. In the end, McNamara canceled half of the F-105 Thunderchief order and substituted the F-4(C) for TAC, while ADC was left with nothing at all.

Chapter Twelve

THE CUBAN CRISIS AND ALERT

A scene that was repeated countless times during the life of the F-106: the pilot running for the jet with the scramble horn blaring and the green scramble light glowing beside the shelter door. (USAF)

Declining defense budgets caused ADC to move the interceptor forces away from central and southern locations to the northern periphery of the United States, where any manned bomber attack from the Soviet Union was expected to be. Meanwhile, basing the interceptor forces at Strategic Air Command bomber bases that would obviously be the first targets for any ICBM attack caused ADC to begin planning to disperse its forces.

Prelude to Crisis

As the ICBM threat grew, the Joint Chiefs of Staff (JCS) became concerned about the survivability of the ADC interceptor force. In 1961 there were 39 interceptor bases in the continental United States (CONUS). Of those, 25 were collocated on SAC bomber bases and 6 more were collocated with a SAGE facility. Since those strategic locations were undoubtedly high on any enemy target list, in June 1961 JCS directed NORAD to develop plans to increase the survivability of the entire air defense system against a ballistic missile and follow-on bomber attack.

One key aspect of the resultant plan included provisions for dispersing the interceptor force. The initial objective was to maintain an increased alert status and develop an all-weather capability to disperse one third of the interceptors located at vulnerable target areas. Upon warning of an ICBM attack, the interceptors would be flushed from their bases, kept airborne as far from target areas as possible, and then either recovered to home base or their designated dispersal site, ready to defeat the follow-on bombers. Permanent alert, maintenance, and weapons storage facilities were to be constructed and continually manned at the dispersal bases. The final objective of the plan was to have four to six aircraft on 15-minute alert at the dispersal bases at all times, with an eight-sortie nuclear capability.

At the beginning of the Cuban Missile Crisis, negotiations between the Department of Defense (DoD) and ADC on the specifics of the plan were still underway. Although an interim dispersal program had been designed, virtually none of the selected fields had received site surveys to determine how adequate they were. Also, negotiations with other services and the Canadian government to use bases controlled by those organizations were just beginning.

On 3 January 1961, President Eisenhower severed diplomatic relations with Cuba, setting off an immediate scramble among DoD, NORAD, and ADC to begin planning how to defend the southeastern United States. Because Cuba had not been considered a threat and budget cutbacks had played havoc with ADC's initial plans to defend the entire country, all of the defensive forces had been deployed along the perimeter coastal areas and northern tier of states, where any Soviet bomber attack was expected to occur.

For the same reason, and at nearly the same time, the last active-duty interceptor squadron based in Florida was just finishing its move from McCoy AFB, Florida, to Westover AFB, Massachusetts. This left no air defense units in the southern portion of Florida at all. With the exception of the training units at Tyndall, on the western panhandle of the state, the only air defense unit between the Carolinas and Louisiana was one Air National Guard squadron flying out of Jacksonville, in the northeastern part of the state.

Two days later, an initial contingency plan for augmenting the air defense of Florida was finished and sent to JCS for approval. On 7 April 1961, JCS ordered a two-week test of the new operations plan, now called Southern Tip. As a result, six F-102s from the training center at Tyndall deployed to Homestead. Located just south of the Miami metropolitan area, Homestead was the home of the 19th Bomb Wing and soon became a hotbed of activity. Two of the F-102s were placed on five-minute alert immediately after arrival, which was five days before the Bay of Pigs invasion of Cuba. The deployment was scheduled to end on 26 April, but JCS ordered it to continue indefinitely, while plans were made to initiate a permanent alert at Homestead.

Because Tyndall could not afford the loss of so many training aircraft, four F-102s from the 482nd FIS replaced them and began alert on 1 July. At the end of the month, VF(AW)-3, the only navy squadron permanently assigned to NORAD, had deployed from their home base at NAS North Island near San Diego, California, and was in place and on alert at NAS Key West, Florida, with eight Douglas F4D-1 Skyrays. That was the air defense situation when the Cuban Crisis began to unfold.

The Cuban Crisis

For the F-106 fleet, the Cuba Crisis began to unfold on 18 October 1962, when HQ ADC notified the 48th FIS at Langley, to prepare to deploy 12 of their aircraft to Patrick AFB, Florida. The unit was to be ready to go not later than 20 October. On 21 October, the deployment order was implemented and the First Fighter Wing (Air Defense), located at Selfridge AFB, Michigan, was notified to prepare to deploy 12 of their Sixes as well.

Here are the stories of two of the 48th FIS pilots: "I was on leave and painting the bedroom of my house when I got the call to pack my bag for deployment and report to the squadron immediately. When I got there, I was told we were deploying to Patrick AFB at Cape Canaveral, Florida, but due to the weather there, we would first go to Tyndall that night and Patrick the next day.

"We arrived at Patrick the following day and organized our operations in the trailers and facilities the base provided. Aircraft were placed on alert and the aircrews briefed on Combat Air Patrol [CAP] procedures and Rules of Engagement [ROE]. Soon, aircraft and personnel from the 1st FIW at Selfridge arrived to supplement the alert and CAP force.

"[My] most memorable [sortie] being a nighttime instrument check in the F-106B while flying CAP off the north coast of Cuba.

Sixes of the 1st FW (AD) on the ramp at Patrick during the Cuban Crisis. While published references all show that the 71st deployed, most of these jets are from the 94th FIS. And it was the 94th that set the record for sorties during the deployment. Note the 30th Air Division badge on the tail of -797, as well as the striping on the external fuel tank. (USAF photo)

When their searchlights swept our aircraft it lit up the cockpit like daylight. They obviously wanted us to know that they knew we were there and could do something about it if they chose to.

"The other memorable thing was the aircrews huddled around the radio listening to President Kennedy's speech to the nation about the crisis and his demands to Cuba and the Soviet Union."

One of the other unit pilots remembers, "We had two to four aircraft on CAP down on the 24th parallel, just north of Cuba. GCI radar would take us down there and put us in a racetrack pattern; we were directed by Data Link [heading, altitude, and speed]. Target commands were sent to my computer and the command bugs would move appropriately on my instruments. If the autopilot was selected, it followed the commands. I could just sit there."

Meanwhile, at Selfridge both squadrons were being recalled but not told anything. Some pilots were told to "report immediately and bring some summer clothing." Those chosen to make the deployment to Florida were not even told where they were going. They were told to preflight their now armed aircraft, put their warm-weather clothes into the weapons bay, and return to the squadron. Then they sat for another 24 hours and waited.

Finally, they were divided into pairs, given a radio frequency, and told to take off in flights of two, at 10-minute intervals. Once airborne, GCI guided them from one sector to another. No contact with the Federal Aviation Administration (FAA) was allowed, and they finally landed at Langley, where they found the remaining aircraft of the 48th armed and on alert. They continued to Patrick and by the time the jets were fueled, they were already receiving airborne orders to man CAP points off Cuba. One CAP was located north of Havana and the other farther to the east.

Although most official histories reference the 71st FIS as being chosen to deploy because they had more aircraft in commission, the wing deployed a mix of aircraft from the two units. It was the 94th FIS that set the record for most F-106 flight hours and sorties flown while flying CAP missions from Patrick.

A few hours prior to President Kennedy's speech, ADC began loading all available interceptors with nuclear armament and bringing all aircraft undergoing maintenance back into commission. At the conclusion of the president's speech, he placed the United States military at DEFCON 3. At the time of the speech, nearly 150 interceptors were already on alert in Florida. One hour later, 10 additional F-106 squadrons began dispersing their aircraft. Of the F-106 units, only the 73rd Air Division at Tyndall did not disperse any aircraft.

Back at Selfridge, most of the remaining aircraft were dispersed to either Hulman Field, Indiana, or Volk Field, Wisconsin, but the instructions they received were slightly disconcerting. Flying for the first time with live atomic weapons caused enough stress, watching the SAC dependents from the KC-97 refueling wing evacuate from Selfridge to Canada while leaving their own families at home did not help, and being told that in case of an emergency, not to jettison the "blivet" (Genie), but to eject and let the weapon crash with the airplane because it would be "easier to find" kind of put a cap on it.

Five hours and forty minutes after the dispersal was announced, 64 additional F-106s (along with 61 Voodoos and 31 F-102s) were in place at the dispersal sites.

Given the preliminary state of dispersal planning, and the fact that none of the locations were notified that nuclear-armed interceptors were about to arrive, the dispersal went amazingly well. However, there were some glitches.

The 11th FIS had half a dozen Genie-armed Sixes scrambled at Duluth IAP, Minnesota, and after being vectored around for an hour, the crews were directed to land at Hector Field, North Dakota, which was the home of an ANG interceptor unit. But instead of being marshaled to the ramp, they were parked on a taxiway and met with a gas truck and the news that they would have to depart immediately

Cocked and ready to go, these Sixes from the 48th FIS are at Patrick AFB, Florida, during the Cuban Crisis in 1962. Note the small squadron badges on the fin, the dark blue and white markings on the speed brakes, and the early external fuel tanks. If airspeed was needed, those would have been quickly "punched off." (USAF)

Most of the remaining 1st FW jets were deployed to either Hulman Field, Indiana, or Volk Field, Wisconsin. Here is a 94th FIS bird at a remote site during the crisis. You can place a large bet that the Genie in the background is a live weapon. (USAF photo)

after being refueled. There were so many other aircraft already on the ground, there was no room for them.

Upon arrival at the Wisconsin ANG's training airport at Volk Field they found the tower closed and deer all over the runway. Several passes over the field with afterburners lit were required to disperse them. After landing, there was no one to park them or chock the aircraft. Since the F-106 did not have a parking brake and all were loaded "wall to wall" with live weapons, this was a matter of serious concern, and pilots had visions of their 20-ton machines rolling uncontrollably downhill and causing a disastrous wreck.

Eventually the crews found a level area to park, shut down the jets, shimmied to the ground, and went looking for rocks or other suitable items to use as chocks. One elderly caretaker was the only person on the field at the time, but fortunately all the buzz jobs over the runway had roused some of the local National Guard people and help was soon on the way.

The 456th FIS arrived at Fresno Air Park, California, under interesting circumstances as well. In the words of one pilot, "The Guard folks did not know that we were coming or that each aircraft was fully armed, nuke and all. When we entered their briefing room they were reviewing a training film that displayed a lot of skin."

Possibly the most alarming event that occurred with an F-106 during the dispersal was when a 71st FIS Six ran off the end of the runway at Hulman Field upon landing after being dispersed from Selfridge. The nose gear collapsed on S/N 58-0767 and bent the nose

of a fully loaded jet. The aircraft was jacked up, de-armed, had the nose cut off, and a replacement from the depot at Sacramento was sent in. The sheet-metal crews spliced the new nose on and the aircraft was eventually flown back to Selfridge, sans weapons, where all of the wiring was hooked up again.

Despite the seriousness of the situation, or possibly because of it, coordination between the notoriously secretive SAC and NORAD was very poor. When SAC dispersed its B-47 bombers without notifying NORAD, things got very, very tense in a hurry. Many intercepts were carried out on SAC aircraft that did not file flight plans, including "having to identify an RB-47 twice in one night because the sector could not, or would not, find out from SAC that there was a B-47 out there. They were blacked out and I was blacked out (no lights) and it was downright hairy," according to one pilot.

Farther up the coast, a nuclear-armed Voodoo from the 444th FIS at Charleston AFB, South Carolina, was scrambled on an unidentified aircraft that was heading directly toward Washington, D.C., from Cuba. It turned out to be a U-2 returning from a reconnaissance flight over the island and intending to deliver its top-secret camera film directly to the authorities. Fortunately, the Voodoo crew was instructed to positively identify the "unknown" prior to destroying it.

Phelps Collins airport, near Alpena, Michigan, hosted at least four full squadrons of Sixes and Voodoos when they were dispersed during the Cuban Crisis. This is typical of one of the dispersal bases. A lonely, cold, and remote place to be stationed while waiting for a call everyone hoped would never come. (SMSgt Jim Koglin)

As the crisis wound down, the interceptor force at Tyndall was allowed to return to a training role on 16 November, and following JCS approval, the dispersal order was canceled on 17 November and aircraft slowly began returning to their home bases. The normal peacetime DEFCON 5 was declared on 27 November 1961.

However, while the immediate crisis may have abated, ADC kept a far larger than normal complement of aircraft on nuclear alert for a time afterwards.

For example, the two squadrons at Selfridge had a combined total of 12 F-106s on alert until the end of the year, all but 2 loaded

Taxiing in front of these early design aircraft shelters, this 11th FIS Six heads to the Duluth runway in 1967. Doors on these buildings slid sideways. If they opened overhead, heavy snow may prevent them from opening quickly. (Ken Hackman, USAF)

Coming out of barn 5 and about to take the high-speed taxiway, this Michigan Guard Six will be airborne in about 45 seconds. Selfridge had a mixture of older alert barns from 1953 and newer rectangular barns built in 1957. With two units based at the field, they also sported an unusual third-floor living area, to accommodate all the additional personnel. In the 1960s, it wasn't unusual for all eight barns to have a mix of conventionally armed jets on 5-minute alert and nuclear armed jets on 15-minute alert. To ease winter operations, the entire alert ramp was also electrically heated to prevent snow and ice buildup. The glassed-in area just above the jet contained a mini command post with hotline telephones to the ODC (operations dispatch center) at the squadron building, tower, and RAPCON, as well as a UHF radio and a teleprinter for the latest weather and NOTAMS. January 1977.

Concrete blast walls between each cell allowed weapons storage and loading to be carried out inside the alert barns, as the Falcons and their caskets in the background demonstrate. Selfridge, November 1974.

This Six is being marshaled out of the later style alert barns at Det 1, 5 FIS at Davis-Monthan in March 1977. Originally, this site was the home of the 15th FIS. Bedrooms are on the top floor in the center of the buildings, while a lounge, dining area, and kitchen occupy the ground floor. ADC personnel spent hundreds of thousands of hours on alert in buildings like this.

Alert shelters at Florida locations were generally just reinforced arches, as seen here behind this 48th FIS Six landing at Tyndall in Dec 1978. In a few minutes it will taxi into the shelter, and a "quick turn" will be in progress to get the jet back onto five-minute alert status.

Leaving the squadron ramp at Castle AFB, California, this 84th FIS jet taxies by the "scramble board" on 17 March 1978. The numbers on the board were matched to a given aircraft. When pilots were sitting cockpit alert, and their light illuminated, that was the signal for a radio silent scramble. When the flashers across the top came on and all the numbers lit up at once, it was the signal for a "flush," a mass scramble of the entire unit. This Six has its IRST extended.

with Genies. But after all of the developmental and initial operational problems, the F-106 had finally demonstrated that it was ready and able to carry out the all-weather interceptor mission.

For anyone interested in reading more of what life was like in the early days of ADC I highly recommend the following books: *Spirit of Attack*, written and published by Bruce Gordon (AuthorHouse LLC 2014, ISBN 987-1-4918-4603-2) and *Spads and Sixes* by Lt Col. Ray Janes (Tattersall Publishing 2011, ISBN 978-1-4507-3885-9).

With the "Black Panthers" emblem visible just behind the exhaust, this F-106A passes in front of the 84th FIS alert barns at Castle AFB, California, in 1978. As the SAC B-52 and KC-135 training base, Castle hosted several different interceptor squadrons or alert detachments over the years.

Although the film is grainy, this typical scene in the day of an interceptor unit was rarely documented. The low winter sun provides little heat inside the "greenhouse" as the two pilots man the Runway Supervisory Unit to monitor landings of the jets. (USAF)

INTERCEPTOR IMPROVEMENT PROGRAMS

This New Jersey ANG Six has the IRST, the later 360-gallon external fuel tanks, and aerial refueling modifications. The high-speed external tanks were longer and slimmer than the early subsonic 230-gallon versions. The natural metal area on the upper spine shows where the aerial refueling receptacle was added, just behind the hot air vent. (Spering/AIR)

With its newest interceptor already well beyond its initially forecast retirement date, and faced with the prospect of no replacements, ADC did the only thing it could: It began improving the fleet. Group I of the Interceptor Improvement Program (IIP), added an IRST system. While the system could not work in moisture, it nevertheless resulted in a huge increase in capability. The system was so sensitive that high-speed targets such as the B-58 or SR-71 could be tracked at ranges beyond 250 miles. It also could verify target azimuth in the presence of electronic jamming. At the same time, the MA-1 system was modified to allow several modes of operation between the radar and IRST. Either could be made "dominant" and slaved to the other or one could remain in search while the other was locked on to a target.

Installation was begun in roughly May 1963 and took around a year to complete. The retractable seeker was mounted just in front of

With the IR seeker extended, and an ECM pod mounted directly on the left external fuel pylon, this 5th FIS Six is taxiing for take-off at Tyndall AFB, Florida. Late in its life, the Six was modified to allow carriage of both the Automatic Identification System (AIS) data pod and ECM pods. (Photo by Don Spering/AIR)

S/N 59-0086 was used as the test bed for the hydraulically tuned magnetron tube. The kill markings show some failures as well as successes. The ducks flying from the pond on the bottom are from when a Genie failed to ignite and landed in a watering pond. (Via Isham)

A close-up view of the two replacement datalink antennas. This is the Six on display at the old K. I. Sawyer AFB, Michigan. The bumper that was added when the tailhook was installed is also distinct. The angled point guards on the sides of the hook point were added after an unintentional approach end arrestment.

Painted in the early markings of the 5th FIS, this is what the underbelly of a Six looked like prior to gaining capability to carry a gun. Six red and white rectangles act as warning placards for the weapons bay doors. Note that these are still one-piece doors with no small NACA-style air scoops. Near the trailing edge of the wing are the dual SAGE datalink antennas and the tailhook. The diagonal joint for the removable tail cone is also clearly visible. (USAF)

the windscreen and the MA-1 system added several new black boxes. Ability to extend or retract the IRST on demand kept it from being damaged by rain or insects. Another modification carried out at the same time was installation of a redesigned radar antenna and additional anti-chaff electronics.

Group II of the IIP, which began in February 1965, shortly after Group I was completed, made two major changes to the fleet. The first was to remove the inadequate Convair B-seat and replace it with the newly designed Weber seat. The second was to add a hydraulically tuned magnetron tube to the radar. The speed at which the radar could change frequencies now made it very difficult to jam. Additional electronic countermeasure capabilities were also added at this time.

Toward the end of 1965, directional datalink antennas were added underneath the aft rear section of the fuselage, replacing the original non-directional ones and the UHF communications antenna was relocated from inside the tip of the fin to an external location on the lower forward fuselage.

Sixes in Paris

On the far side of Le Bourget airport, this 48 FIS Six is ready for its flight demonstration during the 1963 Paris Air Show. A broken starter shaft caused cancellation of the first day's display. Seen on 16 June 1963. (Photo via Norman E. Taylor)

Sometime in late 1962, one of the early F-106 units came up with the idea of sending F-106s to the Paris Air Show. The idea worked its way up the chain of command and ADC approved it. To the chagrin of the originating unit, however, the 48th FIS out of Langley was chosen to participate. Four pilots made the flight and they alternated on each leg between flying and riding along in the C-54 support aircraft that brought the maintenance technicians and spare parts. Because the F-106 did not yet have aerial refueling capability, they flew the North Atlantic route pioneered by the 56th Fighter Group P-80s in 1948, on Fox Able 1.

Departing from Langley, the two F-106s (S/N 59-0124 and S/N 59-0136) flew to Sondrestrom AB, Greenland; Keflavik AB, Iceland; Prestwick AB, Scotland; Lakenheath AB, England; and Ramstein AB, Germany. While at Ramstein, the F-102 unit based there assisted in removing the 230-gallon ferry tanks so that the Sixes could be displayed in a clean configuration. The two jets then continued to Le Bourget Airport outside Paris, France. Aircraft -136 was placed on static display, while -124 was to be the primary for the flying display.

The 48th FIS display pilot was allowed only one five-minute-long practice flight prior to the flying displays scheduled for the weekend. The USAF crews were given strict instructions about the display flying. Due to a B-58 crash at the show two years previously, no passes were made below 300 feet and all low-altitude aerobatics were forbidden.

On Saturday, the starter shaft sheared on the primary jet and, given the tight time window allowed, that flight did not become airborne. According to one of the pilots, "That was not an uncommon thing to happen in those days and we had brought spares, but with the hard takeoff time, I was not able to switch to the spare and make my slot."

On Sunday the flight did get airborne and the demonstration consisted of the takeoff, a high-speed pass down the runway with a pull into rapid vertical rolls, followed by a normal landing. *Aviation Week* magazine described the U.S. displays as "lackluster," but given the restrictions placed on the flying, it was, as the pilot said, "hard to compete with an F-104 making inverted passes at 10 feet."

One-Off Projects

As ICBMs became more of a threat in the early 1960s, the Advanced Research Projects Agency (ARPA) began to study ways of destroying a ballistic missile during its terminal flight phase under the ARPA Terminal (ARPAT) program. As a result, Hughes began investigating the possibility of launching interceptor missiles from an aircraft.

They began by using RB-57F bombers, but when they were grounded due to wing failures, F-106B S/N 57-2521 was bailed from the 456th FIS at Castle to Hughes on 8 April 1964, for use in the program. Since the highly modified AIM-26 missiles needed to be locked on to the target prior to launch, the jet was modified to be able to carry a missile launcher on each of the wing pylons. The aircraft was modified at the Hughes plant at Culver City, California, and then used at Holloman.

The modified missiles were called XHM-81s (a Hughes designation) or Experimental ARPAT Interceptors (EAIs). The aircraft served as the "first stage" of an intercept system, thus allowing a much smaller missile, a concept that was revived again in the Project Spike and in the Defense Advanced Research Projects Agency (DARPA) Rapid (or Responsive) Access Small Cargo Affordable Launch (RASCAL) programs. The missiles were fired in pairs and the program was considered a success, but further development was halted by the Ballistic Missile Defense Treaty. After termination of the tests, the Six was reassigned to the Air Defense Weapons Center (ADWC) at Tyndall on 7 August 1970.

One additional F-106B was pulled out of the fleet about the same time frame, bailed to Convair-Fort Worth, and used to test the radar altimeter and terrain-following radar being developed for the F-111. The early "round-eye" bus (S/N 57-2516) was modified starting 3 April 1964. External camera and instrumentation pod capability was added on the wing stations, in addition to the aforementioned developmental systems. At the end of testing, it was deemed uneconomical to rebuild the Six back to tactical configuration and the jet was passed on to NASA at the Lewis Research Center in Cleveland, Ohio.

Given the long-term decline in the size of ADC's interceptor fleet, and decreasing odds that a replacement for the F-106 would be purchased any time soon, the IIP became more important. By the end of Group II of the IIP, more than 60 F-101B/F Voodoo interceptors had been given to Canada; more Voodoos and even F-106 squadrons were on the table for deactivation. The plan to downsize U.S. air defense assets continued to play out, and the YF-12 seemed to be just a dream, given political bickering and the increasing costs of the war in Southeast Asia.

Meanwhile, U.S. Army Nike Air Defense Assets were also in the budgetary crosshairs. Given that background, continuing to improve the capability and reliability of the remaining F-106 fleet became an ever higher priority for NORAD. In preparation for a multitude of upcoming modifications, one F-106A airframe (S/N 59-0061) was bailed to Hughes in August 1966 for use as a "High Mach" test bed. This was not to increase the speed of the Six, but to upgrade the avionics and missiles to allow higher closure speeds. After receiving

On the Hughes ramp at Culver City, California, this Six was used for anti-satellite testing. Seen here with a modified AIM-26A under the wing, the jet still has the B seat, dating the photo to late 1964 or early 1965. (Via Isham)

Serial number 59-0061 spent virtually its entire life as a test bed. In this 1966 photo, it was serving as a high-Mach prototype while bailed to Hughes. From the number of kill markings on the nose, it was quite effective. Cameras have been faired into the wing near the fuselage to record armament guidance. (Via Isham)

all of the anticipated modifications, it was used for extensive weapons testing at both Holloman and Edwards.

Another project worthy of mention was the Variable Stability Trainers (VST). To make testing and pilot conversion to the ultra-high performance air vehicles such as the X-15 and X-24 lifting bodies safer, and to eliminate the "simulator technique" developed by high-time pilots, two F-106Bs (S/N 57-2519 and S/N 57-2529) were sent to Martin-Marietta in Baltimore, Maryland, during 1966. They were radically modified to allow the rear-seat pilot to see the instrument indications, and receive accurate "stick" and flight responses for the air vehicle that the Six was set up to simulate.

Theoretically, these two jets could simulate anything from a soaring glider to a space re-entry vehicle. It also allowed practicing maneuvers that were potentially dangerous on, say, an X-24, while still remaining safely within the flight envelope of the F-106. The entire program was for the benefit of the USAF Test Pilot School at Edwards.

Modifications included removal of the entire MA-1 system and weapons launchers. A new J75 engine was installed and the weapons bay filled with a large analog computer, a "force feel" system for the rear cockpit center stick, and an autopilot that actually flew the aircraft via inputs from the computer. A "bread board" installation was also located in the weapons bay to enable engineers to vary the control and performance parameters.

Two early F-106Bs were modified into Variable Stability Trainers and assigned to the Air Force Test Pilots School at Edwards. The markings of its previous owner, the 498th FIS, are still visible here on the 19 May 1963 shot taken about six months after its arrival at Edwards and prior to modification. (Frank MacSorley)

The cockpits were also entirely rebuilt. The instructor occupied the front seat and had F-106 instruments as well as the computer-driven indications of the vehicle being simulated. He also had "failure board," which allowed him to simulate nearly any emergency condition for the rear-seat pilot. Both cockpits included a center control stick and a side control stick. With these, the front-seat pilot could "fly" the research vehicle with the side stick or the actual F-106 with the center stick. Functions were reversed for the rear seat.

The redesignated NF-106Bs were initially set up for the following profiles: NF-104 energy management and stability and control profiles, X-15 high-altitude profiles, X-15 high-speed profiles, X-24A lifting body energy management flights, and X-24A lifting-body stability and control flights. Unfortunately, although the intent was sound, the system was so complicated that neither jet could be reliably used within the Aerospace Research Pilot Course and both were relegated to the status of "very sophisticated hangar queens."

Fleet-Wide Modifications Continue

The year 1967 became a watershed, as a plethora of additional modifications began. The F-106 finally began to reach its full potential as three of the most important advances applied to the F-106 up to that point were funded. After a successful feasibility study in 1965 that involved actually flying an F-106A into the "pre-contact" position on a KC-135 tanker and the initial design of an aerial refueling receptacle, on 26 July 1966 SAAMA awarded Convair a contract to produce the first 60 in-flight refueling kits and accessory training equipment.

This eventually led to 269 kits, enough to convert the entire operational fleet. A December 1967 delivery date was specified and

the first test hookups between an F-106A and a KC-135 tanker were conducted on 4 November 1966. The program nearly foundered, however, when the prototype design submitted by the San Antonio ALC could not initially be turned into a production modification at Sacramento. Only a quick response by one of the Convair engineers, who found that the sealant being used to prevent fuel leakage could not be applied over the primer coating applied to the aluminum skin, saved the day. Once the sealant was applied to bare aluminum, the design was finalized and the program was allowed to proceed.

In addition to the new refueling capability, the obsolete subsonic ferry tanks were replaced with new high-speed external fuel tanks that could be flown up to the full speed limits of the aircraft. The new tanks not only eliminated the speed restriction, they generated more lift than drag, essentially becoming "free fuel." To top it all off, each one carried 130 gallons more fuel than the older tanks, adding even more range. With the addition of the supersonic tanks, any advantage the F-101 may have had was completely erased and the remaining Voodoo fleet began to shrink rapidly, leaving the F-106 to shoulder nearly the entire defense of the United States.

Work for the new wing pylons and external tanks was carried out in the field by all squadrons and began in June 1967. The aerial refueling modification began in August 1967 at the Sacramento ALC depot and took around a year to cycle the entire fleet through. Only one squadron at a time received this modification, with the 318th

The louvers for the heat exhaust vent were added at the same time. The door hid the receptacle during normal operations.

This 94th FIS F-106 is approaching the contact position on a KC-135A tanker in 1968 while training for their upcoming deployment to Korea. From the lack of external fuel tanks, the unit is probably deeply into their DACT training program. (USAF photo by Ken Hackman)

Looking down the spine of this F-106B, the new aerial refueling modification is clearly visible. On the B model, the spine had to be altered to allow the boom to engage the receptacle. High-pressure air was used to actuate the system. August 1972.

and 71st FISs being the first two. This led to a period where many aircraft had the new tanks but not the aerial refueling modification.

Several further upgrades were also initiated or installed during the year. In May, Hughes received a contract to design digital TACAN navigation kits to replace the old tube-powered ones. Installation did not begin until 1 March 1970, but at least the change was on the way.

The initial liquid-cooled system for the IR seeker, which had to be serviced after every flight, was replaced starting on 15 June 1967, with a closed-cycle nitrogen system that was far less labor intensive. The original radar scope was replaced with a new multi-mode storage tube (MMST) that was designed to give improved vision during daylight hours beginning at the end of the month.

Both of the latter modifications were done as "Block M," but the biggest leap forward in capability began with avionics "Block N," 1 January 1968, when the antiquated tube-driven Digitair computer was finally replaced with a transistorized version. Overnight, the maintenance man-hours required to keep the MA-1 system operational dropped by an incredible amount. As the capabilities of the new computer were enlarged or taken advantage of over the following years, more of the original "black boxes" of the MA-1 were removed and their functions taken over directly by the computer. This saved even more time and money and resulted in far higher reliability of other systems as well.

This wave of modifications was finalized by replacing the original vacuum-tube UHF communications radio with a more reliable transistorized unit. The Six was now truly the "automated, all-weather interceptor" envisioned in 1948; just in time to head for "hot" parts of the world.

Chapter Fourteen

MOBILITY AND DEPLOYMENTS BEGIN

Early in 1967, the 5th FIS made a "White Shoes" deployment to Alaska. "Balls Six" is shown here high above the snow with an unusual brown radome, 230-gallon external fuel tanks, and early squadron markings. The aircraft forms are in their common position on the left glare shield. (USAF via Isham)

ADC never envisioned that its interceptor forces would deploy away from their home bases, but the rise of ICBMs, the Cuban Missile Crisis, and subsequent world events slowly began to alter that assumption. As a result, planning began to take on a world-wide perspective.

Project White Shoes: The Six Goes North

After the F-102s based at Elmendorf AFB, Alaska, proved to be inadequate to intercept two Soviet TU-95 Bear bombers that overflew Alaska on 15 March 1963, the Alaskan Air Command immediately demanded assistance in the form of higher-performance aircraft and requested F-4 Phantoms. After much inter-command wrangling, a decision was reached so that rotational squadrons of F-106s from the "lower 48" would assist.

JCS decreed that eight aircraft at a time would deploy and that ADC could expect to continue the deployments through 1 October 1965, when a squadron of F-4s would become available. These

deployments were initially known as White Shoes and later as College Shoes; the "College" designation was applied to all ADC Operations Plans. On 15 July 1963, four months after the initial incursion, nine F-106As from the 325th Fighter-Interceptor Wing at McChord AFB, Washington, arrived at Elmendorf. Five aircraft were from the 318th FIS and four were from the 498th FIS.

At that time, the F-106 was using the same subsonic external fuel tanks as the F-102; unless they jettisoned their tanks, the Sixes were no faster than the Deuces they were replacing, but they did add capability, numbers, and longer range. The Alaskan Air Command (AAC) immediately spread out the new interceptors and placed two of them on alert at Elmendorf and the forward operating locations at King Salmon AFB, Alaska, and Galena AFB, Alaska. The first scramble resulting in an intercept occurred on 8 September when the two alert Sixes at Galena found two Tu-16 Badgers over the Bering Sea off the coast of Alaska. Thus started a rotational deployment that continued for seven years, finally ending on 2 October 1970 when the 84th FIS completed the 35th deployment and returned home to Hamilton AFB, California.

With the F-102s of the 317th FIS in the background, these Sixes from the 325th FWG (AD) have just arrived at Elmendorf AFB, Alaska, in this 15 July 1963 photo. This was the first White Shoes deployment, and the crowd on the ramp is wondering what they are getting into. The jets without tail markings belong to the 498th FIS, which had just moved from Geiger Field to McChord two weeks previously. The unit had not had time to apply new markings. (USAF via Isham)

At the beginning, the deployment was seen as a temporary fix while waiting for a TAC F-4 unit to be assigned to Alaska. The initial thought from ADC was that the two squadrons of the 325th FW (AD), and the two squadrons of the 1st FW (AD), would share the rotation, alternating every six months. Since these were the only two F-106 Wings in ADC that had two squadrons assigned, ADC thought that if each squadron within the wing sent four aircraft it would be a bearable burden. Time and many different events eventually proved this to be overly optimistic and the rotational schedule ended up being juggled on a piecemeal basis for years.

In the meantime, the 325th maintained a continuous presence in Alaska until 1 March 1964, when eight aircraft of the 1st Fighter Wing (AD) from Selfridge took over. The 325th Wing returned six months later, on 3 November, but were again replaced by the First FW (AD) only a month later when the 325th Wing aircraft began to be processed through IIP modifications. Continuing with the theme, the 325th Wing returned to Alaska on 30 May 1965, with four aircraft from each squadron. This was supposed to be the last deployment prior to arrival of an F-4 unit. When the 389th TFS, based out of Holloman, and flying F-4C Phantoms, arrived at Elmendorf for what was supposed to be a 90-day temporty duty (TDY), it looked as if the Sixes would be able to return home for good.

Unfortunately, it was not long before they received the bad news that, pending further changes, their stay in Alaska was to be extended until 3 January 1966. TAC had informed ADC that given the increasingly hot war in Southeast Asia, they were going to be unable to meet the Alaska tasking and the F-4s were headed back to the lower 48 by December. That announcement threw a very large monkey wrench into the works. In the end, the 1st FW (AD) was once again in place by 3 December 1965 and ADC planners added the 5th FIS to the mix, to reduce deployment durations to three months per unit.

However, both of the existing two squadron wings were due to be broken up, with each having one of their squadrons move to different bases to cover for F-102 units that were deactivating, so the grand plan had to be juggled again. Due to declining numbers of aircraft assigned to each squadron, ADC decided to share the burden among the eight remaining F-106 squadrons, with each unit providing four aircraft at a time. Eight jets were simply too many for any one squadron to bear, since they were still required to maintain their normal alert commitment as well as fill required training events.

94 F.I.S.
APRIL 15
~ TO ~
JUNE 1
1964

PROJECT WHITE SHOES

OFFICERS
Maj Percy
Maj Shumate
Capt Hauer
Capt Winter
Capt Desing
Capt Horne
Capt Schroeder
Capt Fehlig
Capt Jones
Capt Picard
Capt Pollard
Capt Waldron

F-106 94

When the 94th FIS made their first deployment to Alaska for Project White Shoes, they made up this sign. The White Shoes name came from the white-colored arctic "bunny boots" that were issued to the crews. (USAF via Bruce Gordon)

As a result of many factors, the next round of deployments was most unusual. Four aircraft of the 27th FIS, two from the 318th, and two from the 498th, arrived to replace the 1st FW on 30 May 1966. The 498th was in the process of moving from McChord to Paine Field, Washington, and was not supposed to send any jets on that deployment. However, since Paine was unable to handle the full complement of the 498th aircraft, the simple solution was to send a couple of jets to Alaska while the facilities came up to speed.

Following that deployment, four aircraft from two separate units became the norm for the remainder of the deployments. There appears to have been no serious consideration to having F-101B Voodoo units take part in the rotations. Because the Voodoo was a twin-engine jet and supposedly had longer range than the F-106 it is curious that they were never deployed. Several possible reasons exist for that reluctance, but the main one might have been their inability to maneuver in the face of the MiG fighters that roamed the narrow Bering Straight.

While in Alaska, the deployed units were under the command of the AAC, and the three alert locations at Elmendorf, Galena, and King Salmon remained active until the end of the deployments. When the Six received the new supersonic external fuel tanks in 1968, its range and speed made intercepts of Soviet aircraft possible far to the north of the Alaskan shoreline, and the deployed pilots were scrambled many times on targets as far as 100 miles offshore over the Bering Sea.

The addition of aerial refueling capability also allowed the deployments to be conducted nonstop. The 71st FIS first used aerial refueling when deploying from Richards-Gebaur AFB, Missouri, on 8 January 1968. This worked so well that all successive rotations were scheduled in conjunction with normal weekly SAC

Wearing the medium-blue stripes and yellow band introduced in 1967, these two 456th FIS jets are being serviced prior to another mission over Alaska. Photo taken 18 March 1969. (Norman E. Taylor)

KC-135 tanker rotations to Alaska. About this same time, the name of the Alaskan TDYs was changed from White Shoes to College Shoes.

Additional Tasks for the Six

Operational plans developed by ADC were given the "College" prefix, and the F-106 figured prominently in most of them. College Green was a conceptual plan for F-106s to deploy to both Thule AB, Greenland, and Sondrestrom AB, Greenland, in the event of Soviet harassment of either base and was never activated. Over the years, several squadrons were tasked with responsibility for fulfilling the plan.

College Goose was developed to fill the gap in interceptor coverage when the 59th FIS, flying F-102s, was deactivated in late 1966. It provided for F-106 units to deploy detachments to Goose Bay, Labrador. The 27th FIS at Loring initially had the primary tasking and deployed six aircraft on 17 January 1967. By April the plan had been reviewed and revised. To re-gain the badly needed F-106s and to give the remaining Voodoo force an "opportunity" it would otherwise not have, the tasking was passed to the F-101B force. Thus, F-101Bs of the 52nd FIW replaced the Sixes on 1 June 1967.

However, a short-notice funding cut ended up causing cancellation of the alert rotations on 30 November of that year. But removing the interceptor force did not end forays by Soviet bombers into the Air Defense Identification Zone (ADIZ) and Soviet bomber flights along the east coast of the continent began increasing again in 1968, so a new plan was drawn up.

Beginning on 20 November 1968, Operation College Shaft once again called on the nearest F-106 unit (the 27th FIS at Loring) to provide two aircraft to Goose Bay when needed. On 13 May 1969, the 22nd NORAD Region at North Bay, Ontario, scrambled two of the 27th FIS F-106s, which were directed to proceed at high speed to Goose Bay and refuel there. While the refueling trucks were still hooked up, they were scrambled again, this time against what turned out to be a flight of Bear bombers that was operating off the Labrador coast.

Not expecting a reaction from NORAD, the Bears turned and ran eastbound once they realized that the Sixes had been scrambled against them. After cruising in minimum afterburner and a speed of about Mach 1.25 for a good 15 to 20 minutes chasing the retreating targets, the two F-106s caught up with the "unknowns" 150 miles offshore and proceeded to escort them for another 15 to 20 minutes before returning to Goose. This was the first successful intercept of Soviet aircraft completed by interceptors based in the continental United States. After at least 14 additional deployments, College Shaft ended by 1 July 1970.

With the exception of 12 F-104s sent from California to Taiwan during the Quemoy Crisis in 1958, prior to the Cuban Crisis ADC had been a "stay at home" organization. Since its primary mission was defense of the continental United States, squadrons were neither provisioned nor manned for deployments. In the early 1960s, planning for partial-squadron dispersal to other CONUS locations during wartime was only in the beginning phases, and even then it was envisioned that those locations would be permanently manned and pre-supplied with ground equipment and weapons. The possibility of worldwide deployments, much less the possibility of facing enemy fighters, was not on the "radar scope" of ADC at all. The completely unanticipated dispersal of hundreds of interceptors during the Cuban situation seriously challenged that outlook.

Further JCS-directed deployments brought home the fact that whether they were ready or not, ADC was now a player to provide all-weather interceptor packages anywhere in the world. ADC reacted by forming the concept of a Mobile Air Defense Package (MADPAC) based around a three-squadron wing of F-102 interceptors based at Richards-Gebaur, and providing TDY interceptors on call to worldwide trouble spots. The plan also

A Canadian Voodoo and a 27th FIS Six. The extended development time of the F-106 opened the door for production of an interceptor version of the F-101. Cost differences resulted in 487 Voodoos being purchased for ADC, while only 340 F-106s were produced. But as soon as the Six finally became reliable, the Voodoo fleet began to shrink, with the first batch of "one-oh-wonders" being sent to Canada in 1961. (USAF via Isham)

called for eventual displacement of the F-102 by the F-106, when the latter was equipped with improved external fuel tanks and was capable of in-flight refueling.

This all came to naught when two squadrons of F-102s were removed from ADC control and sent to PACAF in 1966. However, this did highlight the fact that aerial refueling capability was going to be a critical need for the F-106 fleet, and the groundwork that was laid in this early plan provided a firm base for follow-on events.

Two additional major initiatives came out of the haphazard deployments and early planning. First, the College Cadence plan; the formal operational plan (OPLAN) for providing temporary air defense augmentation using worldwide deployments grew out of the earlier MADPAC concept. Second was the realization that ADC assets might have to face enemy fighters as well as bombers. At nearly the same time, ADC received a JCS request to see if F-106s were suitable to act as escorts for F-105s during the Rolling Thunder campaign. The result was ADC taking the lead in developing a dissimilar aerial combat training program, initially under the College Prom and later under the College Dart auspices.

College Prom

The ADC/ADOTT Project 66-1 (College Prom) was the first formal attempt to evaluate the F-106 in a fighter-versus-fighter role and the initial attempt to train F-106 pilots in DACT. Without the shackles of existing philosophies, ADC started with a clean slate to find out what the capabilities of the F-106 really were in the air combat arena and what tactics would be the most effective.

The project took place at Minot, between 22 August and 17 September 1966. F-106s from the 5th FIS acted as fighters, with ADC F-102s and F-104s functioning as adversary aircraft. Priority tasks included basic fighter maneuvers, visual identification of enemy fighters, evaluation of offensive and defensive tactics and the effects of maneuvering on the jet, and determining what modifications would be necessary to the F-106's FCS to engage fighter-type targets. In short, the program was designed to find out if the F-106 would make a good "dog fighter." Because the F-106 did not have an anti-G suit capability at the time, one of the first orders of business was to find out if the pilots would be incapacitated by pulling 5 to 6 Gs in a simulated-air combat environment.

The first portion of the program was merely a warm-up and involved flying tactical two-ship formations and advanced handling maneuvers. Pilots flew to the edges of the flight envelope to accustom themselves to high-pitch attitudes and low-airspeed regimes and to practice avoiding, and recovering from, loss-of-control situations, as well as practicing previously unneeded air combat maneuvers such as rudder rolls and defensive breaks. After completing the initial phase, F-102s and F-104s were used to simulate both early- and late-generation MiG fighters and the Six drivers began to work with four-ship formations.

Seen in early 5th FIS markings, -237 sports a tri-colored fuselage band and a gloss white splitter plate in 1971. External fuel tanks were not always removed for DACT training. (USAF via Isham)

Against many expectations, College Prom proved that the F-106 was a viable candidate for fighter-versus-fighter combat. Already possessing exceptionally well-balanced flight controls, it proved to be extremely responsive to the use of rudder for directional control at high angles of attack, as well. The jet also proved to be stable at high pitch angles, even when flying as slow as 95 KIAS. In fact, all of the F-106 pilots expressed enthusiasm for the superb aircraft response throughout the flight envelope and the lack of undesirable flight characteristics.

Not only was the flight performance outstanding, the MA-1 and Falcons proved themselves capable as well. The MA-1 was able to compute firing solutions against hard-maneuvering targets, something for which it was never originally designed. The final report recommended that a 20-sortie training program be initiated.

The other major recommendation was that the Six acquire a gun. Pilots found they needed a gun when ranges were too close for the Falcons or where an attacker was on the tail of a friendly fighter, as there was no guarantee which aircraft the Falcon would guide on.

One final observation was obvious: The Six needed a clear-top canopy, as the wide bar across the existing canopy seriously obstructed visibility. The two-seat F-106B turned out to be an excellent learning tool; the pilots found that they learned much faster when an instructor first demonstrated the correct way to complete a maneuver instead of relying on the unsupervised trial-and-error method.

College Dart

Following the successful completion of College Prom, DACT training became a priority and a syllabus was drawn up that required a minimum of 12 sorties for pilots to become qualified. Beginning in May 1967, two of the first units tasked under College Cadence, the 71st and 318th, were the first F-106 units to begin qualifying their pilots. Following closely behind, the 5th and 94th FIS were well along by the following year. As more units became involved, more lessons were learned, particularly when fighting the F-104, which had performance and size very similar to the MiG-21. Not only were the Zippers very hard to see, their radar return was so small that the F-106 radar could not detect them at longer ranges.

Some attempts were made to fly against TAC aircraft at Nellis AFB, Nevada, in 1967, but TAC ended that in 1969, ostensibly because of pilot training demands for Vietnam. Given the possible expansion of world-wide deployments and with the enthusiastic support of ADC Commander Lt Gen. Arthur Agan, the Interceptor Weapons School (IWS) at Tyndall began a DACT program known as College Dart. Starting in 1968, the IWS students, as well as the College Cadence tasked units, were scheduled to fly DACT out of Tyndall. Some of the missions were very like those flown in Southeast Asia (SEA). F-104s of the 319th FIS continued to participate and F-101 Voodoos were used as simulated bombers in strike packages escorted by eight F-106s. The F-104s simulated

Returning from a DACT mission over the Pacific, these Sixes from the 460th FIS lead a section of VX-4 F-4 Phantoms back for landing at NAS Point Mugu, California, in 1971. (USN via Isham)

MIGs who attempted to disrupt or destroy the package. Because the F-104s had an extremely small silhouette, Mach 2 capability, and the help of GCI, these practice missions were very realistic and the Six drivers had to be on the top of their game or end up on the Zippers' gun film as "morts."

While the program continued to expand, efforts were made to equip the F-106 with an anti-G suit capability and questions arose regarding structural fatigue due to the increased G-loadings. One F-106 (S/N 57-2502) was chosen to undergo fatigue testing to extend the life of the fleet and to ensure that the simulated aerial combat would not cause structural failure of the aircraft. In the end, the fatigue tests continued so long without any noticeable problems that the test unit began cutting the wing spars, one by one, until they finally managed to induce a failure. The Convair wing proved to be nearly indestructible and the life of the fleet was doubled to 8,000 flying hours.

With the initial success of College Dart, all F-106 units were tasked to begin training in DACT. This resulted in a very large workload, as three units at once were affected by the Korean deployments and all units were continuing to share in the deployments to Alaska, as well as maintain both nuclear and conventional alert lines, not to mention having at least two units changing locations to replace deactivated Voo-

doo squadrons. All units were planned to be qualified by April 1970, just in time for the navy and marines to enthusiastically jump onboard the program.

Far earlier than TAC, the navy realized that it needed an effective DACT program, and by March 1969, the United States Navy Strike Fighter Tactics Instructor Program, better known by its "Top Gun" moniker, was established at NAS Miramar, California. In March 1970, VF-121 at Miramar invited F-106s to attend for DACT training.

Two Sixes from the 84th FIS are escorting a YF-16A back to Edwards in 1977. The 84th maintained an alert detachment at nearby George AFB and could conveniently provide dissimilar training to help evaluate the performance of the "electric jet." (USAF via Isham)

The Six that Landed Itself

This is what the local sheriff saw as he walked up to the freshly landed Six. Ignoring the heavy suction from the air intakes of the still running jet, he looked into the cockpit and found the radar still sweeping on the screen, but no pilot. (USAF)

With the fight knocked off, the instructor pilot (IP) of the element walked the other pilot through the spin recovery procedures over the radio. In the process, the throttle of the spinning Six was placed in idle and the takeoff trim button pressed to return the jet to a neutral trim setting. When the jet had not recovered by 12,000 feet, it was time to eject. When the pilot ejected, the aircraft was in a very stable, very slow rotation, and seemed to the other two jets as if it were simply rotating around its pitot tube.

The second the ejection seat left the aircraft, the nose of the Six dropped, it stopped rotating, and it recovered itself to level flight. In one of the classic radio calls of all time, the IP called over the radio, "You'd better get back in it!" Dangling from his parachute, the pilot was astounded to see his aircraft gliding off into the distance as he descended into the rugged terrain of the Bear Tooth Mountains.

Meanwhile, F-106A S/N 58-0787 set itself up in a gentle glide and seemingly went looking for a suitable place to land. The now-pilotless Six made a couple of gentle turns and then touched down lightly. Seemingly aware of the rock pile in the middle of the field, the jet turned about 20 degrees to the right and went through a barbed-wire fence before coming to rest.

No book on the F-106 would be complete without mentioning the Six that landed itself. On 2 February 1970, the 71st FIS at Malmstrom scheduled a two-versus-two ACT mission that ended up with one of the jets making a nearly perfect landing in an empty wheat field between Box Elder, and Big Sandy, Montana, without the pilot.

The mission started off poorly when one of the jets lost its drag chute on the ramp prior to takeoff and had to ground abort. The remaining three jets took off for a two-versus-one ACM ride. After entering the working airspace and gaining a 20-mile separation, they turned back in. The ROE were that the fight would not begin until the jets passed each other 180 degrees out.

The single ship, knowing that he was at a numerical disadvantage, hit the merge at Mach 1.9, and then went vertical. In that sort of an engagement, he who runs out of airspeed first loses, and the two-ship element was not going that fast. The ensuing fight ended up with a high-G rudder reversal by the single ship that the lower-energy attacker could not match, and the pilot lost control of his Six, which fell into a nearly always unrecoverable flat spin at about 35,000 feet.

The shocked farmer who owned the property immediately called the police and went out to investigate. When law enforcement arrived, they found the jet sitting on its belly with the engine running in idle, and the radar display still steadily sweeping back and forth. The next phone call was to Malmstrom, telling them that one of their fighters was sitting in the field with the engine still running, no pilot in it and, oh, by the way, "How do you shut the engine off?"

That thought was nixed when the heat from the engine melted enough of the snow for the jet to lurch forward a few feet, and a hasty decision was made to just let it run out of fuel, which it did, 1 hour and 45 minutes later. In the meantime, a crowd had gathered, and they watched as the jet continued to turn the snow into slush and inch forward on the slight downhill grade. At first it appeared as if no damage had been done, and there was some thought of simply flying the Six back to Malmstrom, using the road at the edge of the

field as a runway, but further inspection showed that the heavy "stable table" box had broken free from its mounting, and torn a large channel out of the belly as the jet slid forward over it.

In the end, a team from the depot at McClellan AFB, California, was brought in and the jet disassembled in the field and trucked to a convenient railroad spur about a mile away. It was loaded onto a railroad flatcar and shipped to California for repair. The pilot was recovered safely and returned to the base by some Native Americans using snowmobiles.

And -787? It made one more attempt to sit on its belly when the nose gear started to retract during an engine run at McClellan after it was rebuilt. Further investigation showed that two wires had been accidentally crossed in the right wheelwell, and the one that was "hot" was the one that told the airplane that it was airborne. The maintenance technician who was working in the nose wheelwell checking for leaks at the time had his head about 2 inches from the strut when the gear started to retract. Only the fact that the safety pins were installed in the landing gear struts prevented -787 from squashing him flat, and the jet ending up on its belly again. After that final display of pique, the jet went on to fly safely for many more years and is now on display at the National Museum of the Air Force in Dayton, Ohio.

From there, the cross-training program grew at a rapid pace, with virtually all navy and marine air units on both the East and West Coasts becoming involved, to the benefit of all concerned. By the early 1970s, deployments of both USN and USMC units to Tyndall were commonplace, as were F-106 unit deployments to California NAS Miramar, Pt. Mugu, and Oceana.

Have Doughnut

The F-106 was allowed to participate in the highly classified "Have Doughnut" evaluation of the MiG-21F-13 day fighter, with Sixes flying on five dedicated missions in March 1968. Dart flights of from one to four aircraft were flown against the single early-model MiG-21 and objectives included comparing performance of the two aircraft types, determining whether the F-106 would be able to successfully launch AIM-4 Falcons against the MiG and discovering what the best tactics would be.

At the end of the trial, it was evident that the Six could satisfactorily pick up the MiG in a "look-up" situation, launch Falcons, and maneuver for gun kills against the MiG. Furthermore, given its far higher airspeed capability, below 15,000 feet it could engage and disengage the MiG at will. But it was hardly a surprise that the Six pilots had a hard time maintaining visual contact on the smaller jet in a fight, as the bar across the top of the canopy proved to be a real detriment.

The MiG pilot reported that the black radomes of the Sixes really stood out, and that the light gray paint applied to the two Tyndall-based B models for an ADC color evaluation made them much easier to see than the standard Aircraft Gray models. Unfortunately, the results of this evaluation were never passed on to the operational Six crews that ended up facing the North Korean MiGs during their Korean deployments.

In 1969, after the final Have Doughnut report was analyzed, and with an analysis by the Air Force Academy indicating that the F-106 was the only current air force aircraft that could match the MiG-21s maneuverability, the air force decided to see firsthand just how the F-106 would do as an air superiority fighter. The 94th FIS at Selfridge was tasked to send four F-106s and six pilots to the TAC Fighter Weapons School at Nellis for an evaluation against the F-4 Phantom.

In spite of the fact that most ADC pilots had not yet flown any DACT, the results were impressive. After a very brief ground training program and a couple of rides in the back seat of an F-4 Phantom to see what the maneuvers looked like, the Six pilots were on their own. As to be expected, for the first week, the results were poor. But once the Six drivers gained some experience, the tables were turned. Because the F-106 ejection seat reclined slightly, the lack of a G-suit was not that much of a hindrance and the heretofore "babied" F-106 electronics showed no ill effects from the aerial battles. The worst damage was that the lenses of the position lights on the wingtips would pop out due to flexing of the wings.

Never having been appraised of the previous years' Have Doughnut evaluation, the 94th FIS pilots had to reinvent the wheel and found that four F-106s line-abreast was best for visual lookout and offensive attack, but that the finger-four formation was not effective for the Six. And, just as was found in the previous evaluation, given its superior maneuverability at high speed, it was best to keep the F-106 fast. Just below Mach 1 became preferred since the F-106s could go supersonic almost instantaneously through afterburner use. The infrared "boresight" mode of the FCS was also recognized as being highly effective in acquiring the target for a maneuvering dog-fight.

These initial lessons proved to be very timely, because one month later, the same pilots were flying combat air patrols against North Korean MiGs.

Mt. McKinley was a favorite backdrop for photography in Alaska. The 48th and 87th FISs were both deployed to Alaska in May 1969. (USAF)

WORLDWIDE DEPLOYMENT FOR THE SIX: KOREA

Although the markings say 318th, these jets are actually being flown by pilots of the 48th FIS. The reason behind the rectangular paint markings on the leading edges of the wings is unknown. (USAF photo by Ken Hackman)

Events in Southeast Asia eventually led to implementation of the world-wide deployment plans that had been designed by ADC. While F-106 squadrons had been deploying to Alaska regularly, the USS *Pueblo* crisis of January 1968 took them to Korea.

Project Fresh Storm: Operation Combat Fox

As originally envisioned, the College Cadence plan called for a deployment package of up to 24 F-106s, drawn as packages of 6 aircraft. While each cell of 6 aircraft was to remain with its par-

ent squadron during normal times, they were to be prepared to deploy overseas on very short notice. Four squadrons (the 71st at Richards-Gebaur, the 94th at Selfridge, the 95th at Dover AFB, Delaware, and the 318th at McChord) had their allotment of aircraft increased from 18 to 24 to allow them to deploy a package without otherwise harming their readiness for NORAD requirements.

The formal plan was drafted beginning in April 1967 and was published in August. The plan anticipated that the 71st and 318th would have received aircraft modified for aerial refueling and equipped with the new external fuel tanks, and have enough trained crews to be able to deploy starting in January 1968. Training for the crews was set at a minimum of 12 DACT sorties and 4 aerial refueling flights.

While various headquarters within the air force argued about whether ADC could even have a worldwide mission when their guiding regulation (AFR 23-9) emphasized the air defense mission only within the United States, the first two units took it upon themselves to demonstrate their readiness to deploy. First to make use of the new capabilities of the F-106 was the 318th. On 20 November 1967, they flew nonstop from McChord to Tyndall using aerial refueling, then continued on to the ranges over the Gulf of Mexico and conducted live-fire missile shots against drone targets before landing at Tyndall. Not to be outdone, about six weeks later, the 71st deployed four of their aircraft from Richards-Gebaur to Elmendorf on a scheduled College Shoes rotation using aerial refueling.

All of the headquarters bickering about whether ADC was going to be allowed to have a worldwide tasking, and the concept of a "six pack" package drawn from each squadron, ended abruptly on 23 January 1968. Eight days prior to commencement of the TET offensive in South Vietnam, the North Koreans seized the USS *Pueblo*. Fearing this to be a prelude to another North Korean invasion of the South, the U.S. Comander in Chief, Pacific (CINCPAC), immediately sent one of its newly acquired F-102 squadrons from its base at Naha, Okinawa, to South Korea and requested another squadron of all-weather interceptors to replace them.

ADC had already reacted to the situation and ordered the entire 318th FIS to prepare to deploy. Since some of their aircraft were in Alaska on a College Shoes rotation, the 27th FIS was ordered to send four jets to relieve them. They arrived on 29 January, with

Ejection seats were not built for comfort. With pillow in hand this 318th FIS F-106 pilot is greeted by the brass while the Geisha girl waits to welcome him to Naha, Okinawa. The armament placard plainly shows that the Sixes were armed during for the transpac (transpacific) crossing. (USAF)

Once on the ground at Naha, it was unload the C-141 airlifter and get in line. Here is the welcome sign at the entrance to the hangar where in-processing was being handled. (USAF via Foote)

"Sign here." In a scene that would become familiar to ADC Six forces, the in-processing line at Naha seems to be reasonably well organized. A cup of coffee and transportation to quarters are high on the list of desires for these men. (USAF via Foote)

ations within Korea began almost immediately after the pilots climbed from the jets.

Osan was not prepared for the arrival of another squadron of aircraft, but room was made for the F-106s on the D-diamond, an area that had the quickest access to the runway. Crew chiefs and alert pilots lived in trailers near the jets, which were initially parked in the open, since no shelters of any kind were available. Other than a new runway, Osan had sat virtually untouched since the end of active hostilities in 1953. Sand-bag revetments were hurriedly constructed and additional barbed wire was hastily strung around the diamond as additional protection from attack. South Korean military forces manned 40mm AAA sites within the diamond and around the base as well.

Because the other three squadrons tasked with the College Cadence (71st, 94th, and 95th) were in the throes of aircraft modifications and training their aircrews, ADC decided to add another squadron to the mix and chose the 48th FIS. Since the 48th aircraft were not scheduled to be upgraded before they were needed, a novel fix was instituted. First, all 48th FIS aircrews rotated through the 71st FIS to receive the required DACT and aerial refueling training. For the aircraft fix, ADC decided that the two squadrons would temporarily trade aircraft.

The Green Dragons were ordered to leave their aircraft in Korea and return to the United States without them, in the meantime, the 48th deployed without their own aircraft and simply flew the ones on the ramp when they arrived in Korea. When the 318th was back in the CONUS, they flew the 48th FIS jets until another squadron replaced the 48th, at which time the 48th flew the ex-318th jets back across the Pacific, gave them back to their previous owners, and picked up their original aircraft.

The first group of 48th FIS personnel departed the CONUS on 6 June 1968. The second group arrived in Korea on 10 June, and after receiving the appropriate in-briefings, the 48th crews eventually relieved the 318th of the alert commitment on 11 July 1968. Departing 318th crews then returned home via military air transport. Once back home, they picked up the 48th FIS jets, and the first 10 Sixes arrived at McChord on 10 July, with the remainder expected within the week.

the four 318th jets departing for McChord shortly afterward. A quick reaction package of six aircraft was also sent from the 71st FIS to McChord, to relieve the 318th of their alert commitments while they prepared to deploy.

ADC had informed HQ USAF that the 318th was ready to go on 30 January, but movement orders did not arrive until 7 February. Under Operation Combat Fox, and as a part of Operation Fresh Storm, a little more than 24 hours after receiving the orders, 18 F-106s were enroute to Hickham AFB, Hawaii. The squadron reacted so fast that news of their movement had not reached the Hawaiian base prior to their arrival. The first inkling Pacific Air Forces (PACAF) had that something was going on was when the base operations officer tracked down the Hickham commander at the officers club and asked him, "Where do you want me to park the F-106s?" The rejoinder went down in history as, "What F-106s?"

By 11 February, 400 men and 18 aircraft were in place at Naha and the rotation of F-106s to Korea had begun. A week after arriving on Okinawa, PACAF decided that the squadron was better placed at Osan AB, Korea, and the Green Dragons picked up and moved again. Departing Naha on 18 February, four Sixes were on 5-minute alert within 3 hours of arrival at Osan, and briefings on ROE and oper-

F-106 units were assigned to the "D" diamond at Osan AB, ROK, as it was the closest to the runway. Conditions were initially quite spartan as the base had not been used since the end of the Korean War. Mobile trailers and concrete parking pads were the order of the day. Eventually, hardened shelters were constructed for the aircraft. (USAF photo 68-5606)

and in the end, the Sixes in Korea retained conventional armament.

The 48th was duly replaced by the 71st FIS, which flew its own aircraft across the Pacific in three separate increments. Arriving at Osan on 23 December 1968, it made for a less-than-happy Christmas. The unit was immediately put to work when it conducted two intercepts of Tu-95 Bear bombers during a winter snowstorm over the Sea of Japan.

Things heated up in the Korean theater again on 15 April 1969, when North Korean MiG fighters shot down a U.S. Navy Lockheed EC-121M reconnaissance aircraft over the Sea of Japan. Several hours later the 71st started launching four-ship CAP sorties into the area to protect the aircraft now searching for survivors and debris from the downed aircraft. Refueling from KC-135 tankers based out of Kadena AB on Okinawa, these long missions involved two aerial refuelings and identified a

Back in the Pacific Theater, a decision was made that depot maintenance would be carried out at Naha, rather than Osan, and aircraft ended up regularly being ferried back and forth between them.

Deployment of ADC interceptors to Korea gained attention at high levels of command and the ADC Commanders regularly visited the units. Prior to the visit of Lt Gen. Arthur Agan, and in one of the greatest practical jokes ever carried out, the 48th FIS arranged to borrow two multiple-ejector bomb racks from an F-4 Phantom unit based at Osan, along with 12 500-pound bombs. The racks were jury-rigged onto the wing pylons of F-106A S/N 59-0047, which was still resplendent in its 318th FIS markings. When the general came to inspect the unit, the bombed-up F-106 was the first thing he saw.

When the 318th flew to Korea, all of the aircraft were armed with Falcons, but the Genies were left at home. PACAF requested that the AIR-2s be shipped to the theater but the Secretary of Defense nixed the request. The same scenario played out when the 48th arrived,

problem with the new MMST radar tube. The tubes overheated and failed on repeated instances during the 4-plus-hour flights. In three days the 71st flew 76 CAP sorties.

These flights averaged more than 4¼ hours. After three days, the CAP flights were discontinued, but beginning on 3 May 1969 they were reinstituted and continued until 24 May, with the squadron logging an additional 206 sorties during that same period. In the meantime, large numbers of replacement radar tubes had been ordered on a very high priority.

While in Korea, construction had continued apace, and new concrete-reinforced aircraft shelters now dominated the D-diamond. However, concrete was not laid to make them taxi-through capable, and returning interceptors still had to make a 90-degree turn and stop in front of the shelter. Whatever manpower was available was then used to push the 20-ton machines backward into the shelter, a task not made easier by the Korean winter weather.

Hand-operated 40mm Bofors cannons operated by Korean forces were located around the base to protect against air attack. Fencing and ditches were rapidly installed to provide a modicum of safety against a ground assault by North Korean forces. (USAF photo 68-5667)

Under the watchful eyes of the security guard, this Six driver and his crew chief race for the jet to answer a scramble. Within a couple of minutes, the Six will be airborne, and vectored to intercept, identify, and if necessary, destroy, the unknown target. (USAF)

A different view of the "bombed up" Six. It was a great practical joke to play on ADC Commander Gen. Arthur C. Agan when he came to visit the 48th at Osan. (USAF)

Next up in the rotation was the 94th FIS, based at Selfridge. Since flying entire squadrons of aircraft across the Pacific Ocean used inordinate amounts of scarce aerial refueling aircraft, JCS decided to leave the aircraft "in theater" for a year. For the deployment to remain a TDY assignment, and not a permanent change of station, however, the manpower had to be rotated at the six-month point. Since both the 71st and 94th had been based together at Selfridge and shared aircraft between 1960 and 1966, ADC felt that the simplest solution was for the two units to simply exchange aircraft permanently.

So the 94th ferried their Sixes from Selfridge to the 71st base at Malmstrom and boarded a transport to Korea. They arrived on Korean soil and relieved the 71st on 17 June 1969, and for the first time, a Six unit repainted the markings on their aircraft while overseas. The blue alar of the 71st gave way to a simplified version of the previous 94th markings; deleting the old, thin, red stripes, the new markings were a horizontal yellow band outlined with a black stripe above and below.

Fortunately for the newly arrived unit, enough time had passed and enough money thrown at Osan that conditions for the 94th were far improved over those endured by the 318th. However, the mission remained the same, and the scrambles and BARCAP missions to protect the unarmed reconnaissance aircraft continued on a regular basis. Tu-16 Badger bombers, An-12 Cub reconnaissance aircraft, and the occasional Tu-95 Bear bombers were the usual "unknowns" that were identified, but the pilots never knew exactly what they would encounter. Although Barrier Combat Air Patrols (BARCAPs) were originally flown with eight aircraft, they were later reduced to flights of four.

CAPs were located about 20 miles off the North Korean coast, with the U.S. reconnaissance aircraft orbiting farther out to sea.

With corrugated shelters now in place, this aerial shot gives a good view of the 71st FIS MA-1 "Quick Fix" spots at Osan. Even at this late date, the need to be able to rapidly correct preflight deficiencies was obviously needed. (Frank Dutcher)

Going home! A 94th FIS Six is moving forward to the "contact" position while on the transpacific flight back to the CONUS. They will return to Selfridge just in time to pack up and move the unit to Wurtsmith AFB, Michigan. (USAF)

Tankers flew out of Kadena and had an orbit farther south, to which the interceptors proceeded for fuel. Bruce Gordon, in his book *The Spirit of Attack,* has several stories of his time with the 94th in Korea, including a 4-versus-20, F-106–versus–MiG air battle that nearly took place.

"Mr. Bones" became the final F-106 squadron to deploy to Korea. Departing their base at Dover, the 95th FIS flew their aircraft to the West Coast of the United States, then to Hawaii, Guam, Okinawa, and Korea. They assumed the alert commitment on 15 November 1969, and the 94th began ferrying their aircraft home the next day.

Whose jet is it? While displaying the blue tail flash of the 71st FIS, the squadron badges have been removed and the yellow and black crew block on the nose gear door tells us that this is a 94th FIS jet after the swap at Osan in the summer of 1969. (Photo by Bruce Gordon)

USAF photographer Ken Hackman caught this 95th FIS Six over the Korean countryside near Osan AB, ROK. The unit had just arrived and was conducting familiarization flights before taking over the alert commitment from the 94th FIS. (USAF)

"Any questions?" The pre-deployment flight briefing for the 95th FIS is just about to wind up. The lectern and sliding boards were a fixture in many ADC squadron briefing rooms. In a couple of minutes, the pilots will grab their flight gear and prepare to leave Dover AFB, Delaware, on their trip to Korea. (USAF 70-0836)

95th FIS arrival in Korea. (USAF)

But the 94th's last day on alert was an exciting one. Regardless of the departure party that was planned, the unit had eight separate "scrambles" their last day.

Unlike all of the previous ferry flights, which had gone off smoothly, one of the 94th jets made an emergency diversion to Wake Island after experiencing an overheated generator that resulted in a combined AC/DC power failure. Although the divert was successful, the remainder of the squadron continued toward Hawaii, and the unlucky pilot got to spend a week trying to get the jet fixed and find a tanker to drag him home.

Meanwhile, the 95th had picked up the baton only to find that the rotations were now so commonplace that 7th Air Force decided to give them an Operational Readiness Inspection (ORI). In spite of it being unheard of for an HQ to task a TDY unit with an ORI, 7th, apparently having nothing better to do with themselves, decreed that the ORI would take place in spite of unit and ADC complaints. The 95th was the only round-eye squadron to deploy to Korea, and also the only unit to lose an aircraft while there, when S/N 57-2500 was lost on a night mission while preparing for the ORI.

Following the ORI, things did not improve for Mr. Bones and Company. Although ADC had tentatively directed the 460th FIS to prepare to replace the 95th, rumors ran rampant that the 95th would be transferred to PACAF permanently. In the end, a mere two weeks before their replacements were supposed to arrive, JCS canceled the Combat Fox deployments and the 95th became the only squadron to fly their aircraft both ways across the Pacific Ocean, returning home to Dover on 1 May 1970, thus ending the last mass deployment of the F-106 overseas.

Chapter Sixteen

THE SIX GETS A GUN

Seen here firing the Gatling cannon over the Pacific Ocean, the second F-106A modified to carry the gun completes a test profile while flying out of NAS Point Mugu, California, in 1972. (USAF via Isham)

An inquiry by Generals (Jack J.) Catton and (Joseph H.) Moore of the USAF Air Staff about the feasibility of using the F-106 to escort F-105 Thunderchief aircraft during the Rolling Thunder campaign (1965–1968) finally resulted in action on the concept of adding gun armament to the F-106. Following the College Prom exercise, ADC responded with a project to add a 20mm gun, a lead-computing gunsight, and a new clear-top canopy in February 1967. The plan also added a radar warning receiver and ECM capability into the Six, as well as designing a camouflage scheme.

Project Six Shooter gained further traction when F-106s participated in the Have Drill, Have Ferry, and Have Doughnut evaluation programs against the MiG-17 and MiG-21 fighters in 1968. When the Air Force Academy did a study and found that of all the existing USAF fighters, the F-106 was the closest to the performance of the MiG-21, eyebrows were raised across the fighter fraternity.

Further evaluation by ADC found that the Six's radar was quite capable of picking up the MiG, that a snap-up attack with the all-aspect Falcons could be used to exploit the MiG-21's lack of advanced fire control system, and that the F-106 could use its better acceleration to go beyond the MiG's speed limits. A gun was expected to provide better close-in kill potential against any enemy bombers and also increase capability against bombers flying at very low altitudes, as well as reflecting the change in philosophy away from using nuclear defensive weapons. When F-106 units were called to deploy to Korea in response to the *Pueblo* incident, the needs could no longer be ignored, and the majority of the recommendations were approved in 1969.

Another modification that was approved for testing was the Fighter Interceptor Slaved Telescope/Air-to-Air Recognition (FIST/ATAR) system. This device was meant to permit visual identification

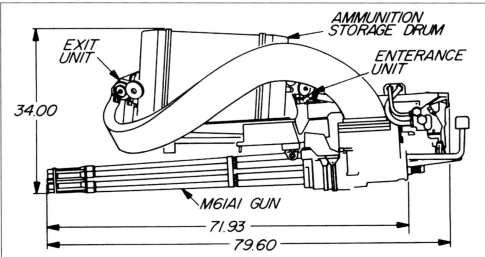

This drawing shows how the gun and ammunition drum were packaged. Only the barrel protruded below the belly of the Six. (General Electric)

This Florida Guard Six shows off the final configuration of the jet. Clear top canopy, yaw vane below the nose, gunsight, 360-gallon tanks, and aerial refueling receptacle show that this jet is ready for a worldwide deployment. (Don Spering/AIR)

Gun testing began on 10 February 1969, when Tyndall-based F-106A S/N 57-0795 was modified with a General Electric M61A1 20mm Gatling gun. The new palletized, hydraulically driven gun system was designed to be rapidly interchangeable with the AIR-2A rocket. It was mounted in the rear of the weapons bay between the aft two Falcon launchers, with only a long fairing containing the barrels protruding underneath the fuselage. Weighing around 200 pounds more than the AIR-2A rocket, the gun carried 650 rounds of ammunition. Due to significant avionics differences between the round-eye and vertical tape F-106A fleet, a decision was made not to modify the round-eye aircraft to carry the gun.

In 1972, some of the modifications projected as part of Project Six Shooter finally began to appear on the Six. Provisions for an anti-G suit capability were added, and a new bubble canopy that finally eliminated the large bar across the top was installed on all A models in 1972. At the same time the optical Genie sight was removed, and the TACAN antenna underneath the forward nose was moved slightly aft and a new Z-axis yaw sensor was added in preparation for installation of the gunsight. Initial modifications to the

of an unknown aircraft out to the limit of radar range. Initial tests were done with a telescope mounted on the lower aft F-106 fuselage. The image was given a 10x magnification and displayed on a television monitor in the cockpit. Since this appeared to meet an SEA requirement as well as an ADC one, PACAF got behind the program and testing was underway at Tyndall by the middle of 1967. The concept eventually resulted in the Target Identification System, Electro-Optical (TISEO), modification applied to many F-4s but was never introduced operationally into ADC.

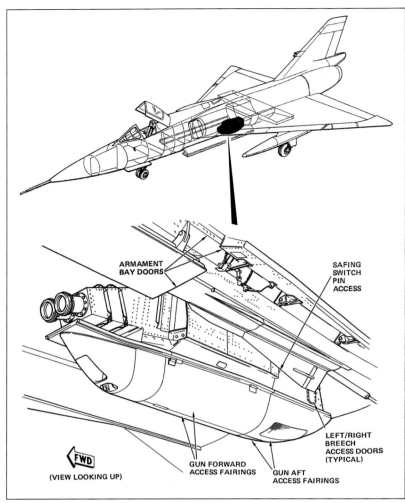

ARMAMENT
BAY DOORS

SAFING
SWITCH
PIN
ACCESS

LEFT/RIGHT
BREECH
ACCESS DOORS
(TYPICAL)

GUN FORWARD
ACCESS FAIRINGS

GUN AFT
ACCESS FAIRINGS

FWD
(VIEW LOOKING UP)

The entire gun system was installed in one piece and was supported by the Genie rack. Two small NACA-type air scoops on the forward interior weapons bay doors fed cooling air to the front of the gun. (USAF)

Adding the gun pod to the Six required modifying the weapons bay doors so that the gun could protrude below the fuselage. The inner doors were pieced so that the aft portions could be removed, and a small fillet was then added to the outer doors to fit around the gun pallet.

What the undersides of a gun capable Six looked like. Note the two NACA-style air scoops and the split section of the inner weapons bay doors. Moving aft, the rotating beacon, keel beam, datalink antennas, tailhook, and aft bumper are clearly visible. (NASA via Isham)

weapons bay doors to allow carriage of the gun pallet and alterations of the hydraulic system to provide for the gun were also undertaken.

Although the gun installation was smooth, the cost of developing a suitable gunsight almost killed the whole project. While the test aircraft carried little more than a World War I–equivalent ring-and-post gunsight, work was underway to design a sight that was compatible with the MA-1. Initial cost estimates from commercial contractors were astronomically high, but a team from the Air Force Academy submitted an affordable bid, and while it faced considerable resistance, it was eventually accepted.

During the summer and fall of 1972, a team led by Lt Col. Albert Pyress from the Air Force Academy (AFA), a group of MIT professors, and the 4750th Test Squadron at Tyndall eventually developed the first funnel gunsight, the most sophisticated gunsight in the world

and something a decade in advance of the sights then in use on the F-15 and F-16. This sight was so effective that the original gun firing rate of 4,500 shots per minute was reduced because so few bullets were needed to destroy a target.

A second jet (S/N 59-0092) was modified by Convair at San Diego beginning in March 1972 and tested at Edwards through

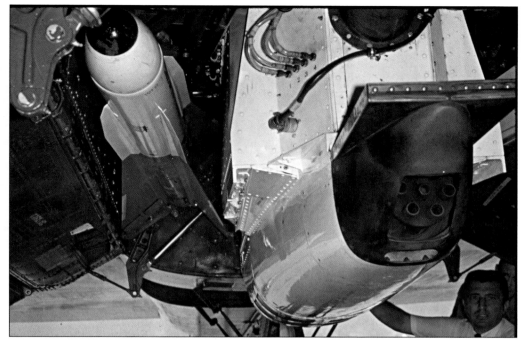

There was not much room between the aft Falcons and the gun, as shown in this September 1969 view of the prototype installation. (USAF via Isham)

In January 1978, these two Sixes from the 5th FIS have both received the yaw vanes on the lower nose, just behind the radome, but addition of the gunsight had been held up by a contract dispute. Both jets carry the Outstanding Unit Award on their fins, while S/N 59-0015 also carries the ADC A Award as well.

Seventy-five guns were purchased for the Six in FY 1975, and the final modifications for all of the vertical tape A models was begun in May 1975. But a lawsuit about the acquisition of the gunsight was filed in 1974 and prevented the sights from being installed in the jets until after 1978, more than a decade after the program was instigated.

Initially, eleven guns were sent to each of the following squadrons: the 5th FIS, 49th FIS, 84th FIS, 87th FIS, and 318th FIS. Two extra guns were provided to the 48th FIS due to their detached alert location at Homestead, which faced a possible Cuban MiG threat. The ADWC at Tyndall received the final seven guns. The original plan was to keep all of the guns with active-duty ADC units because they were subject to overseas tasking. However, with no useable sights, the guns simply sat in the weapons storage areas for several years. Eventually, as units were deactivated or converted to the F-15, more guns were distributed to the remaining active-duty units and Air National Guard units. Both New Jersey and Florida are known to have received them.

Even after sights were installed on the jets, guns were not commonly seen due to the time constraints of recertifying the jets for nuclear carriage when they were removed. After the Genies were retired from day-to-day alert in the mid-1970s, the guns still did not make an immediate appearance, but when the Genies were finally retired in 1984, most units loaded the guns in their place, and vertical tape Sixes were commonly seen sitting alert or flying with the guns installed. There was one small downside to the gun, however: The fairing reduced the top speed of the Six from more than Mach 2.2 to around Mach 1.8.

Although the entire F-106A fleet received new canopies, none of the round-eye F-106As received the modifications to carry either the gun or the sight. But at least six vertical tape F-106Bs were given the yaw vane, had Optical Display Units (ODUs, gunsights) installed, and one (S/N 59-0157) actually received the hydraulic modifi-

September. This jet was also used to fire an instrumented Genie rocket to recertify the configuration of the weapons bay for nuclear weapons carriage, since some physical changes had been made for the gun pallet. It was originally intended that this aircraft be used for the new snapshoot gunsight testing, but the AFA wanted to use a jet that had undergone the Block S avionics modifications, so SAAMA provided an alternate jet to Tyndall.

cations to be able to fire the gun. Unfortunately, that aircraft was lost in an accident shortly after receiving the capability. The F-106Bs known to receive the yaw vanes and ODUs were 57-2513 (SAAMA), 57-2514 (New Jersey), 59-0149 (New Jersey), 59-0155 (New Jersey), 59-0157 (48th FIS), and 59-0158 (48th FIS). The modifications to both the New Jersey and 48th FIS jets were performed at the unit level.

Tyndall and SAAMA continued to run tests on the remainder of the Project Six Shooter proposals, installing Radar Homing and Warning (RHAW) gear on F-106Bs S/N 57-2513 and S/N 58-0902. The F-106B fleet was never considered for a clear canopy and retained the original canopy until the end.

Seen after it was assigned to the B-1 chase fleet, -149 was one of the half-dozen F-106Bs modified to use the gunsight. The yaw vane below the nose and gunsight in the forward cockpit are quite visible here. The ship is the Kittyhawk Flyer, which set an FAI speed record between Dayton, Ohio, and Kittyhawk, North Carolina, to commemorate the Wright Brothers' first flight. (Photo taken 13 Aug 1988 by Marty Isham)

With the angled reflector glass for the gunsight quite evident, this is what the final layout of the cockpit of a vertical tape–equipped F-106 looked like. The thin, vertical view break eliminated reflections off the angled wind screen and was virtually invisible when looking forward. With the pilot's parachute still in the seat back and gloves on the glare shield, this Six will be airborne again in no time. June 1987.

The RHAW antenna housing just above the rudder is very evident in this shot. F-106B S/N 57-2513 was assigned to the San Antonio ALC and was used as the test bed for any modifications proposed for the B model. Note the yaw vane under the nose, which indicates that this is another of the B models to receive a gunsight. (April 1985, Isham Collection)

Last Chances for New Sixes

Thinking that they had at last found a replacement for the F-106, the air force placed an order for 93 new F-12 Blackbird interceptors on 14 May 1965. It seemed as if the Six's day in the sun was passing, and ADC stopped planning upgrades to the Six fleet while awaiting the new manned interceptor. But when Secretary of Defense Robert S. McNamara canceled the Lockheed F-12A interceptor on 9 February 1968 and replaced it with the undefined F-106X and Airborne

On the ramp at Edwards, this Six, assigned to the 4786th Test Squadron, is supporting the YF-12 flight test program. The insignia on the tail reads "Mach III plus" and shows an F-12 launching the advanced XAIM-47 Long Range Falcons. (Isham Collection)

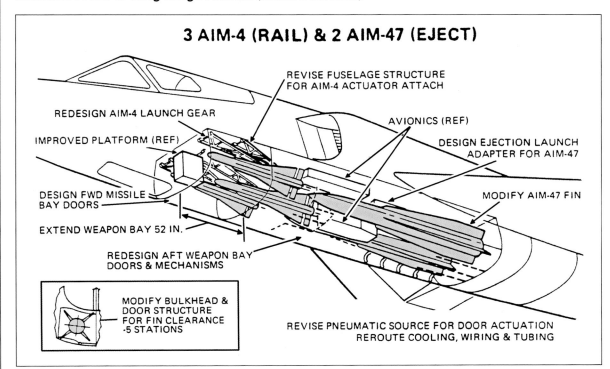

3 AIM-4 (RAIL) & 2 AIM-47 (EJECT)

REVISE FUSELAGE STRUCTURE FOR AIM-4 ACTUATOR ATTACH

REDESIGN AIM-4 LAUNCH GEAR

IMPROVED PLATFORM (REF)

AVIONICS (REF)

DESIGN EJECTION LAUNCH ADAPTER FOR AIM-47

DESIGN FWD MISSILE BAY DOORS

MODIFY AIM-47 FIN

EXTEND WEAPON BAY 52 IN.

REDESIGN AFT WEAPON BAY DOORS & MECHANISMS

MODIFY BULKHEAD & DOOR STRUCTURE FOR FIN CLEARANCE -5 STATIONS

REVISE PNEUMATIC SOURCE FOR DOOR ACTUATION REROUTE COOLING, WIRING & TUBING

One proposal for arming the proposed F-106E/F was to lengthen the weapons bay and add two AIM-47 Long Range Falcons. An avionics pallet similar to that of the F-106B would have been added so that the avionics could be accommodated. (Convair via Kaston)

Warning and Control System (AWACS), it led to yet another round of proposals to upgrade the F-106.

At the request of the air force, Convair dutifully began putting together yet another study on how to improve the F-106. On 3 September, they put forward a set of proposals for an improved interceptor, to be designated F-106E/F. It was planned to be compatible with the new AWACS and over-the-horizon radar net. While keeping the basic airframe, the aircraft would have a new pulse Doppler radar with look-down, shoot-down capability, multiple target tracking, and multiple missile launch capability. A variety of weapons were considered, including long-range missiles with dual-nuclear or conventional warhead capabilities; the AIM-47(M) Long Range Falcon or a modified AIM-7F and medium-range missiles; the AIM-26A/B; or the existing AIM-4F/G.

Adding either of the long-range missiles would have involved extending and redesigning the weapons bay to allow internal carriage of the longer weapons. A high-frequency radio would have been added for long-range communications, with the antenna being placed in the leading edge of the fin. But once again, politics reared its ugly head. The Secretary and DoD wanted the F-106X. The air force and Congress wanted the F-12. In the end, neither saw the light of day.

At this stage, improving the radar of the Six was becoming a significant need. Spare parts and tubes were becoming difficult to source, and failures were becoming more frequent. Several attempts at replacing the radar had been made, and all were disapproved. Fitting the APG-63 radar of the F-15 into the F-106 would have been a very straightforward task, and serious

CONFIGURATION COMPARISON

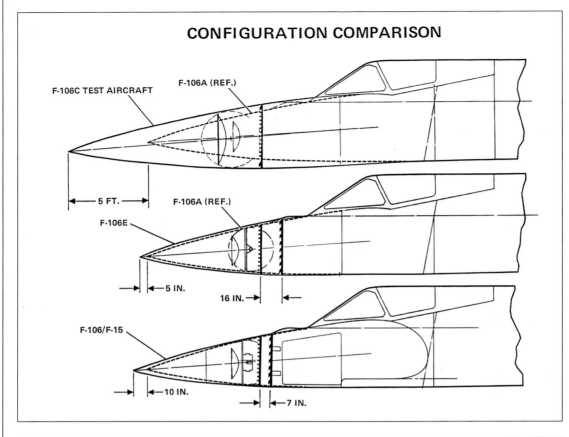

F-106C TEST AIRCRAFT — F-106A (REF.)

5 FT. — F-106A (REF.) — F-106E — 5 IN. — 16 IN.

F-106/F-15 — 10 IN. — 7 IN.

F-106/F-15 AVIONICS TESTBED

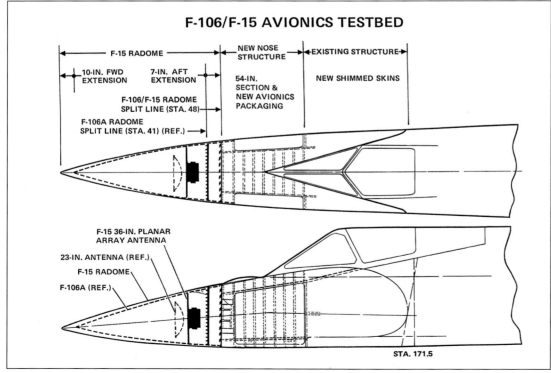

F-15 RADOME — NEW NOSE STRUCTURE — EXISTING STRUCTURE

10-IN. FWD EXTENSION — 7-IN. AFT EXTENSION — 54-IN. SECTION & NEW AVIONICS PACKAGING — NEW SHIMMED SKINS

F-106/F-15 RADOME SPLIT LINE (STA. 48)

F-106A RADOME SPLIT LINE (STA. 41) (REF.)

F-15 36-IN. PLANAR ARRAY ANTENNA

23-IN. ANTENNA (REF.)

F-15 RADOME

F-106A (REF.)

STA. 171.5

This drawing shows how the nose would have been altered for several new radars that were proposed for the F-106. Two of the banana-nose YF-106Cs were built but none of the others went beyond paper planning. Adding the Hughes-designed APG-63 would have been a simple task that would have greatly enhanced the capabilities of the Six. (Convair via Author's Collection)

attempts were made by both ADC and Air Force Logistics Command (AFLC) to replace the old radar, but there were fears within the Pentagon that doing so might cost the air force new fighters then under development. The Doppler radar, although much more advanced, would not be able to guide the old Falcon missiles. Either the radar or the missiles would have to be modified. Yet again, neither survived the political or budgetary processes.

The final attempt at a new F-106 came in May 1971, when a modified F-106, known as the F-106-40, was proposed. This aircraft would use rectangular ramp (F-15) air intakes with canards mounted back on the intakes, as opposed to the earlier proposals that had them on the forward nose. A new P-W F401-PW-400 turbofan (which was eventually unsuccessful) would power the new aircraft. As with all of the prior proposals, this one, too, came to nothing.

With the prospect of the Six having to continue to shoulder the burden of air defense for the foreseeable future, all the Aerospace Defense Command (ADCOM) could do was to continue improving the jet. As a result, the next major change was the upgrade to Block S. Like virtually all of the modification programs to the F-106 after completion of the original Broad Jump program, Block S was run as a Speedline-type modification program. Under this type of program, a special modification center was chosen, staffed, and equipped temporarily.

Only minor sheet-metal modifications would have been necessary to add the radar of the F-15 into the F-106. (Convair)

This beautiful desk model shows the configuration of the F-106-40. As compared to earlier proposals, the canards have been relocated from the nose to the now rectangular air inlets. An extended exhaust also stands out. (Model from John Aldaz Collection, photo by Craig Kaston)

A single F-111 generator replaced the 4 original CSD-driven generators and 24 of the now-obsolete vacuum-tube MA-1 power generation and filtering boxes were replaced with just 3 new solid-state units. At the same time, a major rewiring program was carried out due to all of the changes in the electrical power distribution system. Not only did this modification result in an 88-percent decrease in the mission abort rate for power system–related problems, it decreased the number of spare parts needed by 90 percent. It also completely eliminated five types of expensive and troublesome ground testing (AGE) equipment, eliminated the need for maintenance to run the engine while troubleshooting the system, and saved countless man-hours of work. Reliability of the Six skyrocketed, and by mid-1975, about the only original portion of the electronics left was associated with the radar.

By 1974, the radar was the most unreliable portion of the F-106. Tubes and other electronic components were either no longer available or had to be purchased from countries in Eastern Europe. The Mean Time Between Failures (MTBF) on the radar was down to just two hours, which meant that the radar failed every other flight. A program known as MEISR, the Minimum Essential Improvement for System Reliability, was put forward in the late 1960s. This would have replaced 12 of the original tube-powered black boxes in the radar with 2 solid-state units. It was funded twice but was eventually canceled in 1970. One upgrade that did get approved was replacing the maintenance-prone hydraulic drive for the magnetron tube with an electric unit.

The Last Mods

As the F-106 fleet slowly shrank due to attrition, active-duty USAF squadrons either converted to the F-15 or were deactivated. The original concept of air defense of the United States had also atrophied by the late 1970s. Instead of a force to wage an unrestricted war to prevent hostile bombers from attacking, the mission of air defense had slowly morphed into one of air sovereignty, where interceptors were simply sent out to report back to higher authorities what they found, shadowing drug running aircraft, or providing a show of force by escorting the odd Bear bomber that was flying in the ADIZ. But the mission was still there, and the Six had to be updated to remain flyable.

In 1976, proving again that "blood priority" was still the way to get money for modifications, the F-106 fleet finally received

Aircraft were input, run through the modifications on a tight time schedule, and a new jet was input as a modified one departed. The 84th FIS at Hamilton hosted this program, and it began in July 1972. Much to the joy of the avionics troops, during the Block S upgrade, the existing vacuum-tube Automatic Flight Control System (AFCS, or autopilot) was replaced with a digital unit. In addition, digital ranging replaced many of the tubes in the radar system, and missile antenna positioning was converted as well. The optical sight for the Genie rocket was removed, the firing signals to the forward pair of launchers was altered so that there was a slight delay between Falcon launches, and a composite boresight modification increased capability in a fighter-versus-fighter role.

Completion of Block S left just two major improvements to accomplish: upgrade the radar and replace the antiquated power generation system. Upgrading the radar largely continued to be an exercise in frustration, but after several attempts, a Power Upgrade Program (PUP) was finally funded and installed. Beginning in January 1974 and finishing in June 1975, this modification finally completed the metamorphosis of the Six. Technology had finally caught up to the concept envisioned in 1948. The PUP modification replaced the entire trouble-prone original power generation system with a new generator and microcircuit solid-state components.

lightning protection. Money for that modification was made available after the F-106A flown by Brigadier General James Price, Commander of the 21st NORAD region, received a lightning strike shortly after takeoff from Griffiss AFB, New York, which knocked out all of the electrical power to the jet. The general was killed in the ensuing crash.

Other minor changes in the 1970s included adding three F-4–style rearview mirrors to the A models starting in May 1977 and updating the training missiles. Over the years, the tube-powered MSR had become unsupportable and had its tubes replaced with solid-state components. The WSEMs were likewise updated.

Another batch of significant upgrades began in 1979, when the original stable table for the MA-1 was replaced with the gyro unit also used in the A-10A. Completing the upgrade of the MA-1 navigation, a new stable coordinate reference group (SCRG) was installed, which increased the MTBF from 9 hours to more than 200 hours. A new "universal rack" was also designed. This replaced the worn-out rack in the weapons bay of the F-106B and two other racks with a single unit. In 1980, additional memory was added to the computer as more hardware functions were taken over by software. Thermal electric cooling for the IRST replaced the old nitrogen system in 1981. This again simplified the system by eliminating the need to recharge the nitrogen. It also reduced maintenance by eliminating the need to repair the compressor, water absorber, and associated plumbing.

The final major upgrades consisted of Project Gold Plate where, in the years between 1974 and 1980, the depot rewired the entire aircraft and replaced all of the original, by now corroded, connectors with new ones. Finally, 85 aircraft were chosen to have both their wings reskinned and receive the APG-65 radar receiver and wave guides of the F-18A. Given that the F-106 was designed for a 5-year lifespan with no serious acrobatic maneuvering, it was no wonder that after 25 years of use and 15 years of DACT, much of the skin on the upper wings above the number-one fuel tank (forward third) was starting to crack around the rivets. Carried out by the depot at Sacramento, the fix involved re-skinning the forward portion of the wings with heavier aluminum. The depot became so adept at the repair that enough money was saved to rebuild two additional aircraft and still stay within the original budget.

Likewise, the original radar of the Six was far beyond its designed lifetime. After Hughes had adapted the new receiver to the Six, still using the original plywood F-106 mockup at Culver City, California, the actual work was done via a Speedline setup at Otis ANGB, Massachusetts.

Low over the Florida countryside, this Jacksonville Six shows off the gun pod. The addition of the gun greatly increased the lethality of the Six. (Don Spering/AIR)

Chapter Seventeen

THE ORIGINAL F-106 SQUADRONS: 1959 CONVERSIONS

Proudly displaying the large Mr. Bones squadron badge on their vertical fins, these Darts are from the 95th FIS. As evidenced by the tailhook installed on the lower fuselage of -498, they have already started receiving some of the early modifications. The rotating anti-collision beacons are retracted to reduce drag. Photo from August 1960. (USAF)

Regardless of whether the F-106 was truly ready to enter operational service in 1959, pressure to get the Six on alert was too much for ADC to overcome. New aircraft began to depart Palmdale by the dozens, but they frequently broke down on their delivery flights. Since the Six was brand new, and still highly classified, there was no capability in the field to get them flying again. Not only were many of the maintenance manuals classified, so was the pilot's flight manual. As a result, the broken airplanes had to be left in place until a maintenance team could be put together, and flown out with the needed manuals, parts, and AGE equipment to fix them. In the early days, it was envisioned that the Sixes would never go on cross-country flights. If they had to, they would be armed, so that they would be able to respond to a wartime situation.

ADC squadrons began converting at a pace of one a month. For those units that had previously flown the similar F-102, the conver-sion was only challenging. For those units coming from the F-86L Sabre, the challenge was doubled. For the first few units, the single seat jets arrived at least one or two months before the F-106B models, which made checking out even more sporting. Two factors made the maintenance challenge even tougher.

First, the Technical School for the MA-1 at Lowry AFB, Colorado, was the single longest course in the air force, taking nearly a year to complete due to the extreme complexity of the Six's avionics. Second, the AGE equipment was nearly as complex as the MA-1 it was designed to service. A handful of years prior to the Sixes being parked on the ramp, AGE maintenance was the responsibility of the motor pool. Those personnel were initially overwhelmed attempting to cope with the complicated electronics, pneumatics, and hydraulics in the new AGE equipment designed for the Six.

539th Fighter-Interceptor Squadron

As previously mentioned, the 539th FIS at McGuire was the first ADC squadron to receive the Delta Dart. Paper assignments of aircraft began on 1 May 1959, with the first aircraft apparently not actually arriving until nearly the end of the month. As the first operational F-106 unit, they were immediately tasked to conduct the long-delayed Category III weapons testing. This endeavor kept them busy for another two years and considerably delayed their operational readiness, as much of their time was spent deploying aircraft to Eglin and Tyndall for live fire testing on the Gulf Coast ranges. By the middle of 1960, the 539th had flown more than 1,000 sorties in support of the testing, but progress was disappointingly slow. Only 17 out of the scheduled 49 live-fire sorties at Tyndall had been completed by mid-March 1960. Bad weather and a shortage of targets resulted in 20 unsuccessful missions. Of the 11 missiles or rockets that were fired, 8 were hits.

The good news was that the datalink system was effective 98 percent of the time, in contrast to the poor results other units were having. However, the biggest hurdle was the fact that all of the test benches, ground test equipment, and spare parts at Tyndall had been

As the first squadron to receive the Delta Dart, the 539th designed a Dart-shaped tail marking. Seen here on the McGuire AFB ramp in May 1965, the ADC badge has replaced the original squadron badge on the right side of the fin and the buzz numbers have been removed. The ejection warning triangle is obviously a decal as well. (Frank MacSorley)

procured based on the vertical tape jets that were assigned there. The McGuire-based unit had conventional round-eye jets and virtually none of the test equipment or spares at Tyndall could support them. This was one of the factors that tipped the scales in favor of the subsequent Wild Goose and Broad Jump modification programs. In the interim, both HAC and CV assigned tech reps to all of the new squadrons and the phone lines were kept humming in an attempt to keep the new jets flying.

Showing off the final markings of the 539th FIS, this Six is on display in August 1966. (Ron Picciani Collection)

The 539th designed new tail markings when they transitioned to the F-106. A stylized Delta Dart was applied on both sides of the vertical fin. The wings were dark blue with a white outline and the fuselage was yellow. The squadron badge was placed in the middle of the emblem, on both sides of the tail. A small rectangle of color was later added to the forward portion of the speed brakes to indicate which maintenance flight a particular jet was assigned to.

During this era, ADC units had wide latitude on how they wanted to mark their aircraft, and some units' markings were quite gaudy. Around 1966, the unit changed their markings to a large blue lightning bolt outlined in yellow that covered most of the fin. On the lower aft portion of the fin, some jets had a blue star with a yellow surround, some had a yellow star with a blue surround, and some had no star design at all. Again, this probably depicted the aircraft's maintenance flight.

The only William Tell meet they participated in was in 1961, where they placed third. The unit served at McGuire and kept their initial complement of aircraft until being inactivated 1 June 1967. There were 26 F-106s assigned, including replacements for the 5 losses the unit sustained.

498th Fighter-Interceptor Squadron

The Geiger Tigers of the 498th FIS were based at the joint-use Geiger Field near Spokane. They were the second squadron to receive F-106s, but the first to actually stand alert with the new jets. Their first tail markings were a carry-over from those on their previous F-102s.

While stationed at Spokane, a large Geiger Tiger badge adorned both sides of the vertical fin forward of the rust-colored rudder. A gloss-black fin cap frequently rounded out the design. Although they certainly had some eye-catching markings, they also faced many initial difficulties. Regardless of their highly publicized mass intercept against an "incoming raid" of F-102 interceptors simulating a bomber attack, their maintenance had so much trouble generating flyable aircraft that, as with other early Six units, a large number of their pilots were reassigned to non-flying duties such as Personnel or Supply. Initially, the squadron was assigned to the 4700th Air Defense Wing, the only wing in the USAF to have two squadrons flying two types of Mach 2 aircraft. Their sister unit was the 538th FIS based at Larson AFB, Washington, and flew the F-104A.

The Tigers participated in the 1961 William Tell meet and placed second in their category. Effective 1 July 1963, they moved from Geiger to join the 318th FIS at McChord under the 325th Fighter Wing (AD). Two weeks later they had aircraft in Alaska as part of the initial White Shoes deployment. As a consequence of the relocation, the squadron removed all of the tail markings from their aircraft before eventually joining the 318th in carrying the early two-toned blue North Star marks. Since the 318th had vertical tape aircraft and the 498th had the earlier round-eye jets, the 498th eventually swapped all of their aircraft with the 456th FIS at Castle. This was done to ease maintenance so that both of the units at McChord had identical vertical tape configurations.

On 25 June 1966, the unit moved to Paine where it began experimenting with new tail markings. Initially a somewhat nondescript

These 498th FIS pilots are likely wishing they could be strapping in rather than posing for a photo. Another Armed Forces Day shot, this time on 22 May 1961. (USAF)

At Paine Field, Washington, on a dreary October 1968 day, this 498th FIS jet wears the final paint markings of the unit. (Via Bert Kinzey/Detail and Scale Collection)

red and a blue flash was painted across the lower portion of the vertical tail. Shortly afterward, a third white bolt was added between the red and blue, which were then adorned with white stars, a much more striking design. The squadron badge was placed in a white disc higher up the tail on the left side and the ADC eagle was carried on the right. A little more than a year later, the squadron moved from Paine to Hamilton and passed its assets to the 84th FIS. There were 66 F-106s assigned to the 498th during the 8 years they flew the Dart and they lost an average of 1 aircraft per year during that time.

95th Fighter-Interceptor Squadron

As the third squadron to receive the aircraft, the 95th FIS converted from the F-102 starting in June 1959. They remained at Andrews with a primary mission of defending Washington, D.C., and the surrounding area. The 95th was

Over the Pacific Northwest, this Six from the 498th displays the 325 FW (AD) badge in the early Northern Star markings design. The unit was based at McChord AFB, Washington, when this photo was taken. This Six was the last A model built. (USAF via Isham)

Side by side on the ramp at Andrews AFB, Maryland, on 30 June 1970, both the dark and light blue color schemes of the 95th FIS are depicted here. (Frank MacSorley)

the third and last squadron to receive the early round-eye aircraft, although several other squadrons eventually received them during the many aircraft swaps ADC carried out over the years. Large "Mr. Bones" squadron badges were initially carried on both sides of the fin, but around 1965 the squadron redesigned their markings to a horizontal band on the fin, in either light or dark blue and outlined with yellow. A blue diamond outlined with yellow and located in the center of the horizontal band carried either the ADC emblem or the squadron design. Two white stars were carried in the band, one in front of and one behind the diamond. After the 360-gallon external fuel tanks were added, the unit repeated the tail design on the tanks.

Mr. Bones was relocated from Andrews to Dover on 1 July 1963 and had at least two detached alert sites over the years: Byrd Field, Virginia, and the National Aviation Facilities Experimental Center (NAFEC) near Atlantic City, New Jersey. The 95th was the final squadron to deploy to Osan, there from 15 November 1969 to 1 May 1970. In mid-1972, the 95th transferred its conventionally instrumented jets to the Massachusetts ANG concurrent with gaining vertical-tape airplanes from the inactivating 83d FIS at Loring.

Mr. Bones participated in only one William Tell meet, that being 1972 when the unit was about to deactivate. There were 49 F-106s assigned to the unit over the years, with vertical-tape jets finally being assigned a year before the squadron deactivated and sent those jets to the 177th FIS, New Jersey ANG at Atlantic City, New Jersey.

456th Fighter-Interceptor Squadron

As the first squadron to receive FY 1958 vertical tape jets, the 456th FIS at Castle started conversion from the F-102 to the F-106 on 16 September 1959, when F-106A S/N 58-0761 arrived. Their initial

A very rare shot of the first 456th FIS markings. May 1960. (Isham Collection)

From the beginning, the F-106 was intended for use by the U.S. Air Force Air Defense Command (ADC). Based at Ent AFB in Colorado Springs, Colorado, ADC was the USAF combat arm of the joint U.S. and Canadian North American Air Defense Command (NORAD). As a reflection of the growing importance of the space mission, ADC became the Aerospace Defense Command, or ADCOM, effective 15 January 1968.

By 1977, Congress was pressuring the military to reduce excess manpower. As a result, on 1 October 1979, all of the remaining interceptor squadrons and GCI assets were transferred to the Tactical Air Command (TAC). A new Deputy Commander for Air Defense (ADTAC) reported directly to the TAC commander, and the air defense forces came under ADTAC control. By that date, the 5th, 48th, 49th, 84th, 87th, 318th, and Tyndall-based units were the only active-duty interceptor units left.

Over time, it became apparent that ADTAC was an organizational anomaly. Compared to the rest of the major operational commands, it was essentially a numbered air force. Therefore, on 6 December 1985, the First Air Force (1 AF) was activated at Langley, taking the place of ADTAC. By that date, the only remaining active-duty F-106 units under 1 AF were the 49th FIS at Griffiss and the units at Tyndall.

markings were simply the "Luther" squadron badge on both sides of the vertical fin, but after swapping aircraft with the 498th in 1963, they came up with some striking designs. Virtually the entire upper portion of the vertical fin was painted yellow, with black horizontal stripes across the top and bottom of the design. Five short, black stripes were carried in the rudder. Assigned to the 28th Air Division, they also carried the Air Division markings; as with all other squadrons in the 28AD, a red, white, and blue horizontal band was painted across the lower portion of the fin, with the 28th Air Division badge carried within the bands on both sides of the tail. When

In June 1964, this 456th FIS jet is catching everyone's eye as they walk the ramp. The 28th Air Division stripes have been added to the original markings. (Picciani Collection)

On the ramp at Oxnard AFB, California, this F-106B shows off the later markings of the 456th FIS. (Burgess via the Greater St. Louis Air and Space Museum)

they changed Air Divisions in 1967, new markings were designed. Blue and yellow markings similar to the earlier ones were painted on but carried farther down the tail than the earlier ones had.

106 missions for the F-106. In only 6 hours.

In August 1967, the 456th FIS at Castle was looking at an extended period of minimal flying. With their fleet scheduled for installation of the aerial refueling modification, as well as an IR seeker cooling mod, they were looking for ways to get ahead of the game on their sorties and training. The way they went about it was one for the record books.

They would attempt to fly 106 live-intercept sorties in only 6 hours using their 18 assigned F-106s. Their 2 T-33s would be kept airborne constantly as targets for the interceptors. The attempt was to begin at 0600 on Saturday, 11 August, and end by noon. Rather than ask permission from their Air Division and risk hearing reasons why it could not be done, the unit, under the command of Lt. Col. John C. Marcotte, just went ahead and did it. The unit coordinated with the Federal Aviation Administration's Oakland Air Traffic Control Center to set up a temporary military flying area over the Nevada desert that went from 39,000 to 51,000 feet. That prevented the high-speed interceptor traffic from interfering with normal civilian airliner routes. They also ensured that the GCI stations would have enough controllers ready to go when the first aircraft launched. A T-33 target was actually the first jet to get airborne and was in place by the time the first F-106 launched.

The mission profile for the interceptors consisted of an afterburner climb to 40,000 feet, a supersonic intercept run with simulated weapons firing, followed by a high-speed descent back to Castle, and a quick turn after landing. And then do it again. When the 106th intercept mission landed at 1140, the 456th had set a new ADC and USAF record for the most sorties flown in that time period. To celebrate their accomplishment, a four-ship of Sixes launched later that afternoon to perform a formation fly-by at both Castle and at their Air Division HQ at Hamilton. After being denied their request for a low pass over the field at Hamilton, the Sixes returned to Castle and saluted the maintenance troops on the ramp with a series of flybys and by "beating up the pattern."

The 456th set up a detached alert site at Fresno and deployed at least a half dozen Sixes there during the Cuban Missile Crisis. The unit moved from Castle to Oxnard AFB, California, on 2 July 1968, and shortly after arrival there was inactivated, with its assets passing to the 437th FIS on 18 July 1968. While at Castle, they participated in three early William Tell competitions, placing first in 1961, fourth in 1963, and third in 1965.

An unusually high number of different aircraft were assigned to the 456th FIS, as they swapped jets twice with other squadrons. In 1961 they sent their FY 1958 jets to Selfridge and received brand-new FY 1959 jets, which they kept for another two years. Those jets were then swapped for older FY 1957 round-eyes from the 498th FIS. Flying 67 different aircraft, both conventional and vertical-tape instrumented, the 456th lost only 2.

27th Fighter-Interceptor Squadron

On 1 October 1959 the Falcons of the 27th FIS moved from Griffiss to Loring and became the last squadron to begin conversion during 1959. The 27th initially received a mix of FY 1958 and FY 1959 aircraft, becoming the first squadron to receive the FY 1959 jets. Keeping the markings identical to their previous F-102s, they placed a yellow alar, outlined with a thin black line, inside a horizontal black-and-yellow checkered band on the tail. A black star was placed inside each corner of the alar and the squadron badge was carried on the left while the ADC badge was carried on the right.

They eventually picked up an alert detachment at Bangor AFB, Maine. Under operation College Shaft, the 27th FIS intercepted three Soviet Tu-95 Bear bombers on 13 May 1969. Two F-106s were scrambled from Loring and 2 hours and 33 minutes later, after landing and refueling at Goose Bay, Labrador, they successfully intercepted the Bears after a long tail chase that saw both interceptors cruising in minimum afterburner to catch the retreating Bears. The intercept occurred 150 miles offshore and nearly 700 miles away from Loring. This was the first intercept of Soviet aircraft by interceptors based in the CONUS.

The 27th did not compete in any William Tell weapons meets. Having had 50 Sixes assigned over the years, with 5 losses, the 27th FIS was replaced by the 83rd FIS on 1 July 1971, when TAC took all of the historic First Fighter Group squadrons back under their banner to reform the 1st Tactical Fighter Wing at MacDill.

Showing off the classic markings of the 27th FIS. The leading zero on the serial number denoted an aircraft more than 10 years old. (Don Spering/AIR)

Chapter Eighteen

F-106 SQUADRONS: 1960 CONVERSIONS

Posed on the Selfridge ramp in July 1960, this Six proudly displays the markings of the 94th FIS. This jet is nearly fresh from the factory; still lacking the optical sight and with the interim ejection seat. The large yellow warning placard is unusual, and the comet (not blue!) had the lucky pilot's name in it.

While the three units that converted in 1959 received "round-eye" aircraft, all of the squadrons that received the F-106 in 1960 received vertical tape–equipped jets. The pace of conversion was one unit per month. By the end of the year, all of the original F-106 units had received at least their initial batch of new Sixes.

319th Fighter-Interceptor Squadron

The only squadron to fly the F-106 twice was the 319th FIS, initially based at Bunker Hill AFB, Indiana (later, Grissom). Making the massive conversion from antiquated F-89J Scorpion interceptors to the Mach 2 Delta Dart, the 319th was the first unit to receive F-106s in calendar year 1960. They carried the very recognizable 30th Air Division markings between 1960 and 1963, when they became the first F-106 to convert out of the jet.

In response to the Cuban Crisis, the unit moved to Homestead and transitioned to F-104A Starfighters to counter the Cuban MiG threat. The last Six from the 319th departed Bunker Hill 9 March

Taken on Armed Forces Day 1962, this 319th FIS Six displays the distinctive 30th Air Division markings. (Bob Burgess photo via the Greater St. Louis Air and Space Museum)

1963. The 319th flew the F-104A/B from Homestead from mid-1963 until its inactivation on 31 December 1969.

5th Fighter-Interceptor Squadron

A month after the 319th began their conversion, the 5th FIS "Spittin' Kittens" began equipping the F-106 in February following an administrative "flag move" from Suffolk County AFB, New York, to Minot. Defending the northern tier, the 5th flew the F-106 until converting to the F-15 Eagle in December 1984.

Like other interceptor units, the 5th had several alert detachments over the years. Beginning on 1 January 1963, they began using Billings IAP, Montana, as a dispersal base and detached alert site. This continued through 1 September 1965 when they moved to Hector, where they stayed through 8 January 1966. The records of their detached alert location(s) from then through 1971 have not been found, but on 1 April 1971, they were back at Billings again, staying there until 30 June 1974 when the detachment moved to Davis-Monthan AFB, Arizona, where they stayed until 1 October 1984.

While this photo is showing its age, it is valuable for showing the first markings applied to F-106s of the 5th FIS. Note the lack of black striping around the alars on the nose and tail. F-106Bs were frequently chosen to be display aircraft for Armed Forces Day Open House celebrations.

The detachment moved to Holloman on 1 October 1984 and then to Loring on 1 November 1986, where they remained until transitioning to the F-15A/B. That final alert detachment was closed down on 31 December 1987.

The unit was also famous for having a pair of Canadian Lynx mascots, live Spittin' Kittens, which were kept in a cage and cared for by the life support personnel. But before Spittin' and Kitten arrived, a very interesting set of events occurred between the new interceptor unit and Operation Crowflight, a detachment of U-2 reconnaissance aircraft from the 4080th Strategic Wing based out of Laughlin AFB, Texas. Three U-2s were in place at Minot when the F-106s began to arrive, and the rivalry started immediately. The Crowflight folks had a tendency to paint black crows over anything that was not guarded, and some that were.

One day after its arrival at Minot, one of the very first F-106s was found with a large black crow painted on its tail. That was bad, but the fact that the interceptor had been kept inside a restricted shelter was worse. That was too much for the 5th folks to take,

Shown here in an October 1968 view, this pristine Six shows off the mid-era markings of the 5th FIS. The aircraft forms are jammed on the left glare shield, a very common location for storing paperwork on a Six. (Via Bert Kinzey/Detail and Scale Collection)

and even though the Crowflight hangar was also restricted, shortly thereafter one of the equally highly classified U-2s was found to have a large 5th FIS squadron decal prominently displayed on its vertical tail.

The security implications were such that both unit commanders were summoned to the base commander's office and both HQ ADC and HQ SAC were very interested in what was going on. The two commanders were given very clear instructions that "this would never happen again" and left no doubt about what would happen if it did. Only much later did what really happened leak out. There were no real security violations, but very large quantities of beer did change hands in payment for the zaps.

The original markings of the 5th consisted of the standard 10th Air Force design, in this case a large yellow alar on the tail. The squadron badge was carried on the left and the ADC badge on the right. A small alar was carried on the nose for the crew names and a letter was painted on the speed brakes in black, to show the jet's maintenance flight. After a very short period of time, a thin black outline was added to the outside of the alar to make it stand out.

The unit participated in three William Tell tournaments, taking second place in 1965, fifth place in 1968, and third place in 1980, as well as winning the prestigious ADC A award in both 1972 and 1977. In 1975, the unit became the first ADC squadron to deploy to Germany when they participated in exercise Cold Fire 75, flying out of Hahn AB, Germany. They also participated in seven Red Flag deployments to Nellis and multiple deployments to Miramar to fly DACT against the navy Top Gun classes.

Over the nearly 24 years they flew the Six, 33 F-106s had been assigned, with 9 losses. The 5th began converting to the F-15A/B in the first quarter of 1985, with the first Eagle arriving at Minot on 8 January 1985. Most of the Delta Darts left during the first week of April 1985.

318th Fighter-Interceptor Squadron

The third month of 1960 brought the third unit conversion to the Six, as the 318th FIS at McChord received their first new jet. The 318th had been flying the F-102 and the conversion was relatively smooth. As the nearest F-106 unit to Alaska, the 318th (and 498th) were also the first F-106 units deployed northward after Russian Bear bombers penetrated U.S. airspace and the Alaskan-based F-102s proved to be inadequate to counter the threat. The 318th was also the first unit deployed to Korea in response to the *Pueblo* incident in January 1968.

However, the most unusual event that the 318th was involved with was the D. B. Cooper airliner hijacking incident. In late November 1971, a man calling himself "D. B. Cooper" hijacked a Northwest Orient Airlines B-727 shortly after takeoff from Portland International Airport and threatened to blow up the aircraft unless he was provided with $200,000 and four parachutes. After landing at the

On a drizzly Seattle-area day, this lineup of 318th FIS Sixes shows how the squadron badge was applied inside the early Northern Star tail design. Shortly before the 498th FIS moved to join them at McChord, the squadron badge was moved to the nose and the 325th FW (AD) badge was applied to the tail. (USAF)

Seattle-Tacoma airport to refuel and board the ransom money and the parachutes, the hijacker allowed the passengers to deplane.

When the airliner took off, ostensibly headed for Mexico, the 318th was tasked to scramble two F-106s to shadow it. The problem was that it was the day before Thanksgiving and the entire unit was participating in a formal dining-in event at the time. The actual scramble was to find the two least inebriated pilots and ground crew and get the jets launched, as the squadron had apparently been given permission to stand down from alert for the affair. In any event, somewhere over the wilds of Washington and Oregon, the hijacker parachuted unseen into the night and has never been seen again. From then until the squadron was deactivated, the squadron held a D. B. Cooper Dining-In to commemorate their role in the event.

The unit had several detached alert locations over the years, including Walla Walla, Washington; Kingsley Field, Oregon; and

The Second Attempt

As many veteran F-106 pilots will attest, the Six was quite capable of reaching speeds well above that achieved to set the world speed record in 1959. As the 318th prepared to transition from the Six to the F-15A Eagle, F-106A S/N 56-0459 (the Six originally intended to attempt to set the world speed record) was assigned to the 318th FIS. Many members of the squadron believed, incorrectly, that this was the jet that set the record, and someone came up with the idea to attempt to break the speed record again before the Six was sent to the boneyard, and to prove once and for all just how fast the jet really was.

Rather than involve HQ USAF or HQ TAC, the attempt was a very low-key and "under the radar" affair. Because the unit had some contacts within the USAF Test Pilot School, the jet was taken to Edwards and prepared for the record attempt, while arrangements were made to get the timing equipment, observers, and range time scheduled. It ended up being impossible to completely hide the affair, and once word got out, politics once again reared its ugly head and the word came down that "there is no way on earth we are going to allow a 50-year-old aircraft to set a new world speed record! Congress would be all over us!" In the end there was no official attempt, but what could be a better way to go out than trying to beat your own record?

Flying past an ominous looking Mt. Rainier in the mid-1960s, these 318th FIS Darts display the mid-era version of the North Star tail markings. (USAF via Isham)

This 20 January 1968 view gives a nice look at the mid-era markings of this Six from the 318th FIS. (Morris)

Displaying a TAC badge on the tail, this Green Dragons Six is loaded with the cannon, and has an empty LAU-3 on the wing during William Tell 1982. (Norman E. Taylor)

Castle. The Green Dragons remained based at McChord until converting to the F-15 in early 1983.

The 318th was a regular participant in the William Tell weapons meets, with appearances in 1963, 1965, 1970, 1972, and 1974. On 20 November 1967, 10 F-106s of the 318th were flown nonstop from McChord to Tyndall using aerial refueling. Upon arrival at Tyndall the jets continued to the range and participated in a live-fire event. This was the initial test of the College Cadence plan.

The unit also deployed to Howard AFB, Canal Zone, for exercise Blackhawk '74. As the unit began converting out of the Six in the second half of 1983, their first F-15, a B model, arrived on 22 August. Five-time expired F-106s were sent to the Military Aircraft Storage and Disposition Center (MASDC), with S/N 59-0057 being the first to go, on 2 June. The last two F-106s left McChord for the boneyard on 2 November 1983. The Green Dragons flew 70 F-106s over the years, losing seven of them. Fortunately, they saved S/N 56-0459 as a display aircraft.

94th Fighter-Interceptor Squadron

April 1960 brought the first F-106s to Selfridge as the first of two squadrons in the 1st Fighter Wing based there began its transition. The 94th FIS had already started transitioning to the F-104A Starfighter when the decision was made to give them the Six. In retrospect that was probably the better choice, regardless of what prompted it, because trying to fly the hot Starfighter off a 9,000-foot runway in the northern United States was bound to cause problems. So while the 94th was busily recalling personnel from F-104 schools trying to gain slots for F-106 training and packaging up the Starfighter simulator to gain room for an F-106 sim, the first maintenance training aircraft arrived and the old F-86Ls were sent to other units.

By 18 May 1963, the markings on the tail of this 94th FIS are being painted out, but the external tank markings are still in place. The 94th used yellow as a squadron color during this era. (Burgess via the St. Louis Air and Space Museum)

Rather than receiving new FY 1959 aircraft, the 94th picked up the jets previously assigned to the 27th FIS, as that unit transitioned to all FY 1959 jets. The initial paint scheme carried by the "Hat in the Ring" unit was the thin, horizontal red and white stripes and blue V of the 30th Air Division, with a large 94th squadron badge carried inside the V on both sides of the tail. A yellow comet outlined in black was sometimes carried on the nose with the pilot's name inside. Beginning in early 1961, the 1st FW badge began appearing in the V on the left side of the jet and the 30th Air Division badge in the V on the right side of the tail, but the initial markings were retained on some aircraft through December 1962.

When the AD boundaries were realigned circa late 1963, the 1st FW came under the 34th Air Division and the previous 30th AD markings were quickly removed. For the next four years, only a small squadron badge was carried on the nose, with the ADC badge on the right side of the tail and the 1st Wing badge carried on the left side of the tail. Beginning in 1967, the unit began experimenting with new markings. One jet displayed a large, stylized 1st FW badge on the tail, while another was seen with a green horizontal band with yellow and black outlines with the squadron and ADC badges inside white circles. The design finally chosen was a yellow band with thin red and black stripes above and below it.

The 94th (and sister unit, the 71st) had many problems with their newly acquired Sixes. They arrived with F-102 radar scopes, no trim motors (and other missing parts), and early versions of the vertical-tape displays. There was no documentation on how to use the early displays as they were basically unreadable, and therefore unusable for flight in weather conditions. As a result, small conventional altimeter and airspeed gauges were mounted on the instrument panel temporarily and weather minimums were raised to a 5,000-foot ceiling and 5-mile visibility until upgraded tape displays could be installed.

In late July 1963, the main runway at Selfridge had deteriorated to the point where it was hazardous to fly the hot F-106s there. As a result, it was closed for nearly three months for repaving and the 94th deployed all of their aircraft to Grissom, taking over the facilities of the recently departed 319th FIS until Selfridge was operational again. New concrete did not appear to solve the problem and at least three aircraft were damaged due to deteriorating runway conditions between the end of February and the end of March 1964.

In June 1969, the 94th flew its F-106s to Malmstrom leaving the jets there in a permanent aircraft swap, and then taking a chartered commercial flight to Korea to relieve the 71st FIS at Osan. The 94th became the only squadron to repaint their aircraft in Korea. After taking possession of the 71st squadron's jets, they applied a simpler version of their previous tail marking, applying the yellow band with thicker black outline stripes and omitting the small, inner red edge stripes.

The 94th maintained a dispersal location at Hulman for many years. After the 71st FIS moved from Selfridge to Richards-Gebaur at the end of 1966, the 94th took over the 71st detachment at Niagara Falls IAP, New York, and closed down Hulman, which had always had water problems in the weapons storage area. Approximately two

Winters at Wurtsmith AFB were hard. Enough aircraft shelters were built to protect an entire squadron of interceptors from the conditions. Specially posed for the photographer in April 1970, there is still plenty of snow on the ramp. Note the 94th FIS final markings and yellow F-106–shaped crew legends on the canopy and nose gear door. (Mason)

weeks after their return from Korea, the unit departed Selfridge with a mass flight of all 18 F-106s and 3 T-33s and moved to Wurtsmith AFB, Michigan. Like the other squadrons of the old 1st Fighter Wing, the 94th was replaced by the 2nd FIS on 1 July 1971 when TAC took the squadron number and assigned it to an F-4E training unit at MacDill.

The 94th never participated in a William Tell meet and had 6 losses with the 48 F-106s they were assigned over the years.

Just prior to moving from Kincheloe to Griffiss, the 438th FIS began adding a new design to their aircraft. It is impossible to tell whether the alar is in black or insignia blue in this September 1968 view, but there is no mistaking the (aft facing) Donald Duck insignia on the squadron badge. (MacSorley)

Hooked-up to a tow bar, this 11th FIS Six looks too clean to be going into Depot maintenance. The Red Bulls kept their large squadron badges and tail stripes long after other units had painted them out, and placed an ADC badge on the right fin. January 1966. (Via Bert Kinzey/Detail and Scale)

Another air show photo, this time from May 1966. Note how the 438th FIS style of 30th Air Division stripes stop at the panel line short of the leading edge of the fin. Donald is facing forward on this particular jet, which has the newer main wheels. (Picciani)

438th Fighter-Interceptor Squadron

Continuing the "one a month" conversions to the F-106, the 438th FIS at Kincheloe AFB, Michigan, began receiving the Delta Dart on 12 May 1960. The 438th had been flying F-102s, and both types of jet were marked with the standardized 30th Air Division markings of red and white horizontal stripes with a blue V in the middle. Just to be different, however, the 438th did not carry the stripes all the way to the leading edge of the fin, but stopped them several inches short.

Operating under the Sault Ste. Marie Air Defense Sector, the 438th was charged with protecting the Soo Locks, through which virtually all of the iron ore for the U.S. steel industry passed. Shortly before their deactivation on 30 September 1968, the unit designed new tail markings that consisted of a stylized duck marking in black and white.

There were 29 F-106s assigned to the 438th and they lost 4 due to accidents.

11th Fighter-Interceptor Squadron

The Red Bulls of the 11th FIS at Duluth officially began converting to the F-106 on 23 June 1960. They also transitioned from the F-102, and their initial aircraft markings were also the standard 30th Air Division ones, which they carried until roughly 1966. When they came under the 10th Air Force, they changed marking to a short red alar with black trim. The squadron badge was carried above the alar on the left with the ADC badge on the right.

In an administrative reflagging on 30 September 1968, the 11th was inactivated and replaced by the 87th FIS, which basically kept the same markings. Because all of the men and aircraft remained in place, rather than use the existing 87th FIS emblem, from a unit that had previously been serving at Lockbourne AFB, Ohio, flying F-101B/F interceptors, they simply redesigned the existing Red Bull as its new emblem.

The 11th FIS placed fourth in William Tell 1961 and climbed to second during William Tell 1963. The Red Bulls had 33 Sixes assigned over the years, losing 3 to accidents.

329th Fighter-Interceptor Squadron

29 July 1960 saw the 329th at George AFB begin transitioning from the F-102 to the F-106. Defending Southern California, the squadron initially painted a small red alar on their tails. The 28th Air Division red, white, and blue bands were added shortly thereafter. The 329th received F-106A S/N 56-0467, holder of the world speed record, after the jet was rebuilt during the Test-to-Tactical program. Just a little more than two months after receiving the historic jet, it was

Posing on the ramp at George AFB, California, these brand-new F-106s display the original tail markings of the 329th FIS. Yellow zinc chromate interiors to the landing gear doors and access panels were the order of the day, but many variations were seen later. (USAF)

Shot at George AFB on 22 May 65. This 329th FIS jet has the later-design main wheels and 28th Air Division stripes on the fin. (Courtesy of the Greater St. Louis Air and Space Museum)

destroyed during a landing attempt at Edwards. Rebounding from that accident, in October 1964, the 329th won the Hughes Trophy for Air Defense Excellence, with the highest scores seen in the 12 previous years of the trophy's existence. Fleet attrition led to an HQ ADC decision to close two F-106 squadrons in 1967, with the 329th and 539th being the ones getting the ax. The first F-106 departed in May 1967 and the unit was inactivated on 31 July 1967. The unit did not participate in any William Tell meets and flew 35 aircraft, losing 4 of them.

48th Fighter-Interceptor Squadron

Langley became the next home of the F-106 when the 48th FIS began converting from the F-102 to the Six in early October. As the next-to-last squadron to convert to the Delta Dart, the 48th received a mixture of FY 1959 jets. Defending HQ TAC, and the Washington-Baltimore area for more than 23 years, the 48th converted to the F-15 Eagle starting in February 1982.

The 48th participated in Operation High Speed, and became the first F-106 squadron to send aircraft overseas when they sent two aircraft across the Atlantic Ocean to participate in the 1963 Paris Air Show. The 48th also supported the original seven Project Mercury astronauts (who were assigned to NASA at Langley at the time) in both the F-102 and the later F-106, checking all but one of them out in both types of aircraft. The holdout was John Glenn, who opted to fly the F8U Crusader instead of the Convair Deltas. Two additional Sixes were assigned to the 48th for use by the astronauts both for zero-G weightlessness training and high-speed transports.

The unit had several detached alert locations over the years,

including Wilmington, North Carolina, and Charleston, South Carolina. Under Operation College Sand, the 48th picked up a second detachment, this time at Homestead. Involving six aircraft, this detachment lasted until 1 May 1976.

Early markings consisted of nothing but a small squadron badge on the tail, and either a white or black stripe on the speed brakes to identify the maintenance flight. After 1963, a large squadron badge was applied to both sides of the tail. By 1964–1965, a large white band, outlined in insignia blue, was painted on the vertical tail of their jets, with two additional smaller horizontal bands on the rudder. Initially the large squadron badge was kept, but around a year later it was reduced in size, and the ADC badge replaced it on the right side of the tail. In 1976 the

From the peeling paint, it looks as if this 48th FIS bird has been breaking the Mach, and then some. By 1967, the unit had switched to approved sizes of the squadron and ADC badge on the fin. Notice how much smaller the squadron insignia is on this aircraft when compared with the previous photo. (Geer)

When the 48th FIS added the white band on the tail, they initially placed an oversized version of their squadron badge on the fin. An equally large ADC badge was placed on the right side. (Via Isham)

Caught on final approach to its home field at Langley AFB, Virginia, in March 1976, this 48th FIS Dart shows off its newly designed tail markings. (Picciani)

markings were revised to nine alternating bands of blue and white on the rudder, and a white alar outlined in medium blue on the fin. A colored vertical band on the air intake splitter plate showed the maintenance flight.

The unit placed third in William Tell 1963, and also in 1978. Their final F-106 departed on 9 March 1982, when S/N 59-0123 was towed across the base to the NASA Langley Research Center. Over 22 years, 45 F-106s were assigned to the 48th with 7 lost aircraft.

71st Fighter-Interceptor Squadron

The last original squadron to convert to the Delta Dart was the 71st FIS Flying Fists. Starting in mid-October 1960 they relinquished their F-102s and joined the 94th FIS at Selfridge in flying the Six. As the last squadron to receive the Six, they acquired FY 1958 jets to match their sister squadron, the 94th FIS. While at Selfridge, the 71st first carried the 30th Air Division markings on the tail fin and a squadron badge on the nose, but after the 1FIW was reassigned to the 34th Air Division, the tail markings were removed, and only the squadron badge on the nose and a plain 1st FW and ADC badge on the tail were carried.

The 71st was assigned to Det 2 1st FW at Niagara Falls for their detached alert location. The 71st competed in only two William Tell meets, but they took first place both times, in 1965 and in 1970.

On 2 January 1967, the unit moved from Selfridge to Richards-Gebaur to guard the Kansas City and St. Louis areas, replacing the inactivating 326th FIS, which had operated the F-102 there.

Seen on the Selfridge AFB alert ramp in roughly 1961, this 71st FIS Six has 30th Air Division markings on the fin with the 1st FW badge on the tail and a 71st badge on the nose. Note the difference in design styles between the older 1950s-era barns in the middle and the newer 1960s barns on the outside. (USAF)

The 71st officially assumed alert there on 15 January 1967. Their markings at that time were very plain, with just a squadron badge and ADC badge on the fin.

That move did not last long, however, and barely 18 months later the unit was moved again, this time to Malmstrom. They barely had time to paint a blue alar outlined in black on the tails of their

Seen here on display at an air show in May 1965, this is a rare color view of the markings applied to the five William Tell 1965 competition jets from the 71st FIS. The badge on the tail is from the parent 1st Fighter Wing. (Isham Collection)

Closing up on the tanker, these two Sixes are from the 71st FIS at Malmstrom AFB, Montana. Note how the serial numbers have been masked off, leaving an ADC gray (not white) surround. An earlier iteration of this design had the serial numbers simply painted on the blue, which made them very hard to read. (USAF, May 1970 via Picciani)

jets before they were sent to Korea to relieve the 48th FIS. The 71st deployed in December 1968 with its full complement of F-106s, spending six months at Osan before turning its jets over to the 94th FIS in June 1969. Upon returning to Malmstrom, the 71st took ownership of the F-106s previously assigned to the 94th FIS.

As with the other historical 1st Wing squadrons, the 71st unit designation went to TAC on 1 July 1971, with the unit becoming the third iteration of the 319th FIS. While in Montana, the 71st had detached alert sites at Billings and Spokane. There were 57 aircraft assigned, against 6 losses.

How an F-106 Ended Up at the Air Force Academy

With thanks to Lonnie Berry, 127 WG/CES, Jim Sandvik, and F-106deltadart.com.

Two squadrons assigned to the 1st Fighter-Interceptor Wing (AD) were stationed at Selfridge in the early 1960s. Two of the pilots assigned there almost always struck a wager when they flew a mission together as to who was better at some selected piloting skill. One was assigned to the 71st FIS and the other to the 94th FIS. On this particular day, the wager was which pilot could make the shortest landing rollout.

On recovery after the mission, the 71st pilot made a remarkably good landing and was almost sure to collect the bet.

Now, this was in the early days of the F-106 and the tailhook was unguarded when in the up position. The F-106 in the landing configuration is very nose high with the pilot sitting right over the nose wheel. The tailhook was intended to be put down in the event an aircraft was about to overshoot the end of a runway, and would then engage a heavy wire strung across the runway before the aircraft went off into the overrun and the dirt. This cable was held about 6 inches off the runway by large rubber donuts.

In his attempt to win the bet, the 94th pilot flew a very low-speed, very nose-high final approach and ended up landing in the overrun, short of the runway threshold. When the main gear rolled over the barrier, it bounced up and unintentionally engaged the tailhook, which was still in the up position. This event had never happened before, but was later called an approach end engagement, and it was very similar to a navy carrier landing. Needless to say, the aircraft stopped in a much shorter distance than the rival bird and the 94th pilot won the bet. The aircraft was thoroughly inspected and, fortunately, no damage was found.

Subsequent to this incident, a tailhook modification was hurriedly designed to install a guard around the sides of the tailhook so this could not happen again. In January 1963, this modification was about to be installed by three 1st FIW mechanics on an aircraft that had just been downloaded at alert and towed back to the flight line.

The aircraft was placed into what was then known as "aircraft shelter number 3," part of four contiguous shelters that dominated the main flight line ramp near the base operations building at Selfridge. Two of the airmen were at the rear of the jet, while the remaining airman was instructed to go into the cockpit and release the tailhook. Murphy, doing what he does best, also ensured that the external fuel tanks on the jet were full of fuel, that nobody had replaced the shear pins on the external tanks with steel safety pins, and that the explosive carts on the fuel tanks were not removed or safetied prior to starting maintenance on the aircraft.

As if that were not enough, there were two nearly adjacent buttons on the left side of the instrument panel that were "hot" from the battery at all times, and as luck would have it, he pushed the wrong one. The system worked exactly as designed, and instead of the tailhook being released, both external tanks jettisoned from the jet. They impacted the concrete floor of the shelter, broke apart, and caught fire as the three maintainers ran for safety. The heat was so intense that it melted the steel cables that held the shelter doors open and they slammed shut, turning the aircraft shelter into a giant oven.

F-106 S/N 58-0763 was reduced to nothing but a pile of smelted aluminum, with the remains of its engine sitting on the concrete floor of the shelter, while S/N 58-0761 was so badly heat-damaged that the forward fuselage had ripples in it from the heat. After the accident, it was inspected, found to be unrepairable, and written off.

Meanwhile, the Commander of Air Defense Command and the Commander of the Air Force Academy (AFA) were having drinks at the bar in Colorado Springs and the ADC/CC was enquiring as to why there were no ADC aircraft on display with all the other aircraft on the AFA grounds. Being put on the spot by a senior officer, the AFA Commander did the only thing he could, and said that he would be happy to put one on display if one could be provided.

Shortly thereafter, a crew from the 319th FIS, which was in the process of deactivating, was sent from Bunker Hill to Selfridge to disassemble the jet. It was stripped of all internal equipment, given a new coat of gray paint to cover the burn marks, given new lettering and markings (94th FIS on the left side and 71st FIS on the right), and shipped to Colorado Springs, where it was given *the* prime viewing location on the barracks terrazzo right in front of the Chapel of the Academy. The previous occupant of that location was a very early-model F-100, which was taken to Ft. Carson, Colorado, wrapped in explosives, and dynamited into oblivion.

Whereas the F-100 had been carefully maintained because of its historical significance, the F-106 was just "there" and became a magnet for spirited hijinks. It magically gained new paint jobs (pink!) overnight, and when important athletic events were approaching, significant amounts of graffiti would appear on it.

All of this caused a certain amount of embarrassment among the higher ups and large amounts of work for the maintenance staff, which continually had to repaint the hulk back into something resembling an operational jet. But it was the "Bring Me Men" ramp down to the parade ground that eventually did in the poor Six. A few dozen cadets could easily lift the Six and run with it. And they did. It appeared more than once on the parade ground, and one unfortunate Marine captain learned the hard way that an F-106 coming

A severely heat-damaged S/N 58-0761 is towed out of the ruined shelter at Selfridge AFB, Michigan, on 10 January 1963. The aircraft was cosmetically refurbished and placed on display at the Air Force Academy. It was eventually reclaimed for parts. (USAF)

Accorded a place of honor, this Six was the victim of many cadet pranks and was eventually salvaged after hitting a building while being rolled down toward the parade field one night.

downhill on the shoulders of a crowd is not going to stop, even when you command it to Halt! All attempts to stop the activity were ineffective, and eventually the jet got out of control one night in 1969 when it was being rolled down the ramp, hit one of the buildings, was irreparably damaged, and finally sent to the depot in Sacramento and salvaged.

And that damaged aircraft shelter at Selfridge? It was dismantled and never replaced, leaving a large gap in what once was a continuous structure and becoming one of the very distinctive visual features of the Selfridge flight line. The three remaining shelters were demolished in December 1997, having been in place since April 1958.

Chapter Nineteen

LATER UNITS

"Selfridge tower, Juliet Lima 12 is turning initial with five, straight through." Over Anchor Bay, this flight of Michigan ANG Sixes is setting up for a photo pass over the Six Pack ramp in this April 1978 scene.

ADC went to great lengths to assign notable, historic squadron designators to its interceptor units. As unit designators were transferred to other commands, several units had their identities changed as a result. And as the active-duty forces dwindled due to budget cutbacks and philosophical changes, Air National Guard units began flying the F-106. The Guard eventually became the sole operational users of the Six.

2nd Fighter-Interceptor Squadron

On 1 July 1971, the 2nd FIS was activated at Wurtsmith to take over ownership of the F-106s and personnel of the 94th FIS as the 94th squadron designation was transferred on paper to TAC on that date. During their short tenure in the Six, the Horney Horses competed in William Tell 1972, where they took second place in the F-106 category, earning 13,761 points out of a possible 16,800 over the course of the 18–30 September competition. The unit had really wanted to win the competition because their inactivation had not only already been announced, but was underway.

On 1 October 1972 the unit stood down from alert, and by the end of the year the first jets had already been flown down to Selfridge where they were transferred to the 171st FIS of the Michigan Air National Guard. The 2nd FIS was officially inactivated on 31 March 1973, having sustained no losses to the 20 F-106s that had been assigned to them.

With maps in the cockpit and 781 forms padding where the ladder rests on the fuselage, this Six from the 2nd FIS is on a cross-country flight. The tail design and crew name blocks on the canopy frame and nose gear doors are carryovers from when the unit was designated as the 94th FIS. The black and yellow stripes on the pitot boom are pretty fancy; interceptor units took great pride in the appearance of their aircraft. (Tom Foote)

83rd Fighter-Interceptor Squadron

Also on 1 July 1971, the 27th FIS at Loring was inactivated when the squadron designation was turned over to TAC. The 27th was replaced by the 83rd FIS, which several years earlier had flown both the F-104A Starfighter and the F-101B Voodoo. On 30 June 1972, their 17 F-106s were reassigned to the 95th FIS at Doverand the unit was inactivated.

The unit had been assigned 20 tail numbers during the year it had the Six, and had no losses.

Returning from a William Tell practice mission, this F-106A belongs to the 2nd FIS. Seen here aerobraking after landing at Wurtsmith in August 1972, the unit has only a few months to go before being disbanded.

A very rare view of an 83rd FIS Six. The extended IR seeker means that this jet is about to launch on a practice intercept mission. Photo taken at Loring AFB, Maine, in August 1971. (Brewer via Picciani)

319th Fighter-Interceptor Squadron

The only unit to serve with the F-106 twice, the 319th FIS came to life again on 1 July 1971 at Malmstrom, taking over the F-106s of the 71st FIS, which, like the 27th and 94th squadrons, made a "flag move," administratively moving to MacDill to become an F-4E squadron in the 1st TFW. While in Montana, the 319th had an alert detachment at Spokane. Like the 318th FIS, they were also involved with shadowing the hijacked Northwest Orient Boeing 727-100 during the D. B. Cooper incident.

Initially, the unit simply replaced the 71st insignia on the tail with the 319th Tomcat, keeping the blue alar with black outline that was already on the jets. Shortly before their deactivation, the unit changed the tail markings to a black alar with a yellow outline, added a smaller black alar to the nose, and painted the pitot booms in black and yellow.

After less than a year flying the Six, the unit inactivated on 30 April 1972. All 18 of their jets had been flown to the 460th FIS at Grand Forks AFB, North Dakota, by 24 May, however.

87th Fighter-Interceptor Squadron

On 30 September 1968, the 11th FIS at Duluth was inactivated and replaced by the 87th FIS. This change happened while the unit had four aircraft in Alaska for a White Shoes deployment. Effective 1 May 1971, the squadron moved to K. I. Sawyer AFB, Michigan, with full operations by 23 May.

In addition to Alaskan deployments, the 87th also participated in three William Tell meets. They placed third in 1972, third in 1976, and second in 1984. Of note, was the 87th "shot the gun" at William Tell 1984 that competed head to head with F-15 Eagle teams.

Since all of the aircraft and personnel of the 11th became the 87th, the unit chose to perpetuate the Red Bull identity from the 11th, designing a new version of the emblem rather than adopting the old 87th FIS insignia. Likewise, they initially kept the red alar tail marking of the 11th FIS, but after a short period of time they enlarged it somewhat and the placement of the squadron insignia changed slightly. By 1972 the widely recognized Red Bull tail markings were starting to be applied. Initially, some of the bulls had very

Seen here on final approach to Andrews, the first markings change the 87th FIS made was to extend the alar on the vertical fin farther forward toward the leading edge. May 1972. (Picciani)

short noses, but they were rapidly replaced with longer, more slender ones. At least through 1973, the bull markings also had a white outline. In April 1975, the Red Bulls deployed six F-106s to Luke AFB, Arizona, for DACT with the F-15 OT&E unit based there. In late 1977 or early 1978, a red and black bulls head began appearing on the left noses of the unit jets, with crew names frequently being painted in the lower portion.

On 21 April 1978, eight of the squadron's aircraft departed K. I. Sawyer for Keflavik to assist the 57th FIS in covering their alert while that unit converted from the F-4C to the F-4E. The Red Bulls first Bear intercept was accomplished by Captains Gene Lutz and Bill Thomas about five days later. The deployment ended on 13 May 1978.

When ADC relinquished control of its interceptor force to TAC on 1 October, the 87th had six F-106As deployed to Davis-Monthan for DACT with the A-10 training squadrons based there. Markings changed again once the unit was under ADTAC, with the TAC badge appearing on both sides of the vertical tail and the squadron badge moving to the left nose.

As the F-106 neared retirement from the air force, the 87th stood down from home station alert on 1 February 1985. They ceased alert at their Charleston detachment on 1 July 1985, and inactivated on 1 October 1985. There were 37 F-106s assigned to the 87th over the years with the loss of 6 aircraft.

The painters must have had a bad day when they applied the Bull insignia to this Six as the lower nose is distinctly droopy. In May 1983, these were the final markings of the 87th FIS. The later-style anti-glare treatment was a throwback to the earlier F-102.

437th Fighter-Interceptor Squadron

Far and away, the unit with the shortest amount of time flying the F-106 was the 437th FIS at Oxnard. Beginning its association with the aircraft when the 456th FIS turned its jets over on 18 July 1968, the 437th was subsequently replaced by the 460th FIS just 45 days later, on 30 September 1968, to "give ADC units a more distinguished history."

Badly in need of a paint job, this 87th FIS bus shows off the 1972 "fat nose" bull. Note the white outline and background to the serial number. This early design extends down onto the speed brakes. Later designs did not extend down as far and dispensed with the white. Since the designs were all masked off by hand, many different variations were seen over the years. (Isham)

The 437th FIS did not keep its F-106s long enough to design new markings. The only change was to remove the old squadron badge from the left side of the tail.

460th Fighter-Interceptor Squadron

Taking over where the 437th had left off, the 460th FIS initially began flying conventional round-eye aircraft at Oxnard. With the closure of Oxnard at the end of 1969, the Tigers moved to Kingsley, effective 1 December 1969. That assignment was also short lived, as yet another round of budget cuts forced another move.

Thus, on 16 April 1971, the 460th moved to Grand Forks. The squadron sent all of their round-eye jets to the 186th FIS, Montana ANG, in April 1972, and in their place picked up vertically instrumented jets from the inactivating 319th FIS at Malmstrom.

The 460th participated in one White Shoes deployment and one William Tell weapons meet, taking first place in 1972. The unit was inactivated on 15 July 1974, with the F-106s being divided up between the 144 FIW, California ANG, and the 125 FIG, Florida

The lack of antiskid braking made life difficult for pilots landing on short northern runways in the winter, as this 460th FIS Six demonstrates. Photo taken on 4 December 1970 at Kingsley Field, Oregon. (USAF via Isham)

ANG. There were 54 jets assigned with 1 loss.

Tail markings were initially those of the old 437th FIS, which were, in turn, the same as the last markings of the 456th FIS. Once at Kingsley, however, the unit began experimenting with new markings. Initially the rudder carried a number of thin, alternating yellow and black stripes, but the unit eventually settled on a striking black and yellow alar on the fin and larger black and yellow stripes on the rudder.

Heading out to the Whiskey 470 range over the Gulf of Mexico, this 460th FIS Six is a participant in the William Tell 1972 meet. Note that black and yellow striped pitot tube and the early UHF blade antenna under the nose. (Via Don Spering/AIR)

49th Fighter-Interceptor Squadron

Another unit to be redesignated and reassigned on 30 September 1968 was the 49th FIS, which took over the aircraft and personnel from the 438th FIS. The 49th was stationed at Griffiss and from 1960 to 1968 flew the F-101B/F Voodoo there.

The existing 438th markings were kept for only a very short period of time before the unit began experimenting with new green and white designs based on those the 49th had previously used on its F-101s. Initially, a set of thin green and white stripes that radiated from the base of the rudder was applied. This eventually became the wings of the full Green Eagle design. External tank markings varied over the years, but were commonplace, as were white nose placards for the crew names.

One aircraft carried the name *El Jefe* and four white commander's stripes as the personal mount of General Price, Commander of the 21st NORAD region. This jet was lost when it was hit by lightning and lost all electrical power. The general died in the ensuing crash, and in true "blood priority," all F-106s were shortly thereafter retrofitted with lightning protection.

The 49th flew in five William Tell meets, placing second in 1974 and 1976, first in 1978, fourth in 1980, and first again in 1982. In 1982 the 49th had the distinction, along with the 318th, of being the first to shoot the M61 Vulcan cannon in competition. When the 49th FIS was inactivated on 30 September 1987, they were the last active-duty F-106 unit in the USAF. There were 46 F-106s assigned to the unit, with 9 losses.

Rotating for takeoff at Stewart AFB, New York, in June 1969, these two Sixes are going to perform a fly-over for the cadets at the U.S. Military Academy at West Point. They are painted in the first markings of the 49th FIS. Note how the serial number on the lead aircraft extends on to the green and white, while the presentation on the wingman's jet has been shifted farther forward. (Picciani)

You can still see where the old 438th FIS markings have been painted out on the tail of this 49th FIS Six. (Via Isham)

A Green Eagles Six with TAC markings, 16 April 1984. (Charles Mayer)

Seen here in 1971, this 84th FIS Six has the full markings designed for the 498th FIS. When the unit moved to Hamilton AFB, California, and was redesignated as the 84th FIS, they kept the markings and simply replaced the squadron badge on the fin. (via Isham)

84th Fighter-Interceptor Squadron

The final unit realignment of 30 September 1968 was the 498th FIS becoming the 84th FIS Black Panthers, in conjunction with the unit moving from Paine to Hamilton. The unit kept the striking red, white, and blue lightning bolt design of the 498th, and replaced the Geiger Tiger badge with the Black Panthers emblem. When the 84th returned to Hamilton from their second deployment to Elmendorf on 2 October 1970, they brought the White Shoes deployments to an end.

The 84th competed in only one William Tell event, placing second in 1970. The unit moved to Castle on 15 September 1973, and then made one final return to Alaska, participating in winter exercise Jack Frost '77 before losing their F-106s and becoming a T-33 training unit effective 30 June 1981. The unit lost 4 F-106s of the 43 that had been assigned to them.

The 84th was unique in that it was the only operational squadron to have both round-gauge and vertical-tape aircraft assigned at the same time, which it did between 1974 and 1981. By the mid-1970s, so many aircraft had been lost that there were not enough left to have a full squadron of either type, so the 84th was chosen to have the only mixed batch.

With the Castle AFB alert barns visible in the valley fog, this 84th FIS Six waits on the ramp for the next flight. By February 1981, the markings are much plainer. A TAC badge is on the tail and a small squadron badge is on the nose. The MC-11 air cart and fuel vent catch cans were ubiquitous around a Six. (Charles B. Mayer)

The Six Goes to the Guard

As the philosophy of air defense shifted ever further toward air sovereignty and away from war fighting, air defense forces were progressively shifted from active duty to the Air National Guard. In the 1950s, the Guard stood daytime alert with F-86 day fighters. Then castoffs from ADC, such as the F-89B/C and F-94B, were given to the Guard as ADC moved on to better jets. Those aircraft were replaced by later-model F-89s and F-94s.

Eventually, alert in the Guard became a 24-hour-a-day exercise, and Century Series jets were passed down. This process accelerated during the war in SEA. As the war ate up increasing amounts of the active-duty USAF budget, air defense became a larger aspect of the Guard's duties.

120th Fighter-Interceptor Group
186th Fighter-Interceptor Squadron

Politics has always been a large factor in the Air National Guard, and that may be the reason the 186th FIS at Great Falls was the first Guard unit selected to receive the F-106. Most of their aircraft came from the 460th FIS when that unit converted from round-eye jets to those equipped with vertical tape.

The 186th did quite well in William Tell competitions, winning first place in 1974 and 1976 and second in 1978 and 1982. Topping it off, the unit won the Hughes Trophy as the Best Interceptor Squadron in the air force in 1985. They were also the last unit to participate in a Red Flag exercise, flying as aggressors in Red Flag 87-1. There were 21 F-106s assigned, but the loss rate was relatively high as the unit destroyed 6 of them.

Their Big Sky Blue aircraft markings really stood out, especially when painted with metallic paint. Over time even the cockpit interior was painted light blue, and some jets sported blue interior-exterior carpeting on the floorboards. Individual aircraft numbers were carried on both the nose and tail.

The unit began converting to the F-16A during the second quarter of 1987, receiving their aircraft from the 50 TFW at Hahn as that wing upgraded to the F-16C/D. Montana picked up the alert detachment at Davis-Monthan from the 5th FIS in late 1984 and kept it through the conversion. The first two Delta Darts to depart Great Falls were S/N 57-0246 and S/N 57-2490, which left on 1 April 1987. The last Six to depart was S/N 57-2476, which left on 24 June.

102nd Fighter-Interceptor Wing
101st Fighter-Interceptor Squadron

Next to receive the Delta Dart was the 101st FIS of the Massachusetts Air National Guard. Virtually all of their round-eye jets came from the 95th FIS when that unit received vertical-tape jets in 1972. They intercepted their first Bear on 15 April 1975, off the East Coast of the United States, and participated in three William Tell meets, placing fourth in 1978, second in 1980, and third in 1984.

Like the other Guard units, they came up with very distinctive markings for their aircraft, using light blue to match their unit insignia, and white. They also carried individual aircraft numbers on the jets, and the Cape Cod whaling harpoon design carried on the external fuel tanks really stood out. Their last F-106 departed for the Aerospace Maintenance and Regeneration Group (AMARG; previously MASDC and AMARC, Aerospace Maintenance and Regeneration Center) on 10 February 1988.

Even the ejection seat is painted sky blue on this Montana Air Guard Six as it holds formation in June 1982. Some of these jets even had blue indoor-outdoor carpet on the cockpit floor. Both the active-duty and the Guard units took a lot of pride in their jets, but the Guard had more latitude in displaying it. (Brian Rogers)

Departing Pease AFB, New Hampshire, in August 1972, S/N 57-2494 is in the early markings applied to 102 FIS Sixes. (Ron Picciani)

From the very nose-high attitude of this 101st FIS Six, you can tell the pilot has had to slow way down to stay with the camera ship. Fortunately, the Six had excellent slow-speed handling. (Mass ANG)

Caught at the exact moment of liftoff, this Six from the Massachusetts Air Guard gets airborne in August 1987. (Alec Fushi)

177th Fighter-Interceptor Group
119th Fighter-Interceptor Squadron

Third in line to convert to the Six was the 119th FIS of the New Jersey ANG. Flying out of NAFEC Atlantic City, their first jet arrived on 3 October 1972 from the 95th FIS.

Their only appearance in a William Tell meet came in 1984. This was the last meet featuring the F-106 as competitors, and the Jersey Devils took home first-place honors in the F-106 category. Alongside the 87th FIS they competed in the Profile V gun mission. There were 29 Sixes assigned over the years with no losses.

The squadron made one major change in markings, that occurring in June 1980 when they switched from relatively plain red horizontal striping to a large red and white alar design with a large "NEW JERSEY" carried on the upper part of the tail. They added an individual aircraft number to the aft fuselage when the markings changed. The 119th had the honor of being the last F-106 unit in existence and hosted a memorable Dart Out event before sending their final jets to the boneyard in Arizona on 1 August 1988.

This New Jersey ANG shows off the earlier unit markings, after the round ANG badge was replaced with the later style. That red-painted pitot boom matches the rest of the unit colors as well. (Undated photo by Don Spering/AIR)

For many years, the Soviet Union deployed both Bear D Maritime reconnaissance and Bear F submarine hunting bombers to Cuba. Deployment and reconnaissance flights off the U.S. coast frequently resulted in interceptions by U.S. interceptor units to identify the "unknown" radar tracks. (New Jersey ANG via Isham)

191st Fighter-Interceptor Group
171st Fighter-Interceptor Squadron

Michigan became the fourth unit to receive the F-106, beginning conversion from the RF-101A/C in December 1972 and acquiring the aircraft that had been assigned to the 2nd FIS at Wurtsmith. Most of these jets had originally been assigned to the 71st FIS when they were based at Selfridge in the early 1960s. They were subsequently swapped with the 94th FIS when those units exchanged aircraft while on TDY to Korea, and then returned to Selfridge, some 14 years after they first arrived from the factory.

Exactly how the 171st got their Sixes is a story in itself. Since the two collocated units of the Michigan ANG had been flying identical aircraft types since the 1950s, there was a movement to separate the units into different missions, and a meeting was arranged at the Guard Bureau in Washington, DC, to discuss which unit would receive the F-100 and which would receive the F-106. On the day of the meeting, the 171st attendees flew a T-33 while the 107th members flew in RF-84Fs. The weather at Andrews was poor but the T-33 managed to land there. The RF-84s had to divert to Byrd Field and secure ground transport to Washington. By the time they arrived, the meeting was virtually over, and

These four Sixes proudly display the later markings of the 177th FIS. (Don Spering/AIR)

"Defiance" in all its glory. Shot with a 55mm lens, the pilot of S/N 58-0772 has backed down and aft somewhat at the photographers request to better frame the photo. There is not much separation between aircraft in standard fingertip formation. 171st FIS in April 1978. INSET: One of the more famous pieces of Six nose art was "Defiance," which graced S/N 58-0772 of the Michigan ANG. The mouse has a surprise waiting for that hawk. Note how the art actually goes up onto the anti-glare panel.

the 171st had been assigned the F-106, leaving the F-100D for the 107th squadron.

The black and yellow checkerboard rudder, horizontal black band with a large "MICHIGAN," and dual alars on the fin made the Michigan F-106s really stand out from the crowd. Unfortunately, continued losses within the F-106 fleet necessitated that one F-106 unit convert to a different aircraft type to keep the other units at full strength. Much to their dismay, the Six Pack was chosen to convert to the F-4C. Flying the Six for less than six years, with no losses, they sent their final jet back to an active-duty unit, the 84th FIS, on 16 August 1978.

The summer of 1974 saw a major F-106 force structure realignment. Concurrent with the shutdown of the 460th FIS at Grand Forks, the air force planned to convert two ANG F-102 units, the

125th FIG at Jacksonville and the 144th FIW at Fresno to the F-106. However, the 460th's contingent of airplanes would only give the ANG units about 9 F-106s each.

To stand up two new units while closing only one, the force structure planners reduced the number of authorized aircraft (Unit Equipment, or UE, in that era; Primary Authorized Aircraft, or PAA, in later years) to 15 for each of the 6 ANG F-106 squadrons, 13 F-106As, and 2 F-106Bs. Michigan and New Jersey each gave up some of their vertical-tape jets to Fresno and Jacksonville, while Montana and Massachusetts each transferred a few round-dial airplanes to ADC's 84th FIS at Castle, freeing up a few more vertical-tape birds for the two new Guard units. The ANG F-106 units stayed at the 15-aircraft level until 1981 when the 84th FIS gave up its F-106s and switched to the air defense adversary mission with T-33s.

The 1950s fire station and 1930s hangars leave no doubt that this is the main ramp at Selfridge ANGB. The MD-3M power cart is running, and from the intake covers, it appears as if this Michigan Six is about to undergo an engine run. F-106 ramps were always full of AGE.

The missing aircraft shelter was a fixture for many years at Selfridge Field. Note the rectangles painted on the ramp indicating placement for the Falcon missile coffins and other equipment. (Spering/AIR)

This Six Pack jet is on takeoff roll at Selfridge 29 April 1978.

144th Fighter-Interceptor Wing
194th Fighter-Interceptor Squadron

The last two units to receive F-106s were the 194th FIS of the California ANG and the 159th FIS at Jacksonville. Both units converted nearly simultaneously during May 1974. Flying out of Fresno the 194th competed in two William Tell meets, taking first place in 1980 and fourth in 1982 before converting to the F-4 in 1983–1984.

At first, the only marking applied to the F-106s was the two-digit NORAD call-sign number, much like the 194th had used on its camouflaged F-102s. By 1976, the vertical tails were painted like the California state flag: white overall, a red stripe across the bottom of the fin with "CALIFORNIA" in black lettering, and a bear in the middle of the tail above the tail numbers. In 1982, the state flag tail gave way to a simple horizontal blue stripe high on the fin, again with "CALIFORNIA" in the stripe. They applied the squadron emblem to the right side of the fin and then put the TAC emblem on the left side, becoming the only Guard F-106 unit to display that insignia.

The unit lost one jet (S/N 58-0777) in the Pacific Ocean on 18 July 1979 and began converting to the F-4D Phantom during the fourth quarter of 1983. Since most of their Sixes were not due for depot maintenance, they were redistributed among the remaining Six units. The last jet to leave was S/N 58-0774, which departed on 19 January 1984, but the unit did keep S/N 59-0146 for display purposes.

Descending into the Southern California haze, this four-ship formation from the California ANG has the boards out to keep from accelerating above the 250-knot low-altitude speed limit in May 1978.

SAC B-52s frequently trained with interceptor units. May 1978.

A plain blue band and TAC badge were the final markings of the 194th FIS. Compare the spine of this A model with the Montana F-106B parked behind. Tyndall, 23 October 1982.

125th Fighter-Interceptor Group
159th Fighter-Interceptor Squadron

Gaining their first F-106 on 29 May 1974, the 159th conversion from the F-102 was rapid. In William Tell 1976, the unit finished fourth during their only appearance as competitors. For William Tell 1986, they painted their aircraft in several unique paint schemes to serve as targets and range support aircraft.

The unit began converting to the F-16A during the first quarter of 1987 and received their new jets from the 50 TFW at Hahn. On 23 March 1987 they marked the departure of their last F-106, as S/N 57-2509 left to become a part of the B-1B bomber chase program at Palmdale, California.

There were 43 F-106s assigned to the Florida unit with 2 losses. Unit markings consisted of a blue tail band outlined in white, with a white lightning flash inside the band. Individual aircraft numbers were carried on both the nose and tail.

Florida ANG F-106A was captured while on takeoff roll in May 1987. The conical camber applied to the leading edge of the wing is very evident here. (Alec Fushi)

Returning to Jacksonville after an intercept mission. Florida jets carried the group badge on their fins and the ANG badge on their external fuel tanks. (Don Spering/AIR)

Chapter Twenty

TYNDALL AND F-106 MARKINGS

Making a photo flyby of Panama City, Florida, this bus was the personal mount of ADWC Commander Gen. James Price. It shows off the markings he designed for the unit when he was assigned there in 1968. The hump added to the spine when the aerial refueling modification was added is very evident here. (USAF)

The story of Tyndall AFB, Florida, deserves a book in its own right. The interceptor equivalent to TAC's Nellis, Tyndall hosted all formalized F-106 training, including both transition and the Interceptor Weapons School (Fighter Weapons School equivalent). Tyndall was the home of the Air Defense Weapons Center, the longtime host of the biennial William Tell weapons meets, Combat Pike and Combat Archer live-fire exercises, and Copper Flag air defense exercises.

With a huge airspace over the Gulf of Mexico that was suitable for all types of live-fire missile testing, the history of Tyndall was joined with the history of the F-106 from the arrival of the first F-106A (S/N 58-0778) on 26 October 1959 until the last two F-106Bs (S/N 58-0900 and S/N 58-0902) departed on 9 April 1984. There were 79 F-106s assigned to units based at Tyndall over the years, and 13 were lost to accidents.

The following Tyndall units were involved with the F-106 over the years: 73rd Air Division, Air Defense Weapons Center, 4756th Air Defense Wing, 4756th Air Defense Group, 4756th Air Defense Squadron (weapons), 4756th Combat Crew Training Squadron, USAF Interceptor Weapons School (IWS), 4750th Test Squadron, 475th Test Squadron, Southern Air Defense Scramble Section (SADASS, aka the Dixie Darts) 319th Fighter-Interceptor Training

Squadron, 2nd Fighter-Interceptor Training Squadron, 325th Fighter Weapons Wing, 325th Tactical Training Wing, 475th Weapons Evaluation Group, 82nd Tactical Air Target Squadron, and 83rd Fighter Weapons Squadron (QF-106 drones).

All F-106 squadrons had to deploy to Tyndall at least annually to participate in Combat Pike exercises. As a nuclear-capable aircraft, each individual F-106 had to live fire an ATR-2 at least once a year to recertify the aircraft's nuclear capability. This Weapons System Evaluation Program (WSEP) gave units two weeks at Tyndall to shoot both the Genie and Falcons against the BQM-34A/F Firebee drones and BOMARC missiles.

As the home of the ADC's 4750th (later, 475th) Test Squadron, many "one of a kind" modifications to the F-106s were tried out. Two of the most interesting were the Simple High Accuracy Guidance (SHAG) project and Project Spike. Running in the 1970s, the SHAG project involved modifying an F-106A (S/N 58-0778) to carry missile launchers on the wing pylons (replacing the external fuel tanks) and developing one of the first helmet-mounted sights. Wearing one of the Honeywell-developed helmet sights, the pilot could launch either modified radar-guided AIM-26B or IR-guided AIM-4D Falcon missiles off boresight, which meant that he could simply turn his head and look at the target without having to maneuver the

Assigned to the 4756th Test Squadron, this F-106B was caught on the Pete Field ramp on 7 October 1960. (Burgess via St. Louis Air and Space Museum)

Displaying the markings of the 73rd AD on its tail, -783 sits on the Tyndall ramp in about 1964. (Via Isham)

At Tyndall 22 September 1972. (MacSorley)

Six to point at it. The guidance package in the missiles used data processed by the MA-1 in the aircraft and sent via radio to the missiles.

ADC once again led the way with Project Spike. This 1971 project was the second attempt to put an anti-satellite missile on an aircraft. An AGM-78 Standard Anti-Radiation Missile (ARM) was modified to carry a kinetic-kill homing vehicle. Test flights usually saw the missile carried under the right wing. Although no live tests were carried out and the project was not pursued, it laid the groundwork for the later F-15–launched the Anti-Satellite Weapon (ASAT) program.

Far too many other test programs were carried out at Tyndall to be able to list them all here, but several paint schemes were evaluated over the years to see what might be an effective camouflage color at altitude. Over the years, Sixes were seen painted gloss white, light pink, and shades of light blue. None of these were ever adopted for the fleet, and all operational jets were always painted FS 16473 gloss Aircraft Gray, which was commonly known as ADC gray. One final test worthy of mention is the one F-106B modified to use electroluminescent "tape" formation lights, which was seen at Tyndall in late 1978.

When other forces canceled due to weather, the air defenders kept flying. As he pulls the chocks prior to launch, the crew chief is hoping that this training mission taxies away quickly and he can get indoors before the cloudburst arrives. Tyndall AFB, Florida, in August 1975. The markings are typical for all units during the Plain-Jane era.

On a training mission out of Tyndall in November 1978, this ADWC Six has successfully intercepted an uncooperative T-33 target at low altitude, over land. The T-bird was loaded with chaff and ECM, and the student in the Six had to work hard for this "Mission Accomplished."

Displayed inside a hangar at Tyndall alongside a Ryan Firebee drone, this Six was the test bed for the gun modification. The two small air scoops, one below the crew name block on the forward fuselage and the other just aft of the beacon on the upper fuselage, were replaced by NACA scoops on the weapons bay doors for the fleet modification. The jet also has an early z-axis yaw vane mounted in front of the UHF antenna below the nose. (USAF)

Seen here in 1971 carrying an inert AGM-78 Standard Arm modified for Project SPIKE anti-satellite tests, this Six was also the prototype for the Vulcan cannon modification. (USAF)

SHAG was another test program run at Tyndall during the 1970s. AIM-26 Falcons were modified for use with a Honeywell-developed helmet-mounted sight. Guidance data was sent via the aircraft to the missile. Forty years later, a similar system is now operational on virtually all U.S. fighters. A camera pod is carried under the left wing. (USAF via Isham)

Undergoing another very mundane, but rarely documented procedure, this bus undergoes some corrosion control, a fancy way of saying it is getting washed, at Tyndall in December 1978. However, it is the presence of the electroluminescent "tape" formation lights that caused the photographer to record the scene. This Six seems to have been the only one to receive this modification.

Into Storage

Although Tyndall-based units began transitioning to the F-15 in December 1983, the first Sixes had already departed Tyndall for storage in April of that year. The last transition course for the F-106, class 84CBT, graduated from training on 6 April 1984, and this marked the end of formal F-106 training at Tyndall. That was also the date the last F-106s departed the Florida base enroute to Davis-Monthan. F-106B S/N 58-0900 was the last Six to leave Tyndall.

The very first F-106 retired to AMARC was S/N 59-0116 from the 48th FIS, arriving on 12 January 1982. That and the second aircraft, S/N 59-0122, also from the 48th, were virtually the only 2 Delta Darts that arrived for storage with their squadron markings painted out. Most of the early retirees were jets that were out of time and needed expensive depot maintenance. For the remainder of 1982, only 2 more Sixes went to the boneyard, both from the 49th FIS, and none followed until March 1983. During that year, 23 jets were retired. The years 1984 and 1985 each saw another 37 Sixes arriving at the boneyard. Only 6 went into storage in 1986, but 60 were sent to the desert in 1987, and the final 27 were sent in 1988.

F-106 Unit Markings, Bicentennials and Boss Birds

Throughout the nearly 30 years that the Six flew in active service, several themes were evident in the unit markings. Since interceptor squadrons were usually based alone and frequently in isolated northern areas, ADC went to great lengths to improve squadron morale and *esprit de corps*. Assigning squadron numbers that had significant historical honors and allowing them great license to decorate their aircraft were two ways to accomplish that. Since the command was defending North America, all of the interceptors remained over friendly territory, and there was little need to disguise or subdue the markings painted on the aircraft; indeed, the signature orange flight suits that ADC crews wore were designed to be as visible as possible to assist in rescue should they have to eject in remote areas. The four basic themes of markings were: the "big badge," Air Division–specific markings, the Plain Jane era, and individual unit designs.

Several of the early Delta Dart units converted from the F-102 and simply carried over their previous markings. In the cases of the 456th FIS, 95th FIS, 498th FIS, and to some extent, the 48th FIS, this amounted to applying a large squadron badge to both sides of the vertical fin. The 498th kept the brick red-orange rudders of their earlier jets and frequently added a gloss-black fin cap as well. The 48th came late to the "big badge" party, starting with smaller squadron badges and only making the change around late 1964. By 1960, ADC regulation 66-23 stipulated that the ADC badge be placed on the right side of the vertical fin, but until the mid-1960s this was widely ignored; the 95th FIS in particular kept its squadron insignia on both sides of the fin through at least 1965.

A few higher echelons of command went one step further and designed common markings for all of the interceptor squadrons within their area of responsibility. The 28th Air Division, which generally covered California; the 10th Air Force, which covered the Northern Tier; and the 30th Air Division, which was responsible for Michigan and the upper Midwest, all came up with unique designs. The 28th AD added horizontal red, white, and blue bands to the lower portions of the interceptor tails and placed their Air Division patch inside it on both sides of the fin. Other than that, each squadron could decorate their aircraft as they chose.

On the ramp at Andrews in May 1964, here is an example of a large squadron badge, in this case the 48th FIS. (Ron Picciani Collection)

All units within the 10th Air Force placed a colored alar on the fin; each squadron was assigned its own color combination. For example, the 5th FIS used a yellow alar with a black or insignia blue outline, while the 11th FIS, after transferring from the 30th AD, used a red alar with a black outline.

The 30th AD came up with some of the most striking markings ever applied to the interceptor force. Alternating red and white horizontal bands were applied to both sides of the tail, broken in the middle by a blue V. Beyond that, each unit was free to embellish or alter the design to their taste.

For example, the 438th did not bring the bands all the way to the leading edge of the fin, instead stopping them a few inches back. The 11th FIS used roughly half the number of bands the other units did. The 94th FIS put a large "Hat in the Ring" badge on both sides of the tail, while their sister unit, the 71st, placed the squadron badge on the nose just behind the radome. At least some of the 1st Fighter Wing Sixes were seen with 30th AD badges inside the V on the left side of their tails during 1962.

When the Air Division boundaries were realigned in late 1963 or early 1964, some units transitioned to new divisions. The 11th at Duluth transferred from the 30th AD to the 10th Air Force and eventually switched markings from the red, white, and blue to the red alar. Most of the units within the old 30th AD then came under the 34th AD. Possibly as a result of a 34th AD edict, virtually all units removed their old markings and never applied anything beyond a squadron or wing badge and ADC insignia on the tails for the next four years.

When they were finally allowed to apply new markings, the 94th FIS tried out at least three designs before settling on one, while the 438th went to the black and white alars, which resembled a stylized duck. The 456th FIS responded to an Air Division boundary

This 329th FIS Six displays the thin horizontal red, white, and blue stripes with the 28th Air Division badge inside. The early main wheels are also very evident here. This shot was taken in February 1967. (Via Bert Kinzey/Detail & Scale)

Caught in December 1969, this Six from the 71st FIS shows off a typical 10th Air Force–style alar marking, in this case medium blue with a thin black outline. The serial numbers on the tail are the later style, with a thin surround of the Aircraft Gray paint to set them off. (Jack Morris)

It is no surprise that the Squadron Commander's jet for the 456th FIS would be S/N 57-2456. Seen at Elmendorf on 18 March 1969, the new blue and yellow tail markings and commander's stripes stand out. That is an air conditioning hose plugged in below the air intake. All those tubes in the avionics generated an immense amount of heat, and even in Alaska, cooling air had to be supplied anytime radar work was being done. The MC-11 high-pressure air cart below the wing tip was used to start the jet. (Norman E. Taylor)

change in mid-1967 by replacing their black and yellow tail markings with even larger medium blue and yellow ones.

Remaining units were free to design their own markings and every one of them did. As the first F-106 unit, the 539th FIS initially designed a marking that consisted of an insignia blue Delta wing with a yellow fuselage and afterburner. The squadron badge was carried inside this design on both sides of the fin until the regulation change in 1963, at which time the ADC badge replaced the squadron badge on the right side. A small rectangle of color was carried on the lower rudder of some of the jets, to indicate its maintenance flight. Shortly before they were deactivated, the unit designed new markings, which consisted of a very large medium-blue lightning bolt with a yellow outline.

A late-1973 decision by the ADC Vice Commander, Lt Gen. Royal N. Baker, brought an abrupt end to the color. The official reason given was that it was to save money and manpower. The unofficial reason is that at least one high-ranking SAC general reportedly said, "If my units cannot have individual paint on their aircraft, nobody can have individual paint schemes." Given the gaudy F-86 that Gen. Baker flew during the Korean conflict, my guess is the latter one was the real cause for the change.

In any case, all of the individualized paint was removed from the interceptor fleet, leaving nothing but a small squadron badge on the left and a small ADC badge on the right. This was also probably the reason that the first ANG units that transitioned to the F-106 started out with nothing more than a small, colored horizontal band on their tails, a marking that would have been right at home on a TAC F-100.

Within a couple of years, though, the Guard units began painting some very colorful markings. The Six Pack from the Michigan ANG designed and painted a striking set of black and yellow markings. The fact that it took several days to hand cut and apply the masks, and additional time to paint the tails, was unimportant; the unit was proud of their jets and more than happy to take the time to show them off.

The units in Florida and California also responded with very attractive schemes. The blue and white tails of the Jacksonville-based unit and the stylized California state flag applied to the tails of the Fresno unit left no doubt who owned those jets. Montana and Massachusetts eventually redesigned their markings into far more attractive and distinctive ones as well. For the active-duty fleet, the arrival of the American Bicentennial brought the Plain Jane period to an end.

As the prohibition against color was slowly lifted, units started experimenting with markings. Some simply returned to their old marks, possibly with minor alterations, such as the 5th FIS. Some, such as the 48th FIS, designed completely new markings, but three units decided to show their patriotism by painting one of their aircraft into a showpiece. The 318th painted S/N 58-0776 into *Freedom Bird* and the 49th FIS painted S/N 59-0076 into *Spirit of '76*. That particular aircraft sported at least three variations of bicentennial markings, with the Eagle tail markings originally staying in green and white. They were later repainted into red and

In perfect position on the boom, this is the 49th FIS Bicentennial jet in its final markings, with the red lightning bolt and rudder stripes. (USAF via Isham)

The earlier Bicentennial markings of the 49th FIS retained the original colors for the squadron markings. A 13-star flag was carried on this side, while a 50-star flag was carried on the right. (Spering/AIR)

Carrying a Freedom Bird logo on the external fuel tanks, and a Spirit of '76 on the tail, the 318th showed their Bicentennial spirit on S/N 58-0776. The large artwork on the fin made it necessary to move the serial number to a nonstandard location. Note the pilot's helmet resting on the canopy rail. (Spering/AIR)

Seen here on 13 June 1976, far and away the gaudiest Bicentennial celebration aircraft was the City of Jacksonville, which was assigned to the 159th FIS of the Florida ANG. In addition to the upper colors, the lower fuselage and wings were painted with wide red and white stripes. (Ray Leader/ Flightleader)

white, and for a short period the aft fuselage was adorned with a large painted logo as well. Florida took it to extremes, however, with their *City of Jacksonville*. The entire aircraft was painted gloss white, with a blue nose that trailed up and back along the spine to blend into the tail. White stars were painted inside this area. The remainder of the tail was red and white and the entire underside of the jet was painted with wide red stripes that ran from front to back.

Through the years, pitot booms were frequently painted in squadron colors in various forms of stripes and spirals, and external fuel tank markings were common. Although some units did not bother, many took the time to design striking markings. Some of the earliest designs were on the subsonic tanks of the Sixes of the 94th FIS; they carried a yellow nose that slimmed down into a horizontal stripe.

Under the influence of Col. James Price, in 1968 the 498th FIS designed some of the flashiest external tank markings. After the unit was redesignated, the 84th FIS carried on the tradition, although somewhat subdued from the original design. When Col. Price transferred to Tyndall, he promptly redesigned both the aircraft and external tank markings. When he was reassigned to command the 21st NORAD Region, he had one of the 49th FIS jets painted as his "commander's jet" as well.

Several units applied commander's striping to some of their aircraft over the years. Traditionally, one stripe was assigned to a Flight Commander's aircraft, two stripes indicated the Squadron Operations Officer, three stripes designated the Squadron Commander's jet, and four stripes meant a Senior Commander. Two of the first jets marked with command stripes were S/N 59-0148, which was marked with three bands for Lt. Col. Price, commander of the 456th FIS, for the 1961 William Tell weapons meet; and S/N 57-0231, marked in an unusual set of diagonal red and white stripes on the rear fuselage for squadron commander Lt. Col. Utterback in about 1962.

The 11th FIS Squadron Commander's jet displays a very unusual form of command striping in this 16 May 1965 view. Both the location and presentation of the stripes are unique. The word "UTTERBACK" on the tail is the commander's last name. The 11th was unusual in using fewer horizontal stripes on the tails than other units within the 30th Air Division. (Via Isham)

While the 11th FIS bird was a one-off, several Darts from the 456th received a varying number of command bands through the years. No other units used them until Col. Price took the reins at Tyndall. Arriving there in 1968, the F-106B assigned as CINCNORAD's personal mount received command markings. Following ADWC commanders continued the tradition with varying numbers of aircraft. The 5th FIS painted one of their jets in a three-colored command band in the mid-1970s, and then joined the 87th and 49th FISs in the 1980s by decorating several of their aircraft. The only ANG unit that applied command stripes was Montana.

El Jefe. You are not left wondering who owns this particular Six; it belongs to the commander of the 21st NORAD Region. Less than two weeks after this photo was taken, Maj Gen. James L. Price lost his life in this jet after taking a lightning strike shortly after takeoff from Griffiss AFB. Shortly thereafter, the Six fleet finally received lightning protection. The "Blood Priority" never fails. (Jack Morris photo 3 March 1973)

One of the very few ANG Sixes to receive command stripes, this Montana bird not only has stripes, but the NORAD numbers are painted in metallic blue with white outlines. Photo taken 19 June 1982. (Brian Rogers)

When TAC took over the assets of ADC, the colorful squadron markings were allowed to remain, but the TAC badge was placed on both sides of the tail. Squadron badges usually migrated to the left side of the nose, and the ADTAC badge began to appear on the right nose of the jet. Within the Air Guard, only the California unit changed their markings, replacing their distinctive red and white tails with a very plain medium-blue band across the tail. They were also the only Guard interceptor unit to display the TAC badge on their aircraft. By the time ADTAC became the First Air Force, the 49th FIS was the only active-duty F-106 squadron left in existence, and thus they became the only one to display the 1st Air Force badge on the right nose of their Sixes.

Nose art was seen sporadically over the years. The 11th FIS originated it on the Delta Dart fleet, and between 1960 and 1962 every one of their jets was adorned with an individual design. The practice fell out of favor until the 87th FIS put nose art on the jet they sent to William Tell 1972. The Michigan Six Pack followed suit shortly thereafter with a few of their aircraft receiving artwork. The 48th FIS later painted a few of their jets with variations of the well-known Tazlanglian Devil design developed by Dick Stultz.

The New Jersey ANG used one of their F-106Bs to set a new FAI world speed record between Wright-Patterson and Kitty Hawk, North Carolina, the location where the Wright Brothers made the first powered aircraft flight. This aircraft was painted with special nose art to commemorate the event. This same jet was used to fly astronaut Gordon Cooper from Edwards to the F-106 retirement ceremony in New Jersey. His name was added below the rear cockpit, while the Faith 7 name of his space capsule was painted on the nose-gear door.

The unit also decorated one of their F-106As in a salute to the Six. Artist and photographer Don Spering and several assistants designed

The entire squadron of the 11th FIS is lined up and ready to go for a mass launch and flyby for departing Sector Commander Brig Gen. Harrison R. Thyng in July 1963. All of the squadron jets carried nose art between 1960 and 1963. The tail of -460 shows how the crew names were applied to the jets. (USAF)

and painted historical references to the entire aircraft, and all of the unit was allowed to sign their names in dedicated areas on the fuselage. As the Six neared retirement, the depot at McClellan allowed participants in their departure ceremony to use black markers to sign their names to the final Six to roll out of depot maintenance.

Unlike most aircraft sent to the desert boneyard at Davis-Monthan, virtually all of the Six units left their squadron markings on the jets rather than painting over them. When the Sixes were pulled out and sent to the drone program, many traces of their earlier markings remained. The Six went out with style.

A little more than a year from their deactivation, this 49th FIS Six shows off the new 1st Air Force badge on its nose as it taxies in to parking at Selfridge ANGB, Michigan, in June 1986. At this point, carriage of the gun was standard.

Chapter Twenty-One

EXERCISES AND COMPETITIONS

As the rocket cleared the belly of the jet, a lanyard attached to the jet pulled out of a plug, which caused motor ignition. The rocket exhaust burned through nylon cords across the back of the rocket, which caused the fins to extend. An accelerometer allowed the timing signal to detonate the warhead. Simple and unstoppable. A Genie launch in a nutshell. (USAF).

Over the years, F-106 squadrons participated in many events, ranging from the biannual William Tell weapons meets to Flag exercises, Air Division exercises, and others. This chapter is only a brief overview of activities the Six fleet was involved with.

William Tell

At the top of any list recounting F-106 participation in exercises is, undoubtedly, the bi-annual USAF Worldwide Air-to-Air Weapons Meet, more commonly known as William Tell. The first appearance of an F-106 on the ramp at Tyndall was as a display during the 1959 meet. The competitions included more than just missile and rocket firing over the Gulf. Units were judged on the appearance of their aircraft, and personnel and teams went to great lengths to look good.

A Weapons Load competition was held to see which team could complete a weapons load in the shortest amount of time while complying with all checklist items. Inspectors watched like hawks while

the clock counted off seconds. In addition, many of the profiles were handled like actual wartime scrambles, with the crews "cocking" their aircraft and placing them on alert status and then waiting in the flight-line shacks for the scramble phone to ring.

By the 1961 meet, four F-106 units had participated in the competition. In those days, there was no overall champion; instead winners from each category were named. The honor of winning the first F-106 competition in William Tell went to the 456th FIS. Since the Genie was considered the primary weapon for the F-106, three out of the four firing profiles used the MB-1T rocket. The fourth profile was flown at night and used an IR-guided Falcon. Targets were Q-2C Firebee drones, and the top F-106 weapons load team was the 456th FIS.

Of the remaining F-106 teams, the 498th FIS placed second, the 539th FIS placed third, and the 11th FIS came in on the bottom. But even losing in the competition still left a unit a leg up on other units. If your unit was selected for the competition, the other guys stayed home to watch.

A subsonic BQM-34A Firebee drone is displayed in front of the prototype gun-modified F-106A, while its supersonic cousin, the BQM-34F, and a TDU fiberglass towed target are behind. This first Six gun has two small air scoops that were replaced by NACA scoops in the weapons bay doors for the production version. (Via Don Spering/AIR)

Far offshore, this EB-57B from the Vermont ANG has gotten outside of radar coverage and will soon start its "faker" run, simulating a possibly hostile intruder. Two ALE-2 chaff tanks under the wings augment the onboard electronic jammers. Both ground-based and interceptor radars could be jammed simultaneously.

Every interceptor squadron had two or three T-33s assigned as target support aircraft. Unless a radar reflector was hung on the lower fuselage, their small radar cross section made them very difficult targets. While not supersonic, they could reach 505 KIAS, or Mach 0.8. This T-bird from the New Jersey ANG has an ECM pod loaded under the left wing, and probably a chaff tank hung on the right side. The Sixes are in the early markings of the 177th FIS. (Don Spering/AIR)

The 11th FIS Squadron Commander's jet on the ramp at Tyndall during William Tell 1963. A large green shamrock decorates the nose. In the background are aircraft of the 456th FIS. (USAF via Isham)

Spectators are already on the ramp as this 71st FIS Six parks at Bradley Field, Connecticut, on 16 May 1965. It has already been painted up with the special William Tell 1965 paint scheme worn by the five participating jets. Checkers are medium blue and white with a red apple, yellow arrow, and black feathers and point. (Tom Hildreth)

FIS, which placed second; the 48th FIS, which placed third; and the previous winners, the 456th FIS, which finished in fourth place.

Many changes were instituted for the 1965 William Tell competition, as the Six had matured greatly over the intervening years. This was the first competition in which the Six used the newly upgraded radars, which featured the rapid-tune magnetron and parametric amplifier. The interceptors launched ATR-2A Genies and both the radar-guided and infrared-guided AIM-4F/G Falcon missiles.

For the first time, frontal attacks were made against drone targets using the Falcons, and new targets appeared in the form of EB-57 electronic jammers (at medium altitudes) and TDU-9B towed targets (at low altitudes). New tactics also entered the mix and the two-minute alert scramble was also introduced instead of units meeting a pre-planned takeoff time. Once again, four F-106 units participated, and this time the 71st FIS based at Selfridge won the overall category, as well as the Top Load Crew and Top Weapons Control Team honors. Coming in second was the 5th FIS out of Minot and the 456th and 318th FISs placed third and fourth, respectively.

For the 1963 William Tell competition, some new teams were on the ramp and a new winner was crowned. Although flying the same profiles as the previous meet, a new category of competition was added, that of the best Weapons Control Team, thus allowing the GCI controllers that normally worked with each competing team to be part of the competition as well. The Green Dragons of the 318th FIS won the F-106 category going away, winning both the Top F-106 Load Team competition, the Top F-106 Weapons Control Team competition, and outscoring the other interceptors by a wide margin in the flying. Also competing that year were the 11th

After a five-year hiatus due to the war in SEA, a very austere meet was held in 1970. The big change for this event was that, rather than being a carefully controlled test setup, firing parameters were not absolutely dictated. F-106 teams competed in a GCI-controlled environment using TDDL (datalink) communications.

Each team was scheduled for three live-firing missions conducted during daylight hours and one ECM mission conducted at night. All four team aircraft were charged with a firing attempt for each mission. Points were awarded for making assigned takeoff and recovery times and for the use of proper intercept control procedures. Mission profiles now began emphasizing Falcon employment, and only one Genie launch was conducted.

Once again, the 71st FIS took home top honors. They also won the Top Maintenance award, the 84th FIS took home the trophies for Top Load Crew and Top GCI controllers, and the 318th FIS placed third.

A larger event was held in 1972, with five F-106 teams competing. Once again, four intercept profiles were flown, with only minor changes from the 1970 event. When the dust settled, the 460th FIS was the overall F-106–category winner. The 318th had the Top Controller Team and also won the Load competition but placed fourth overall. The 2nd FIS, in their swan song before being deactivated, took second place, with the 87th FIS third, the 5th FIS fourth, and 95th FIS at the bottom of the leader board. Like the 2nd FIS, the 95th FIS was also in the process of being deactivated and had already removed all their squadron markings from their aircraft prior to passing them to the New Jersey Air National Guard and had to quickly design and repaint the five jets that they sent to the meet.

The first year that an Air National Guard F-106 unit participated was in 1974, and the 120th FIG from Montana promptly took home the honors, leading the second-place 49th FIS by a little over 300 points. Only three F-106 teams competed this year as the Air Defense fleet continued to shrink. The 318th was the third team.

The 120th FIG repeated their victory in the 1976 William Tell meet flying against the 49th FIS from Griffiss, the 87th FIS out of K. I. Sawyer, and the 125th FIG out of Jacksonville.

The four teams participating in William Tell 1978 were split evenly between active duty and the Air National Guard in the final competition hosted by the ADC. This time around, the 49th FIS emerged victorious, with the 120th FIG from Montana placing second, the 48th FIS from Langley placing third, and newcomers 102nd FIW from Otis placing fourth. The competition profiles were altered to be much more challenging. Automatic Identification System (AIS) scoring pods made their first appearance, as did the supersonic Firebee drone, and for the first time, PQM-102 drones were used as targets.

With the demise of ADC as a flying command, 1980 saw the William Tell meet hosted for the first time by TAC. Award categories were expanded and

Any military veteran alive will recognize this scene. It is called "hurry up and wait." Seen on the ramp at Tyndall during a William Tell meet, the pilot rates a folding lawn chair while the maintenance folks rest on the ramp in front of this Montana ANG Six. A rarely seen sun screen has been placed on the glare shield. (USAF via Isham)

the F-106–category winner was the 144th FIW based at Fresno. The Massachusetts Guard moved up a notch, taking second place, while the active-duty squadrons, the 5th FIS and 49th FIS, placed third and fourth, respectively.

The 1982 competition brought a measure of revenge for the ADTAC units, with the 49th FIS taking the F-106–category honors over the 120th FIG, 318th FIS, and 144th FIW. A new profile was added to the competition for the gun-equipped units.

In 1984, the last year the F-106 participated as a fighter-interceptor, three units were selected to participate. The 177th FIG, home-based at Atlantic City won the final event, taking home the Top F-106 team and Top Maintenance awards. The 87th FIS took home the Top Weapons Controller Team and Top Load Team awards, with the 102nd FIW from Otis, rounding out the field.

For competition profiles, all of the old targets were gone, replaced by QF-100 drones and a towed gunnery target. The profiles themselves were also far different from those faced by crews in the early days. With the retirement of the Genie rocket, gone were the high-altitude fly-up/snap-up profiles.

For this event, Profiles I and II were live-fire, two-ship element attacks against a maneuvering QF-100. The interceptors launched in pairs at a scheduled time to a CAP, each with one radar and one IR missile; at the CAP the flight lead declared who would shoot which. Tactical lead fired the radar missile in a front cutoff (Profile I) and the wingman then converted to a stern IR shot (Profile II). The shooters reversed roles for the next mission.

Profile III was a cold mission using WSEMs. A two-ship element was scrambled against unknown targets. They had to identify the target and kill it in minimum time on the ACMI range.

Profile IV was another cold mission using WSEMs. This time it was a four-ship area defense against a mass raid employing ECM, chaff, and evasion. The profile called for a total of 12 targets consisting of a combination of F-106, T-33, B-52, and F-111.

Profile V was the gun profile. A TAC F-4 unit towed a low-cost tow target (LCTT) equipped with the DSQ-40 electronic bullet scoring system. Shooters were loaded with 300 rounds of 20mm.

Other Exercises and OPLANS

The F-106 fleet was an integral part of many operational plans, most of which were designed to reinforce the defensive shield on the southern perimeter of the country. College Tap would have taken up to 24 Sixes from the training units at Tyndall and used them operationally; College Sand was an alert detachment at Homestead, usually manned by the 48th FIS. Although the original intent of that plan may have been directed toward Cuba, most of the scrambles were on drug-running aircraft from the Caribbean.

College South was another OPLAN designed to defend against any incursions by Cuban aerial forces; College Key, which placed interceptors at Key West had the same mission. College Green, on the other hand, was designed to protect the installations in Greenland from Soviet harassment or attack. With the exception of

With the bleak topography of the Reykjanes Peninsula in the background, this 87th FIS Six is a long way from home. Seen here in April 1978, the unit was assisting the 57th FIS while the latter unit converted from the F-4C to the F-4E. The IRST ball was not normally left extended while the jet was parked. (Photo by Baldur Sveinsson)

With the aircraft shelters of the 57th FIS and TDY sub hunting navy P-3 Orions in the background, this 87th FIS Six has just gotten airborne on the north-south runway at Keflavik, Iceland, on 1 May 1978. The 87th deployed half a dozen Sixes to help out while the 57th converted from the F-4C to the F-4E. (Photo by Baldur Sveinsson)

Although of poor quality, this is one of the few photos showing an 87th FIS F-106 intercepting a TU-95 Bear bomber while deployed to Keflavik, Iceland, in April 1978. (USAF photo via Isham)

College Sand, none of these OPLANS were ever activated except on a short-term test basis, if then.

In the spring of 1974, the 318th FIS deployed to Howard in support of Black Hawk '74, a joint task force exercise designed to evaluate the air defense capability of the Panama Canal Zone. The second Six squadron to cross the Atlantic Ocean was the 5th FIS when they deployed from Minot to Hahn to take part in exercise Cold Fire '75. In April 1978, the 87th FIS deployed from upper Michigan to Keflavik to help cover alert duties while the Black Knights of the 57th FIS converted from the F-4C version of the Phantom to the E model. Several TU-95 Bear bomber intercepts were accomplished while the Red Bulls were flying from "the rock."

Beginning with Red Flag exercise 76-02, which began on 28 February 1976, F-106 units participated in a total of 28 Red Flag and Green Flag exercises, which were held at Nellis. Only one unit participated at a time and the interceptors were always part of the "red" forces. The last two units to participate were the only two Air National Guard F-106 units to participate: the 119th FIS from New Jersey and the 186th FIS out of Great Falls, Montana. They were present for Red Flag 86-02 and 87-01, the latter of which finished on 22 November 1986.

Six units also participated in three Maple Flag exercises, which were held at CFB Cold Lake Alberta, Canada. The 87th FIS attended exercise 02-79; the 318th was there for exercise 05-80; and the 84th FIS rounded out the trio, participating in exercise 06-81, which was held in October.

In 1982, ADTAC came up with the idea of an Air Defense Flag exercise, which became known as Copper Flag. It was held at Tyndall and a test

of the concept was held using ADWC assets in April 1982. After refining the concept somewhat, the first official Copper Flag, 83-1, was held starting 21 February 1983 with the 5th FIS and 194th FIS being part of the "blue" forces.

As night fell over the Gulf of Mexico, Goat Hill (the portion of the Tyndall flight line devoted to parking deployed units) came alive as the squadrons scrambled to meet the threat over the Gulf. Night, weather, and ECM were the "meat and potatoes" of the exercise, and targets included everything from T-33s running lights out at 500 feet and acting as cruise missiles, to Voodoos and Sixes flying at Mach 2 at 50,000 feet and above. The Canadian Armed Forces deployed their Bombardier Challenger jamming platforms.

The author well remembers acting as Supervisor of Flying for the Blue Force one evening and watching the local 11 p.m. TV weathercast. A radar picture was on screen and the entire operating area over the Gulf of Mexico was one solid shade of gray, with various loops and patterns around the edges. It was all radar reflections off the airborne chaff drifting downward. The weathercaster's words were something to the effect of, "Don't worry folks, that's not a hurricane; it's just the air force out playing in the Gulf tonight."

Frequent periods of autonomous operation were also part of the scenario, during which time the GCI controllers simply stopped transmitting target information, and it was then up to the interceptor forces to organize themselves to cover their assigned lanes and find any targets on their own.

Ten Copper Flag exercises were held before the event was canceled and two F-106 units were usually in attendance as "blue" forces, while the Tyndall-based 325th FWW also provided F-106 targets for the "red" force on three occasions. The final Copper Flag, 86-1, ended 14 December 1985.

The midday lull during a Red Flag exercise at Nellis. The jets are being turned while the morning aircrews debrief the mission and the afternoon crews get ready to launch. Aug 1978.

One additional exercise in which F-106 units participated was the annual Amalgam Brave event that was held between 1980 and 1986 at the NATO low-level training base at Goose Bay, Labrador. Sponsored by the Canada East NORAD region, one deploying unit acted as the host and helped coordinate which units would attend as either "blue" or "red" air. These were primarily low-altitude training events, usually with significant ECM support. Air refueling units, AWACS, and even the U.S. Navy Big Crow jamming platform participated, as well as U.S. Navy Carrier Air Wings doing their final workups prior to deploying to a carrier. In addition to deployed ANG A-7D and RF-4C units, the German Air Force R/F-4, RAF Vulcan bombers, and Tornado units deployed to Goose also acted as "red" air. One Canadian Armed Forces F-101B Voodoo unit was always present, as well.

Although records for the earlier events are missing, the 101st and 119th FISs of the Massachusetts and New Jersey ANG attended in June 1983, the 5th and 87th FISs deployed in June 1984, and the 159th FIS of the Florida ANG participated in the June 1985 event. One additional deployed Amalgam Brave was conducted between 10 and 18 May 1987 when seven F-106s of the 101st FIS, Massachusetts ANG, participated in an event based at Elmendorf.

With a wave for the photographer, this 5th FIS Six taxies out for an Amalgam Chief mission in June 1984. The overcast at Goose Bay, Canada, won't present a problem for this sortie, as most of the action took place below a thousand feet. F-15 "Eagles" of the 318th FIS are parked behind the taxiing Six.

With typical 1950s USAF wooden buildings in the background, this F-106A from the 87th FIS sits on the ramp at Goose Bay, Canada, in June 1987. The pilot is attaching the parachute leads and chatting with his crew chief before climbing up the boarding ladder for another Amalgam Brave mission. This Six has typical late-era markings, with the F-102–style anti-glare treatment on the nose and an ADTAC badge below the windscreen. The Red Bull insignia was carried on the left side.

Chapter Twenty-Two

NASA AND FINAL DUTY

Keeping an eye out for trouble, -513 chases a new Rockwell B-1B bomber. Even with its long "legs," it still took two of the Delta Darts to chase one Lancer acceptance flight. (USAF via Isham)

In spite of the F-106's role as an interceptor, NASA was both the first and last operator of the Six. The large volume of the weapons bay, coupled with its high performance made it an outstanding test platform and NASA utilized the Six to its fullest.

B-1 Chase

As B-1B Lancer supersonic bombers began rolling off the final assembly line at the Rockwell International manufacturing facility at Plant 42 in Palmdale, California, Detachment 15, Contract Management Division of AF Systems Command, stood up to support the acceptance test flight program. Beginning in March 1986, they initially borrowed Edwards' F-111s and F-4s for photo and safety chase duties. When those were not available from Edwards, they even leased civilian T-38 Talons. But cost and availability constraints meant that the B-1 program started slipping behind schedule due to unavailability of chase planes. The nearly four-hour-long acceptance flights covered the entire flight envelope of the B-1B. The first half was flown between 15,000 and 20,000 feet and the final portion was flown at around 200 feet above ground and Mach 0.85 (about 640 mph). Heat rising off the desert made that portion extremely turbulent.

A chase plane that had both long endurance and high speed was badly needed. Since F-106s were becoming available as the fleet was being retired, they were chosen to become the new dedicated chase aircraft. Between 10 October 1986 and 6 July 1990 eight Sixes were used. Even with external fuel tanks, it took two Sixes to chase one B-1 acceptance flight. About half of the fleet was based at Palmdale and the remainder flew out of either Kirtland AFB, New Mexico, or in support of flights out of the B-1B depot at Tinker AFB, Oklahoma.

Several iterations of tail markings were applied. As the first arrival, S/N 57-2513 retained its ALC markings of high-visibility orange on the vertical fin and wingtips. Shortly after arrival, a black silhouette of a B-1 and the words "B-1 Chase" were applied in black above the serial number. This jet apparently retained its high-visibility markings throughout the chase program but later received a large white outline of the markings subsequently applied to the other jets, with the word "CHASE" at the bottom of the fin. S/N 59-0061 was similarly marked when it arrived from Kelly, and the jets from Florida and New Jersey arrived with their old squadron markings still in place.

F-106s Used for B-1 Chase Aircraft

Serial numbers included the following:

Aircraft	From	Arrived Palmdale	To AMARC	Tail Color
57-2513 (B)	Kelly	10 Oct 1986	25 Jun 1990	orange
58-0795	ADWC	30 Oct 1986	03 Mar 1987	light blue
59-0008	**Florida**	**12 Dec 1986**	**18 Mar 1987**	**none**
59-0060	Florida	24 Jan 1987	27 Jun 1990	light blue
59-0061	Kelly	06 Feb 1987	06 July 1990	hi-vis/light blue
57-2535 (B)	Florida	03 Mar 1987	03 Apr 1990	dark blue
57-2509 (B)	Florida	23 Mar 1987	24 May 1990	dark blue
59-0149 (B)	New Jersey	02 Aug 1988	14 Jun 1990	red

New tail markings, consisting of silhouettes of both a B-1 and the F-106 flying in formation with exhaust trails and shadow shaded in white, were designed by one of the crew chiefs and applied to all of the aircraft in three colors. A small Air Force Systems Command (AFSC) badge was applied just above the rudder. S/N 58-0795

After its retirement, the New Jersey commemorative F-106B went to the B-1 Chase program. Seen here at Palmdale, California, on 13 August 1988, it still carries its nose art. The gunsight is also visible in the original slide. Several variations of markings applied to the Six chase fleet are visible. Those massive MA-3 air conditioning carts are still needed to keep the avionics cool while working in the California heat. (Isham)

received a unique small-radius rounded demarcation between the anti-glare panel on the nose and the radome. As B-1 production wound down or their airframe times ran out, the Sixes were passed on to AMARC where they were stored pending conversion to drones.

NACA/NASA and the F-106

Due to its cavernous weapons bay, large avionics compartments, and high performance, NACA, and later NASA, made greater use of the F-106 than any other Century Series aircraft. A wide variety of research was carried out using the Six. In fact, NASA was the first

Showing how the two Pratt & Whitney J85 engine configurations were different, N516NA is shown in flight during 1969. The front-seat pilot flew the aircraft and navigated while the rear-seat occupant operated the two additional engines and collected data. (NASA photo C 69-2870)

actual user of the F-106, with SN/57-0235 arriving at the NACA Ames Laboratory 4 September 1958, quite literally straight out of final assembly at Palmdale. Between then and 14 December 1959, the NAS Moffett Field lab used this early MA-1 jet primarily to evaluate the integration between the MA-1 AWCIS and the automatic flight control system, with special emphasis on the human interface and system performance after radar lock-on to a target.

Astronaut Use

At the beginning of Project Mercury, the Space Task Group (STG) astronauts were based at NASA Langley. Established in 1958, the STG originally used the F-102s and T-33s of the 48th FIS. When the 48th converted to the F-106, the unit received two additional airframes for NASA to use. The two Sixes were used for proficiency, high-speed transportation, and chase duties. According to instructors from the 48th FIS, of the seven original astronauts, only John Glenn did not check out in the F-106. As a navy pilot, he preferred to fly an F-8 Crusader, which he borrowed from nearby Oceana.

Because NASA was reluctant to advertise the fact that the astronauts were flying combat-capable aircraft, very little was done to publicize the fact, other than one photograph of the original Mercury Seven astronauts standing in front of an unmarked F-106B. One B model (S/N 59-0158) and one A model (S/N 58-0782) were assigned, but apparently the astronauts used whatever aircraft was available at the 48th. The aircraft record cards for the two jets are somewhat enigmatic as well, with the B model showing as belonging to the 48th FIS and the A model showing as being assigned to the 73rd Air Division at Tyndall.

A very rare shot of S/N 57-0235 while assigned to NASA Ames in May 1959. This Six was used to evaluate human interface with, and operation of, the automatic mode of the FCS. (Isham Collection)

When the STG moved to Houston, the two Sixes were apparently transferred to Ellington AFB, Texas, but the aircraft record cards continued to show no bailment or assignment to NASA. In fact, the cards show that -782 was reassigned from the 73rd AD to the 94th FIS on 6 April 1962.

NASA Workhorse

The next Six assigned to NASA was F-106B S/N 57-2516. This jet had an interesting career. As one of the very early, "barely tactical" B-models, it never received a full T-T-T modification. After a short stint with the AFFTC at Edwards, it was sent to the 95th FIS at Dover on 17 June 1959 to assist in their conversion to the F-106. On 23 February 1960 it was transferred to the Sacramento ALC to receive the Broad Jump modification and have its early-style cockpit modified to the later configuration with higher side consoles.

Following release from rebuilding, the jet was sent to Kelly Field on 4 June 1960, where it was used by the San Antonio ALC for test work. With the exception of a three-month loan to Tyndall, the jet spent the next four years as a test bed at Kelly.

On 3 April 1964, the jet was bailed to the Fort Worth Division of General Dynamics and modified for use as a test bed for the new F-111. The jet received the radar altimeter and terrain-following radar of the F-111 and flew in this configuration for the next two years. At the completion of Aardvark testing, it was deemed uneconomical to return it to tactical configuration and was passed on to the NASA Lewis Research Center in Cleveland, Ohio, on 31 October 1966 for use in Supersonic Transport research.

Seen here on the ramp at Selfridge ANGB, Michigan, on a very chilly day in early 1973, N616NA has just been towed out of the hangar in preparation for a test mission. This aircraft and N607NA were frequent guests at Selfridge, as the base had an ANG F-106 unit and closer access to the restricted area over Lake Huron than the NASA base at Cleveland.

Burn marks on the side of the fuselage give an indication of just how many lightning strikes this Six suffered in the course of research. It is at NASA Langley on 27 October 1982. From the smooth upper spine, it is evident that this bus has never received the aerial refueling modification.

Preparing to land at Langley in May 1982, N816 is seen late in the lightning test program. (Ron Picciani)

Huron, and less traffic than the commercial Cleveland airport, both -516 and its counterpart -507 frequently resided in the old 1930s-era brick hangars at Selfridge.

At the conclusion of the SST research, -516 was planned to go to NASA Dryden at Edwards, but it was later transferred to the NASA Langley Research Center and given the civilian registration N816NA instead. The two J85s and their pylons were removed and the elevons returned to their normal configuration, and -516 began a new career as a Storm Hazards research vehicle.

Specifically, -516 was used to assess how aircraft with digital electronics and composite structures responded to lightning strikes. For this research, the aircraft was extensively "hardened" against high-current electrical charges using lightning protection devices, electromagnetic shielding of electrical power and avionics systems, and JP-5 fuel versus the normal air force JP-4. Electromagnetic sensors were installed; a shielded recording system was installed in the weapons bay; and several video, still, and movie cameras were added to visually record the strikes; as was a special weather radar that could display either airborne- or ground-based images of the weather. Finally, an air-sampling system and a new, composite fin cap were added. The airframe was stripped of paint in 1983 to further enhance its electromagnetic hardening.

While most of the later thunderstorm research flights were conducted near Langley or the NASA Wallops Island, Virginia, facility, initial flights in 1980 and 1981 were flown in the vicinity of the National Severe Storms Laboratory at Norman, Oklahoma. Between January and March 1984, N816NA was used to compare the electromagnetic effects of lightning with those from a nuclear explosion. During this period the jet was mounted on the special test stand at the Air Force Weapons Lab at Kirtland. Over the course of the storm hazards research, the jet made 1,496 thunderstorm penetrations, experienced 714 direct lightning strikes, and provided invaluable data for designers of new-generation aircraft. This program ended in 1985.

Once at Lewis, this Six received civil registration N616NA and became a research test bed. Since the proposed new generation of supersonic transports had Delta wing platforms just like the Six, the aircraft was chosen to be a full-scale test vehicle to augment wind tunnel testing. Two GE J85 jet engines were added to new mounts located on the aft ends of the wings. The right engine was used as a reference for noise, drag, and thrust, while the left engine tested a wide variety of intake and exhaust designs.

For the next three years this Six flew from either Cleveland or Selfridge conducting research in subsonic and supersonic cruise and noise reduction. Since Selfridge was nearby, had an active-duty F-106 squadron (and later, an ANG F-106 unit) to aid in maintenance, easy access to a giant restricted area running most of the length of Lake

During the lightning tests, N816NA was flown out to Kirtland AFB, New Mexico, and placed on the EMP test stand to see how it withstood high-energy radiation. (NASA photo)

New Aerodynamic Research

Following completion of the lightning research -816 became the test bed for a new aerodynamic concept, the vortex flap. In an attempt to improve the overall lift-to-drag ratio of a wing, the Langley lab designed a specially shaped leading edge to the wing of the F-106. This vortex flap was designed to both generate and trap a vortex of air along the leading edge and thus reduce drag across the entire airspeed

Variations of the vortex flap leading edges were comprehensively tested in the wind tunnel before being applied to the F-106. (NASA)

On its first flight with a vortex flap modification, the pressure transducer locations are very evident on the wings of N816.

N816 is being modified for the Vortex Flap Project at Langley in 1982. The right wing from S/N 57-2507 lies on the ground prior to installation in the full-size wind tunnel. Note the slight upward reflex at the tip, showing that this was a Case XIV wing.

regime of the aircraft. Initial flight tests with N816 were begun in February 1985, simply to test the visualization system. To visualize the airflow over the wings, the jet was modified so that the airflow was mixed with heated propylene glycol vapor, which was ejected from a probe mounted under the leading edge of the left wing.

A specially installed mercury vapor light mounted on top of the fuselage projected a sheet of light across the top of the left wing and illuminated the airflow and vortex pattern. These patterns were filmed by video camera and recorded for later use; initial flights were made on moonless nights to optimize the images. After finalizing the recording system, flights to establish the performance baseline of the original unmodified wing were conducted in August and September 1987. Once the baseline had been established, the newly designed leading edges (the result of more than 3,000 hours of wind tunnel testing) were installed.

The vortex flaps were ground adjustable with the right wing being instrumented to measure surface pressures and the left wing being instrumented with accelerometers and strain gauges to monitor structural loads and deformation. After a series of high-speed taxi tests, the first flight with the vortex flaps installed was on 2 August 1988. Over the following 2½ years, 93 research flights were made to determine the aerodynamic performance of the flaps. Following completion of this research, this aircraft was donated to the Virginia Air and Space Center, where it is currently on display.

The Prototype Bus Goes to NASA

After spending most of its career as an ejection-seat test aircraft and proficiency trainer at the AFFTC, the prototype F-106B (S/N 57-2507) was transferred to NASA's Lewis Research Center in Cleveland on 26 September 1972. Given the civilian registration N507NA, this jet was initially used as a chase aircraft for N516. Given its lack of an MA-1 system, the huge amount of available internal space led to N507 being given the solar cell calibration duties formerly carried out by a Lewis-based B-57. The aircraft was then fitted with air-sampling pods and joined the Global Air Sampling Program (GASP). N507 was not flown extensively but did deploy to Alaska for 10 days in early 1977. One of its final duties in this role was to monitor ash and air quality following the Mount St. Helens volcanic eruption in May 1981.

N607NA/57-2507 was used to chase the three engine test missions, and is seen here on the Selfridge ANGB ramp prior to an air show in July 1976. (El Mason)

Next the jet was fitted with a special color scanner and used to monitor the water quality and pollution levels of the Great Lakes and Lake Okeechobee in Florida. The airborne measurements were compared to water samples obtained from research boats to see if aerial pollution monitoring was viable. At the end of this program, the aircraft was transferred to NASA Langley on 12 May 1981.

After little use, in 1984 the jet was selected to assist in the Vortex Flap Program as the full-scale wind tunnel shape. Since the entire aircraft would not fit into the tunnel, it was carefully cut in half down the length of the centerline in what was known as the F-53 project. Once in place, it had variations of the vortex flap mounted on the leading edge of the wing so they could be tested prior to manned flight. NASA project reports on these tests clearly state that the prototype F-106B had the early Case XIV wing.

Two other F-106 aircraft were acquired by NASA very late in the game. S/N 59-0123 was towed across the field from the 48th FIS to NASA Langley in March 1981 and used for parts to keep N816NA flying. F-106B S/N 57-2545 was sent to Langley on 30 January 1985, possibly to provide replacement leading edges for N816NA once vortex flap experimentation was complete. It was never done due to budgetary constraints and the jet was later returned to Tyndall for use as a drone.

Project Eclipse

In 1996, Kelly Space and Technology (KST), the USAF, and NASA Dryden teamed up to determine if a reusable space-launch vehicle would be practical. In this proof of concept, a modified NC-141A was used as the tow aircraft and an F-106 known as the *Delta Dragger* was the towed article. Two F-106s (S/N 59-0010 and S/N 59-0130) were taken from the drone program at Holloman and flown to Mojave Airport, California, during August and September 1986 for initial modifications and maintenance work. Approximately one year later, both jets were flown to the NASA Dryden facility at Edwards to begin the tests. S/N 59-0130 had

With its Pratt & Whitney J75 at idle to power the flight controls and avionics, the first tow flight of Project Eclipse is underway on 20 December 1977. The Lockheed NC-141A Starlifter belonged to the AFFTC's 418th Flight Test Squadron. The program ended on 6 February 1998, marking the last mission for a Six other than delivery to AMARC. (NASA via Isham)

The tow attachment for Project Eclipse used a modified drag chute release mechanism from a B-52 bomber. A small video camera is located inside the small circle of rivets, and the squadron badge from the previous owner, the 5th FIS, is prominent on the ejection seat inside the cockpit. (NASA via Isham)

a modified B-52 drag chute release mechanism mounted in place of the IR seeker on the nose while S/N 59-0010 was used as a spare.

After conducting flights to determine the effects of wake turbulence between the two types of aircraft, six towed flights were conducted with release altitudes occurring between 10,000 and 25,000 feet. A 1,000-foot length of vectran liquid crystal polymer rope connected the two jets for takeoff and tow. Once flight test objectives were completed, the rope was severed and the F-106 returned for landing at Edwards. The last tow flight was completed on 6 February 1998 and the jets were ferried to the boneyard at Davis-Monthan on 30 April and 1 May 1998, with the latter possibly being the last manned flight of an F-106.

FAREWELLS

As the Six left operational use, a series of Farewell events were held to commemorate this superb interceptor's illustrious history.

Dart Depart

In mid-January 1986, the depot at McClellan had a going-away event that coincided with completion of the last F-106 to undergo Programmed Depot Mainte-

nance. F-106B S/N 59-0149, assigned to the New Jersey ANG, was the last Six to roll out. A public event was held with attendance consisting mostly of Sacramento ALC employees, their families, contingents from the last operational F-106 units, and Southern California aviation photographers. Medal of Honor recipient and F-106 pilot Bernie Fisher attended, while a single-seat Six did a flyby. At the end of the event, the ropes were lowered and the crowd was allowed to autograph the bus using black markers.

Dart Out

In contrast to the rather low-key event held in California, the Dart Out held at Atlantic City, New Jersey, on 10–11 June 1988 was a large and well-attended event. The transient ramp was full of jets, and several KC-135s full of attendees arrived as well. Families, photographers, and Six pilots and maintainers walked the ramp and inspected the displays inside the hangar.

Friday night started with a flight suit party at the club, with one attendee stating, "I have never seen so many orange flight suits in one place in my life." A single Six was launched at dusk and made some very low passes over the party. Fortunately for the pilot, the light was too poor to take photographs of the pine trees swaying from the wingtip vortices as the Six blasted past.

Saturday 11 June was the big public day and Atlantic City launched the fleet, with twelve Sixes taking to the air. An eight-ship formation made passes, as well as a single Six doing several flybys,

S/N 59-0043 shows off its commemorative paint job. Markings on the external fuel tank read "Last of the Sport Models," while the aft fuselage markings pay tribute to the world record speed holder. Seen at Atlantic City, New Jersey, in June 1988. (El Mason)

"The Ultimate Interceptor." Even in the twilight of its career, the Six was still a beautiful and competent machine. Many war stories were told of operational Sixes achieving speeds well in excess of the official speed record. It is too bad the jet was never given a second chance to prove what it was really capable of. (Don Spering/AIR)

While maintenance folks signed a large area on the right fuselage, the drivers signed inside the box on the left. The angled reflector for the gun sight and the three rearview mirrors are clearly visible as well. (El Mason)

Prior to the "Dart Out" at Atlantic City, Don Spering and a crew of helpers painted farewell markings on S/N 59-0043 of the 177th FIS, the last operational F-106 squadron. This close-up of the nose not only shows those markings, but clearly shows the z-axis yaw vane, located just behind the shark mouth marking. (Mason)

A close-up view of the commemorative markings on the left nose of F-106B S/N 59-0149 as seen on the B-1 Chase support ramp, 13 August 1988. (Isham)

including one with the jet rolled up on its side with the weapons bay doors open so that the crowd could clearly see the four Super Falcon missiles and gun pod. As befitted a unit transitioning from old to new, one of the Atlantic City Sixes led one of their new F-16As on a close formation pass as well and the East Coast F-16 demo from Shaw AFB, South Carolina, also performed.

That evening a large banquet was held in one of the Atlantic City casinos. The unit had flown in Mercury Seven astronaut and test pilot Gordon Cooper for the event, giving him a final ride in the back seat of an F-106B. Remarks were made by the New Jersey Adjutant General and the Commander of the 1st Air Force before remembrances from some of the attendees and a slide show on the history of the Six began.

When the event was over the last of the operational Sixes were slowly ferried out to the boneyard at Davis-Monthan to await con-version to drones. The last three jets departed Atlantic City on 1 August 1988 and the planned five-year-long service life of the Six, one that in reality lasted 30 years (by far the longest first-line use by any of the Century Series) finally came to a close only a few miles from where the first Six was originally acquired by the very first operational squadron in 1959.

NASA Retirement Ceremony

The final farewell event occurred on 17 May 1991, when the NASA Langley Research Center retired S/N 57-2516/N816NA in an event attended by none other than Dr. Richard Whitcomb, who was in many ways directly responsible for the success of the F-102 and F-106. At the end of the affair, the aircraft was donated to the Virginia Air and Space Center in Hampton Roads, Virginia, where it is currently on display.

Chapter Twenty-Three

A WARRIOR'S DEATH

At Holloman AFB, New Mexico, on 20 October 1996, S/N 58-0791 is the spare for a mission launch. The canvas-protected area on top of the yellow drone control van parked behind the Six is where the pilot controlled the takeoff and landings. (Jack Calloway)

Like the F-102 and F-100 before it, after its retirement, the F-106 fleet was chosen to become Full Scale Aerial Targets. Most of the remaining airframes were converted to drones, with the remainder staying in the desert boneyard to provide spare parts as needed.

The QF-106 Pacer Six Drone Program

Like the F-102 before it, the F-106s were also destined to become Full Scale Aerial Targets (FSAT) with 194 converted. Three years before the last Sixes were delivered to AMARC, Flight Systems Inc. (FSI) began converting the first Darts into what became known as the Pacer Six program. After being returned to flyable status at Davis-Monthan, the jets were flown to Mojave Airport, California, where FSI began the initial work.

The first flight of the converted QF-106 occurred in July 1987, but the remaining conversions were very slow, with the final aircraft not completed until 1990, around two years after the last Six had entered the boneyard. All following drone conversions were carried out by the air force, in conjunction with American Electronics Laboratories (AEL). The 188 following aircraft were returned to flight status at Davis-Monthan and some of the initial work was also done

there, then the jets were ferried to AEL at East Alton, Illinois, just outside of St. Louis, Missouri, where the remaining work was done. That program also slipped, with the initial planned delivery date of May 1991 delayed until September.

In late 1991, the Pacer Six program really got going and the first QF-106s began operating as FSATs with the 82nd TATS (later, 82ATRS) at Tyndall and with a detachment at Holloman. Given the conversion cost, every attempt was made to extend their lives.

Earlier F-100 drones used IR burners on the wingtips to decoy heat-seeking missiles, and an attempt was made to mount similar devices on the pylons under the wings of the Sixes. Unfortunately, the large Delta wing shielded the device from any upper hemisphere attack and that attempt was fairly quickly abandoned. In an attempt to save some of the drones from damage, small IR burner pods were developed and installed on the wingtips of a few Sixes.

The low-cost Firedrake program took commonly available travel pods made from the shell of small napalm canisters, mounted ALE-40–type chaff and flare dispensers pointing downward from the bottom, and designed new sequencing units that allowed both higher dispense rates and more variability than the original ALE-40 programmer. These were loaded on the wing pylons of the drones.

Seen at Tyndall on 3 August 1983, S/N 59-0026 has an IR burner mounted to the left wingtip. When mounted on the external pylon location, the wing tended to shield the heat source, making it ineffective. (Brian Rogers)

Being prepped for a launch at Holloman AFB, New Mexico, this B model sports the L-shaped "Bullwinkle" ECM antenna on the nose and a Fire Drake pod on the wing pylon. Several antennas related to unmanned operation have been added on the lower nose, aft fuselage, and vertical fin. 11 February 1997. (Jack Calloway)

as targets for air-to-air missile firings by later model fighters. Profiles included use of the AIM-120 AMRAAM or various models of AIM-9 heat-seeking missiles, and the Sixes could even be flown in remote-controlled formations. On some occasions the Six would simply refuse to die, and at least one survived a hit by an AMRAAM follow-on 20mm gunfire and then a direct hit by an AIM-9 heat-seeking missile before finally crashing into the Gulf of Mexico.

Missions flown from Holloman were generally in support of the U.S. Army, and the most common missiles used were either U.S. or Russian hand-held, heat-seeking missiles, such as the 9K38 Igla (SA-18/Grouse) man-portable, infrared homing surface-to-air missile. Regardless of the location, unmanned drone flights were chased by a manned F-106 to assess any damage before attempting to recover the Not Under Local Operation (NULLO) flight.

On 20 February 1997, F-106B S/N 57-2524 became the last QF-106 to be shot down at Holloman and the program then shifted to the QF-4 Phantom. At the end of the Pacer Six program at Tyndall in January 1988, three of the flyable survivors were flown back to Davis-Monthan and were once again interned in the boneyard (S/N 59-0158, S/N 59-0043, and S/N 58-0774), while S/N 59-0023 was flown to Dover to become a museum display aircraft.

Seven damaged and non-flyable airframes were left at Tyndall and became known as the Swamp Things due to their location on the airfield. Their serial numbers were 57-2509 (B), 57-2517 (B), 57-2543 (B), 57-2545 (B), 58-0786, 59-0047, and 59-0105. They were eventually purchased and, after a series of legal challenges, shipped by truck to El Paso, Texas, where they have been partially restored and are being sold to museums.

Many of the surviving Sixes at AMARG were also allotted to museums across the United States, but some damaged airframes were either dumped into the Gulf of Mexico to become artificial reefs or trucked to the Goldwater bombing range near Gila Bend, Arizona, to be used as ground targets. (See Appendix 5 for a list of survivors.)

Alternatively, a standard LAU-3 launcher could be mated to the pylon and either an AIS scoring pod carried or an ALQ-167 ECM jamming pod. Some of the QF-106s received an equivalent internal electronic jamming system and these were identifiable by the "Bullwinkle" horn antennas on both sides of the nose located just behind the radome.

The final conversions were completed during the fourth quarter of FY 1994. Flights from Tyndall varied between testing new upgrades to existing air-to-air missiles and providing a full-size target for Fighter Weapons School classes, but most were programmed

Under tow at Holloman on 17 December 1996, -155 has had its ejection seats removed, sports the Bullwinkle ECM modification, and has a new countermeasures pod hung under the wing. (Jack Calloway)

The Final Proposal: MF-106A RASCAL Satellite Launcher DARPA

With the Six seemingly finally condemned to the boneyard at Davis-Monthan, one last attempt was made to inject new life into the jet. In November 2001, DARPA began soliciting requests for proposals on a RASCAL program. In February 2002, HMX, Inc., and subcontractor Destiny Aerospace responded with a proposal that would have initially used two F-106s updated with pre-compressor cooling, reaction jets, a thermal protection system on the leading edges of the aircraft, and a modified weapons bay to launch payloads of up to 150 kg into low-earth orbit.

The two aircraft proposed were F-106A S/N 59-0130 and F-106B S/N 59-0158. The modified Sixes were to reach speeds up to Mach 3 and remain in a powered climb up to 100,000 feet. After the engine flamed out, reaction control thrusters would allow the pilot to continue controlled flight up to 200,000 feet, at which point the payload would be ejected from the enlarged weapons bay and the accompanying rocket would have boosted the payload into orbit.

Although Destiny won a Phase II development contract, in the end DARPA did not follow through with the concept. Rumor has it that once again politics had raised its ugly head and that the mantra "No 45-year-old 'has been' is going to show up our new fighters!" was the bottom line.

Ending where it began. Fittingly enough, this Project Eclipse Six flies over Edwards, a little more than 41 years after the prototype first took to the air at the same location. Little did Convair or Hughes realize just how capable and versatile their design would turn out to be. (NASA via Isham)

Silhouetted here by the setting sun, the F-106 will forever hold a place in the hearts and souls of those who flew and serviced this magnificent aircraft. (Don Spering/AIR)

F-106 CONTRACTS

No F-102B or F-106 contract was ever a supplement to, or part of, an order for any other F-102–type aircraft. The entire contract numbers had the prefix AF41 (600) and then the individual numbers below.

30169 covered the first 17 F-102Bs (S/N 56-0451 through S/N 56-0467), approved 4 April 1956. These aircraft were redesignated as F-106A on 29 June 1956, prior to assembly.

30169 Supplement 1 was for 18 F-106As (S/N 57-0229 through S/N 57-0246), approved 14 December 1956. All except the last were initially dedicated to testing.

33808 covered the first 54 tactical F-106As (S/N 57-2453 through S/N 57-2506), approved 31 December 1956.

30169 Supplement 2 was for the first 7 F-106Bs (S/N 57-2507 through S/N 57-2513), approved 25 May 1957. Again, all were initially used for test work.

33808 Supplement 1 was for 34 tactical F-106Bs (S/N 57-2514 through S/N 57-2547), approved 3 May 1957.

34814 was initially written to purchase 140 F-106As (S/N 58-0759 through S/N 58-0899), approved 30 April 1958. It was later revised to eliminate serials -799 to -899, which resulted in only 40 single-seat aircraft being purchased. It also initially included a large order for F-106Bs. The complete details have been lost, but it may have covered S/N 58-0900 through S/N 58-0950. In any event, only five B models were built and the remainder of the contract was canceled as part of a force cutback.

36546 initially called for 240 F-106s (S/N 59-0001 through S/N 59-0240). Of these, 75 airframes were canceled and S/N 59-0001 through S/N 59-0148 were built as F-106A models, while S/N 59-0149 through S/N 59-0165 were built as F-106Bs.

11333 covered all of the aircraft in the T-T-Tprogram rebuild. Of the planned additional purchases, including the 350 F-106C/D planned for FY 1960 and on, none ever reached the contract stage. Notice that contract number AF 30169 only covered developmental aircraft, most of which were later rebuilt to tactical standards under the T-T-T program.

F-106 MODEL NUMBERS AND DIFFERENCES

Given the large amount of confusion and misinformation surrounding the early F-106s, the following information has been included for historical accuracy. Seven Convair model numbers were applied to the F-106 fleet, as follows:

Model 8-20 were prototypes and were never intended to carry the MA-1 nor F-106A weapons suspension equipment. They had access doors below the fuselage to access test instrumentation in what later became the weapons bay.

Model 8-21 had a weapons bay with space and provisions for weapons launchers and both provisions and space for the MA-1 AWCIS to be added at a later date.

Model 8-22 aircraft had a complete weapons bay, including weapons launchers as well as space and provisions to be able to install the MA-1 AWCIS at a later time.

Model 8-23 jets had a complete weapons bay, weapons launchers, and a pre-production MA-1 AWCIS.

Model 8-24 aircraft had a complete weapons bay, including launchers and production model MA-1 AWCIS.

Model 8-25 was applied to the (Y)F-106C.

Model 8-26 was applied to the F-106D, the two-seat variant of the C model.

Model 8-27 was applied to all F-106Bs no participating in the T-T-T program.

Model 8-31 was applied to those F-106As that came out of the T-T-T program.

Model 8-32 were the F-106Bs that underwent the T-T-T rebuild.

THE FIRST 50 SIXES

CV Model, Version and Production Number	USAF Serial Number	Planned Production Number	Actual Production Number	USAF Block Number	Date Accepted or Ready	Notes
FY 1956 Prototype Aircraft						
8-20-1	56-0451	1	1	-05	29 Dec 1956	side stick
8-20-2	56-0452	2	2	-05	26 Feb 1957	side stick
FY 1956 Production Aircraft						
8-21-1	56-0453	3	3	-10	31 Aug 1957	
8-21-3	56-0455	5	4	-10	30 Nov 1957	
8-21-4	56-0456	6	5	-10?	31 Oct 1957	
8-22-2	56-0458	8	6	-15	30 Nov 1957	
8-22-3	56-0459	9	7	-15	30 Dec 1957	CV engine test
8-22-4	56-0460	10	8	-15	31 Jan 1958	
8-22-5	56-0461	11	9	-15	13 Jan 1958	
8-22-6	56-0462	12	10	-15	18 Mar 1958	1st A/C scheduled for production center stick
8-21-2	56-0454	4	11	-20	31 Mar 1958	
8-23-1	56-0463	13	12	-25	30 Apr 1958	1st A/C scheduled for pre-production MA-1 prior to delivery
8-27-1	57-2507	B	13	-05 (B)	21 Apr 1958	1st B model and only one with a case XIV wing
8-22-1	56-0457	7	14	-30	28 Apr 1958	This A/C not scheduled to have either weapons launchers or MA-1
8-23-2	56-0464	14	15	-35	18 Jan 1958	
8-23-3	56-0465	15	16	-35	30 Jun 1958	
8-23-4	56-0466	16	17	-35	28 Jun 1958	
8-22-7	56-0467	17	18	-40	30 Apr 1958	AF engine test; the last F-102B and the first actually built with the Case XXIX (29) wing?
FY 1957 Production Aircraft						
8-23-5	57-0229	18	19	-45	28 Jul 1958	
8-23-6	57-0230	19	20	-45	18 Jun 1958	
8-27-3	57-2509	B	21	-10 (B)	09 Jul 1958	
8-23-7	57-0231	20	22	-45	26 Jul 1958	
8-24-1	57-0232	21	23	-50	30 Aug 5 1958	1st A/C to receive production MA-1 prior to delivery
8-27-4	57-2510	B	24	-15 (B)	30 Sep 1958	
8-24-2	57-0233	22	25	-50	29 Aug 1958	

8-24-3	57-0234	23	26	-50	30 Jul 1958	
8-27-2	57-2508	B	27	-20 (B)	19 Sep 1958	First aircraft scheduled to receive production AN/ASQ-25 (MA-1)
8-24-4	57-0235	24	28	-55	30 Aug 5 1958	L/D ratio tests
8-27-5	57-2511	B	29	-25 (B)	29 Sep 1958	
8-24-5	57-0236	25	30	-55	13 Sep 1958	First aircraft originally scheduled for the Case XXIX Wing
8-27-6	57-2512	B	31	-25 (B)	Nov 1958	
8-24-6	57-0237	26	32	-55	23 Sep 1958	8-32-6
8-27-7	57-2513	B	33	-25 (B)	18 Nov 1958	
8-24-7	57-0238	27	34	-55	01 Oct 1958	First A built without wing fences
8-27-8	57-2514	B	35	-30 (B)	31 Oct 1958	
8-24-8	57-0239	28	36	-60	31 Dec 1958	Converted to YF-106C
8-27-9	57-2515	B	37	-31 (B)	31 Dec 1958	
8-24-9	57-0240	29	38	-60	19 Dec 1958	Converted to YF-106C
8-27-10	57-2516	B	39	-31 (B)	17 Jan 1957	First tactical B model, to 95 FIS and later NASA
8-24-10	57-0241	30	40	-60	15 Sep 1958	
8-27-11	57-2517	B	41	-31 (B)	03 Jun 1959	
8-24-11	57-0242	31	42	-60	--	Crashed 27 Oct 1958 before delivery
8-24-12	57-0243	32	43	-60	20 Oct 1958	
8-24-13	57-0244	?	44	-60	19 Dec 1958	
8-24-14	57-0245	?	45	-65 (Planned)	29 Nov 1958	
8-24-15	57-0246	?	46	-64	20 Mar 1959	First block-64 and first tactical A model
8-24-16	57-2453	?	47	-66	29 May 5	First A model in initial production contract, to 498 FIS
8-24-17	57-2454	?	48	-66	25 May 1959	to 539 FIS
8-24-18	57-2455	?	49	-66	01 May 1959	to 539 FIS
8-27-12	57-2518	B	50	-35 (B)	28 Aug 1959	to 498 FIS

Appendix Four

PROTOTYPE F-106 TEST AIRCRAFT ASSIGNMENTS

56-0451

Assigned to Convair at Edwards. First flight on 26 December 1956. The prototype initially differed from production models in having the YJ75-P-1 engine (which had the same thrust as the P-9, but higher fuel consumption) and different inlet ducts. The ducts on the prototypes were initially 50 square inches larger and aligned parallel to the aircraft reference line; production inlets drooped 5 degrees downward.

Follow-on flights conducted instrument calibration, flutter investigation, Air Turbine Motor (ATM) evaluation, takeoff performance, speed brake operation, and emergency landing gear extension. Engine inlet vari-ramp and aircraft performance testing were conducted from mid-February through early March 1957. The aircraft was then put into maintenance to install the fuel transfer system and to replace the side stick with a center stick.

After returning to flight status in early April, testing was devoted to flutter investigations. Follow-on testing evaluated the wing fences, nose-wheel steering, and roll coupling. Air Force Phase II testing began in the latter part of May and lasted through June. The aircraft was then used for aft CG and low-altitude flutter tests, which ran through July, at which time the aircraft underwent a 25-hour engine inspection and a 50-hour airframe inspection.

Flight testing resumed with general systems evaluations, flight performance testing, hinge moment evaluation of the elevons, rudder buzz evaluation, and hydraulic temperature tests, with flutter testing continuing through the first part of November. On 20 November 1957 the jet was ferried to San Diego for spin-test modifications. It was ferried back to Edwards at the end of January 1958 and put into layup status while instrumentation calibration, rework of the fuel valve installation, rocket catapult (ejection seat) modification, and various minor aircraft discrepancies were repaired.

Taxi runs to evaluate the spin-parachute modification were conducted in late February and investigated things such as inadvertent chute deployment. Preliminary stall-and-spin testing was conducted in March and the first part of April 1958. After the initial stall testing, the wing fences were removed and the slotted leading edges installed. Stall testing was then repeated to compare the two configurations. Spin demonstration flights were begun in April, and after an engine change, stall testing continued through May. The stall program was expanded to investigate the post-stall gyrations that were encountered on early stall and spin entry tests. Testing was conducted with various CG locations and post-stall gyration testing was completed in July.

Later projects included tailhook evaluation, 230-gallon external fuel tank performance, and flight evaluation. This jet was donated to the National Museum of the Air Force on 27 March 1960. Having no navigation equipment installed, it was led across the country by two F-106As that were being delivered to the 27th FIS.

56-0452

Assigned to Convair at Edwards until 10 April 1957, at which time it was handed over to Pratt & Whitney. The aircraft was used for power plant and performance testing through 30 June 1962, when it was sent to the 3320th Maintenance and Support Group at Amarillo Technical Training Center, Texas, as a ground trainer.

After its first flight and acceptance on 26 February 1957, the aircraft was immediately put into maintenance to add the instrumentation necessary to evaluate thrust and power plant components. Flight testing began the second week of April 1957 and continued through the latter part of May when the aircraft was again put into work status to perform a hot section inspection of the engine, replace the side stick controller with a conventional center stick, recalibrate the instrumentation, and prepare the aircraft for the Air Force Phase II evaluation.

In late June the aircraft was flown to San Diego where it remained until 14 August 1957. While at Convair, the aircraft had another engine hot-section inspection, had the original straight cylindrical ejector replaced with a cylindrical-divergent one with a modified tail cone, had a modified fuel control installed, and had the air inlets thinned and modified to represent the production standard of 1,000 square inches. Flight tests revealed that thinning the inlet lips alone reduced drag by 1,200 pounds at Mach 2 and 35,000 feet. After being returned to flight status and flown back to Edwards, it was immediately grounded again while instrumentation calibration was conducted.

Performance testing resumed in the latter part of August and continued through September, before going back into work status for yet another engine hot section inspection, more modifications to the ejector (nozzle), and engine shroud and instrumentation changes. Performance evaluation flights resumed in October and cruise, climb, maximum power acceleration, and manual vari-ramp operations at supersonic speeds were conducted to evaluate the effects of the changes.

During late October, the aircraft was modified again, this time receiving a short convergent-divergent ejector configuration and slotted vari-ramps in place of the original perforated ramps. During takeoff on 12 November 1957, the right-hand main tire blew out while the aircraft was nearing takeoff speed. Considerable wing damage was sustained from shrapnel thrown from the wheel and brake assembly, and the aircraft was put back into maintenance for repairs.

By the end of November, 20 test flights had been made, which evaluated 9 ejector and vari-ramp combinations. The short convergent-divergent ejector nozzle was deemed the most effective and was adopted as the production configuration. While in work status during late December due to a broken vari-ramp operating mechanism, a new J75-P-9 engine was installed and the production-type short convergent-divergent (CD) ejector and engine shroud installation was completed. The wing fences were also removed and the slotted leading edges installed. The aircraft finally returned to flight status at the end of February 1958.

Testing that month consisted of noise investigation, wing-slotted leading-edge evaluations, pneumatic controller evaluation, performance testing, and power plant characteristics. Several flights were conducted to determine inlet duct buzz limits at varying supersonic speeds. This testing found that the overall drag was unaffected by installation of a production J75-P-9 engine and the production CD ejector. Testing also revealed that replacing the wing fences with the leading-edge slots reduced drag by 1,400 pounds at Mach 2 and 35,000 feet.

During March and April 1958, flight testing revolved around determining the most effective tail-cone installation, and five variations were evaluated. Configuration I was the prototype tail cone with a 6.4-inch extension (the basic configuration). Configuration II was the prototype tail cone. Configuration III was a gloved tail cone with a 6.4-inch extension. Configuration IV was a gloved tail cone with a length identical to the prototype. Configuration V was the prototype tail cone shortened by 4.6 inches. The gloved tail cones were found to cause excessive noise and Configuration V was chosen for production because of the best overall characteristics.

Several fuel controls were also evaluated during these tests, as well as tail cone pressure surveys, an evaluation of a vari-ramp slot plug to find its effect on subsonic noise, and forward CG flutter point tests. Following these flights, the jet was once again placed into maintenance, and over the next two months instrumented variable-ramp gimbals, an electronic vari-ramp controller with production-type shock mounts and an electrical noise filter, a vari-ramp slot seal, and a replacement fuel control were installed.

In addition, the J75-P-9 engine was modified to increase the area of the first-stage turbine by 4 square inches and the second-stage tur-bine by 10 square inches (the 4 plus 10 modification). Instrumentation for investigation of the yaw-buzz program was installed and the vari-ramp actuators were replaced. Yaw-buzz flight testing began in June 1958 and continued throughout the month, leading to replacement of the engine. Continuation of the yaw-buzz tests continued after engine replacement and basic transonic/supersonic drag flight testing was completed in early August 1958. Testing in September 1958 included afterburner performance and convergent-divergent ejector tests to evaluate the cookie-cutter configuration inserts to prevent yaw on takeoff.

At the end of the test program, this aircraft had the following characteristics:

- J75-P-9 engine with the 4+10 turbine modification
- Updated Hamilton-Standard fuel control with P-17 trim
- Short convergent-divergent ejector (nozzle) with cookie-cutter inserts
- Configuration V tail cone
- Slotted throat vari-ramps
- Prototype 1,050-square-inch inlet
- Case XIV wing
- Wing leading-edge slots with fences removed

It deviated from the final production F-106A in the following ways:
- Production inlet cowl lips had additional thinning with the same inlet area.
- Production inlets had a 5-degree droop.
- Later production aircraft had the Case XXIX wing.

Even with all of the modifications, the best speed this airframe managed was Mach 2.07 at 35,000 feet. Time to accelerate from Mach 1.0 to Mach 1.9 was 3.5 minutes.

56-0453

Assigned to Convair at Edwards. First flight in late August 1957 followed by layup for instrumentation installation through September. Then used for sub-systems evaluation in the first part of October. Placed into maintenance for installation of additional instrumentation required to evaluate the Sunstrand Constant Speed Drive system and stability and control. Returned to flight status at the end of November.

December 1957 testing investigated dynamic longitudinal and lateral directional stability, use of the ram air turbine, airspeed calibration, and cabin temperature control response. In layup for the first part of January 1958 for repair of stability instrumentation and activation of bleed valves. Flights were conducted for longitudinal feel system evaluation and snap-up attack testing during the middle of the month. An engine hot-section inspection was carried out at the end of the month. Four flights were carried out in the first half of February 1958 to evaluate the longitudinal feel system, dynamic lateral stability, turn coordinator, and takeoff and landings.

The aircraft was then modified for Air Force Phase II testing. Testing was conducted in April to check the aircraft configuration changes and instrumentation. Functional check flights were carried out to evaluate the slotted vari-ramp and vari-ramp controller. Following that, the engine was changed out and instrumentation rework done.

In early May 1958 the aircraft was used for additional ram air turbine testing, and evaluation of the all attitude tank of the CSD and the vari-ramp controller. The aircraft then went back into maintenance for a change of vari-ramp controller and drive cables. Instrumentation required for turn coordinator tests was also activated.

During June, ram air turbine testing and CSD testing resumed to evaluate a new flow control valve for the RAT. Tests were also conducted with the landing gear extended to see what effect that would have on the RAT. Turn coordinator testing followed for the remainder of the month. This aircraft was sent to Sacramento for storage on 11 May 1959 and returned to San Diego for the T-T-T modification on 7 January 1960.

56-0459

CV - EDW. J75-P-17 power plant test, exhaust nozzle and performance testing. Conditional acceptance 30 Dec 1957. Ferried from Palmdale to Edwards 2 January 58. Evaluated J75-P-9 performance, including compressor stalls and afterburner re-light characteristics. During March 1958, it received the 4+10 engine mod, bleed-valve changes, and new fuel control. Flight testing in late March was for production airspeed system calibration, angle-of-attack (AOA) transducer calibration, refrigeration unit tests, and engine cooling tests.

On 19 April, the jet was ferried to San Diego for inlet duct, vari-ramp, and fuel system modifications, as well as installation of the J75-P-17 engine. Then back to Edwards for additional engine tests. In October 1958, the jet received the "cookie cutter" modification to the ejector fairing.

Used for performance and aircraft systems testing through November 1959. It was the primary aircraft for the Project Firewall speed record attempt but had continuing problems with high-speed yaw and resulting compressor stalls. After rebuild during the T-T-T program, no further yaw problems were noted.

F-106 SURVIVORS*

Actual S/N	Displayed S/N	Markings	Location	Remarks
56-0451	59-0082	171 FIS Mich ANG	Selfridge Air Museum Selfridge ANGB, Michigan	Mid inlets Old canopy
56-0454		PQM-106	Holloman AFB, New Mexico	
56-0459		318 FIS	McChord AFB, Washington	
56-0460		5 FIS	Minot AFB, North Dakota	On pole
56-0461	57-0231	87 FIS	K. I. Sawyer AFB, Michigan	
57-0239		159 FIS	Jacksonville IAP, Florida	
57-2513 (B)		B-1 Chase	Yanks Air Museum, Chino, California	
57-2516 (B)	N816NA	NASA	Air & Space Center, Hampton, Virginia	Hanging from ceiling
57-2523 (B)		177 FIS NJ ANG	NAFEC Atlantic City, New Jersey Entry to NJANG	Pole, extended IR *Genie* and *Falcons*
57-2533 (B)		59 FIS	Kelly Field Annex, San Antonio, Texas	On a pole
57-2545 (B)		PQM-106	St. Louis, Missouri	In pieces
58-0774				Movement in progress from Hill AFB to Yankee Willow Run A/P, Belleville, Michigan
58-0786				Movement in progress from El Paso, Texas, to California Science Center, storage/restoration in Victorville, California
58-0787		49 FIS	National Museum of the Air Force wright-Patterson AFB, Ohio	Indoors Cornfield bomber displayed with Falcons, Genie, MF-9 and Falcon dolly
58-0793	57-2456	456 FIS	Castle Air Museum, Atwater, California	Gun pod, Falcon
59-0003		5 FIS	Pima Air Museum, Tucson, Arizona	
59-0010		5 FIS	Aerospace Museum of California, McClellan A/P Sacramento, California	
59-0023		95 FIS	Air Mobility Museum, Dover AFB, Delaware	IR extended
59-0093	59-0005	5 FIS	Dakota Territory Air Museum, Minot, North Dakota	Indoors
59-0047		PQM-106	St. Louis, Missouri	In pieces
59-0069	57-2492	186 FIS	Great Falls IAP, Montana	

59-0086		48 FIS	Pacific Coast Air Museum, Santa Rosa, California	White band, tail markings
59-0105		159 FIS	Camp Blanding Museum, Florida ANG. Starke, Florida	On pole
59-0123		48 FIS	Museum of Aviation, Warner-Robins AFB, Georgia	Blue white Genie, Falcons
59-0130		PQM-106	AMARG, Davis-Monthan AFB, Arizona	Last Six in the boneyard
59-0134		48 FIS	Pete Field Museum, Peterson AFB, Colorado	Original canopy
59-0137		49 FIS	Evergreen Aviation Museum, McMinnville, Oregon	
59-0145		ADWC	Tyndall AFB, Panama City, Florida	
59-0146		194 FIS	Fresno Air Park, Fresno Air Terminal, California	
59-0158 (B)		329 FIS	Century Circle, Edwards AFB, California	
59-0146 (B)			Timmerman A/P, Milwaukee, Wisconsin	Forward fuselage only, for mobile display

* As of 1 January 2016

Wingman's view of an F-106B beginning to roll in a formation takeoff with its Pratt & Whitney J75 turbo-jet in full afterburner.

INDEX

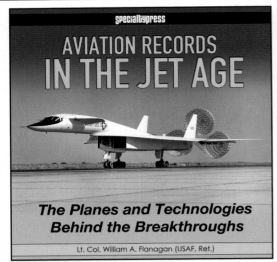
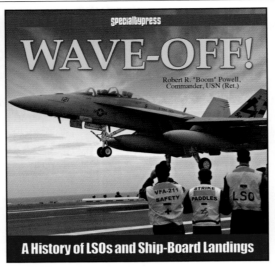

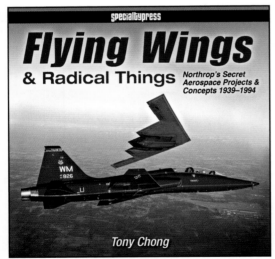
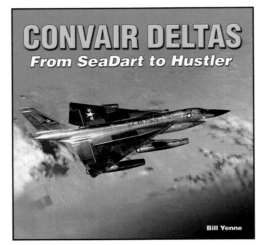
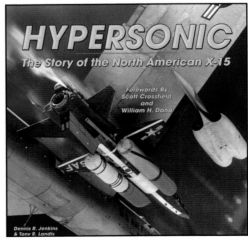

F·102 B INB

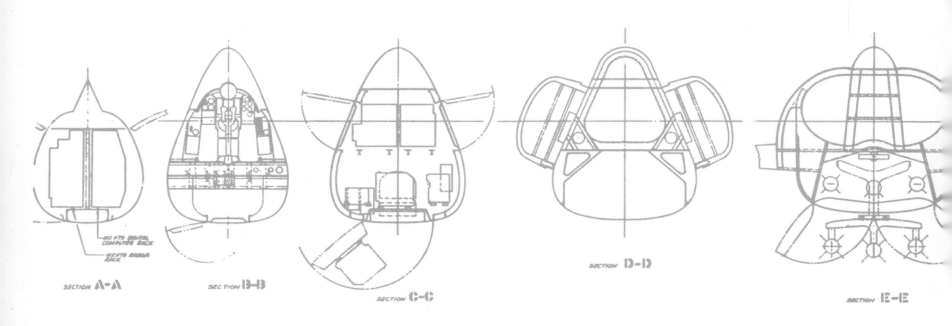

SECTION A-A SECTION B-B SECTION C-C SECTION D-D SECTION E-E

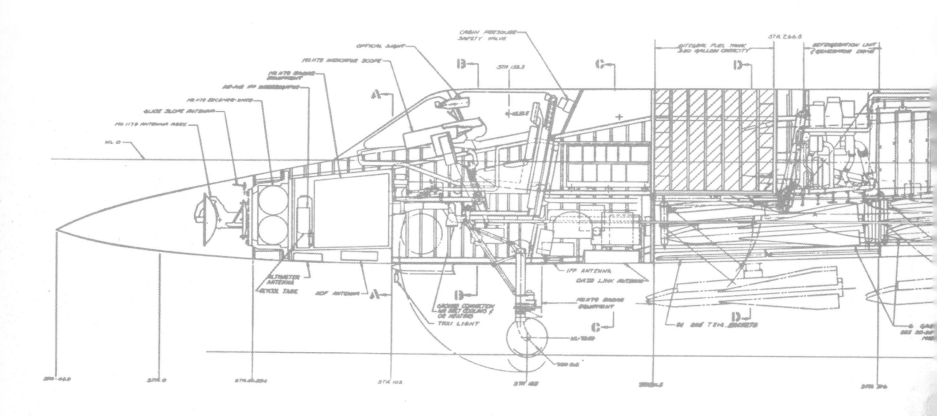